EGYPT IN
BIBLICAL PROPHECY

WILBUR M. SMITH

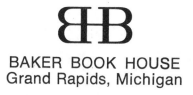

BAKER BOOK HOUSE
Grand Rapids, Michigan

To

ROBERT P. DUGAN

able business executive,
munificent donor to many evangelical causes,
always displaying the Christian virtue
of graciousness,
this book is gratefully dedicated.

PUBLISHER'S PREFACE

It is interesting to note that this book was written before the present crisis in the Near East. This enabled the author to write objectively, with his eye fixed on Scripture. This also gave him a clear view of some of the prophecies concerning Egypt made in post-Biblical times. Such a viewpoint makes this a fascinating book to read at a time when Egypt is so much in the news.

It is only natural that a book such as this one should have come from the pen of Wilbur M. Smith. He is everywhere recognized as a student of Biblical prophecy. The publishers are grateful to him for enabling them to make this thorough and comprehensive study available again.

PREFACE

Serious students of the Word of God—and, indeed, many who are only superficially acquainted with the Scriptures, but are dimly aware that they contain prophecies relating to the end of our age—cannot learn of any major contemporary event occurring in the Middle East (the lands of the Bible, and of Biblical prophecies) without asking the question, "What took place in Biblical history in the specific area in which this new crisis has burst upon our world?" Indeed, many cannot refrain from asking further, "Is there any statement, or statements, in the prophecies of the Bible that bear upon the role of this area at the end of the age?"

Personally, I must confess that when this recent crisis (of 1956) occurred in Egypt, I was driven to examine, for the first time in years of study of Biblical prophecy, the whole subject of Egypt in Israel's history and in the Old Testament predictions concerning certain other nations of that part of the earth. Had someone placed before me, six months ago, an examination covering Egypt in Biblical *prophecy*, I would have "flunked" it, even if the questions were not of a technical nature. However, when newspapers were recently filled with reports from Egypt day by day, I was unable to escape a desire to review the whole theme of Egypt in the Biblical writings, both historical and prophetical.

From the study in which I have been engaged during the past few months, I have had four definite experiences of surprise. The first of these was in discovering that there are approximately 250 verses in the Old Testament which, *at the time they were uttered,* were prophecies of events yet to take place in Egypt. A subject to which the Scriptures give 250 verses is one about which those who claim to be Bible students ought to have some knowledge. Many of these prophecies have been fulfilled, of course, since the time of their utterance, e.g., the predictions of the wars of the Ptolemaic kings in Daniel 11.

My second surprise came in realizing that some passages in this catena raise tremendous problems, such as the historical certainty of Nebuchadnezzar's invasion of Egypt (inasmuch as the secular historians of Greece and Rome never referred to what must have been a very important historical event). As we shall observe later, there are some sentences contained in these prophecies about which no one can really be dogmatic.

A third surprise was in discovering that *the area around Suez* was definitely referred to by Isaiah. Though the word "Suez," a modern term, does not occur in the text, all commentators agree that it is to the vicinity of the present city of Suez that one particular Isianic prophecy points.

Finally, I was surprised to realize that no one has attempted (as far as I have been able to ascertain) a full investigation of the *prophecies* of the Old Testament relative to this ancient kingdom, and the future of this geographical area. To illustrate: In the two massive bibliographies of material on Ancient Egypt available in the New York Public Library, over sixteen thousand items are listed, many of them relating to "Egypt and the Bible," yet there is not a single reference, either to articles in periodicals, or to books, to Biblical prophecies about Egypt.[1] Furthermore, the New York Public Library informs me that in all the literature which they have acquired since the final supplement to this bibliography was issued (in 1942) there is still no reference to this subject.

In one area of literature, I have been prevented from carrying on the research that I wished it had been possible, and that is the searching of the great prophetic periodicals of Great Britain of the early part of the nineteenth century. Of the possible one hundred and eighty bound volumes of twenty-two different prophetic journals, I have been able to consult only about thirty volumes. What is in the others, I have no idea, but certainly buried somewhere in this literature must be articles on the subject of Egypt in prophecy. I only wish that when in England in the summer of 1955, I had known that this subject would be engaging my attention.

In the realm of the interpretation of Biblical prophecy, more foolish things have been said—as well as some very worthwhile and profound things, of course—than in any other one area of Biblical exegesis. For example, this whole wretched business of date-setting, though condemned repeatedly by the failure of these chronological schemes, always finds a few men still engaged in such folly. Many attempts have been made to relate events contemporary with the writing of a given volume to certain Biblical prophecies—the fall of some government, the destruction of some famous city of the Near East, the enlargement of the boundaries of the British Empire (we perhaps will not hear too much about this in the future), etc. Many authors have lived long enough to regret some of their unjustified and strained interpretations. I trust that nothing in this volume will be considered fantastic, or unwarranted by anything that the Word of God has said on the topics discussed; although many may not agree with some of the statements made here. Nowhere in this work have I attempted to relate the decline of the influence of Britain in the Near East to any Biblical prophecy; nor have I anywhere undertaken to tell what the status of Egypt might be next year, or the year following. I find nothing in the Scriptures which would give any indication of what, e.g., Nasser's next move might be. This volume simply represents an endeavor to get at the basic teachings of the major prophecies of the Old Testament that bear upon this once marvelous land of the Pharaohs, a land that is again agitating the thought of the whole world.

I have had considerable help in the preparation of these pages. First of all I wish to thank the Rev. Wilbur Helmbold, then Librarian of Providence Bible Institute, who, in a long day of research in the library of Yale Divinity School, was able to uncover a number of passages in early missionary literature directly concerned with missions in Egypt. Colonel F. B. Miles kindly sent me two articles from his own pen, on Egypt in prophecy, of a general nature. My friend Mr. S. Kingsley Miner, of the Harper Memorial Library of the University of Chicago, has been most co-operative in making available many books, invaluable help which he has extended to me over a period of twenty years. A colleague, Dr. Gleason L. Archer, generously placed at my disposal his own full, accurate, annotated translation of Jerome's Commentary on Daniel, the only complete translation of this writing I know of, a work which some publisher should be printing. Dr. Archer also made for me a careful study of the relevant pages

PREFACE

of the Latin commentary on Isaiah by Vitringa (1659-1722)
(because after forty years of neglect my own Latin is so rusty).

I am indebted to Mrs. Carl F. H. Henry for a translation of
Luther's comments on Isaiah 19 and Daniel 11 (works that
have never been translated into English). Miss Rosalie Edmis-
ton, Secretary of the United States Council of the Egypt
General Mission, has been of invaluable help in placing in
my hands some biographical material on American missionaries in Egypt which otherwise I would not have seen. From
the great university library of Amsterdam, the Administrator
has graciously loaned me the biography of Hermanus Willem
Witteveen, by Dr. J. H. Gunning. Miss Clara B. Allen,
Librarian of Fuller Seminary, has given unfailing assistance
in securing needed books from various libraries throughout
the country.

1. I refer to the two volumes by Ida E. Pratt, *Ancient Egypt, Sources of Information in the New York Public Library* (New York, 1925) and the supplement, *Ancient Egypt, 1925-1941*.

CONTENTS

11

CONTENTS

I

GEOGRAPHICAL FACTORS
IN BIBLICAL PROPHECY

One of the primary characteristics of the Bible which distinguishes it from the basic texts of other world religions is the absolute dependence of its ethical and religious teachings upon historical events involving historical personages. The two great epochs of ancient India are *The Ramayana* and *The Mahabharata,* the former describing the adventures of a banished prince in the wilderness of southern India, and the latter based on legends of some major conflict among the races of northern India. Authorities on these texts admit that they have much in common with the *Iliad* and the *Odyssey* and "the two together comprise the whole of the epoch literature of the ancient Hindus." But the heroes of these stories were born of gods, supposedly fourteen or fifteen centuries before Christ, and are thus fictitious.[1] In Greek literature, while the gods are said to reside on Mount Olympus, and we know where Mount Olympus was (and is), we also know that no god or goddess ever lived there: what is related of these deities cannot be located in any chronological scheme. No one ever saw "the Elysian fields." The philosophical works of Seneca and Plotinus have nothing to do with geography. The same can be said of the Koran in which not one great city of Europe, or Syria, or Asia Minor, is mentioned by name.[2] And Boston plays no part in *Science and Health.*

13

Immediately upon opening the Scriptures, however, we find ourselves in a garden surrounded by four named rivers, two of which are still known by the names assigned to them in the ancient annals of Israel. Following the record of the Flood, we are introduced to the famous table of nations in Genesis 10, which Professor Albright has said, "shows such a remarkably modern understanding of the ethnic and linguistic situation in the ancient world in spite of all its complexity, that scholars never fail to be impressed with the author's knowledge of the subject." [3] Indeed, the Old Testament literature is so predominantly historical, and its records so dependable, that in the third volume of the *Cambridge Ancient History*, entitled "The Assyrian Empire," one of the three indexes is devoted to Biblical passages exclusively. In the Index to Names in this volume there are 23 references to Herodotus, 7 to Thucydides, 5 to Strabo and 1 to Pliny; but there are 1104 references to 1002 different passages taken from 34 Old Testament books! [4]

In two early passages of the third Gospel, Luke the historian relates his account of the life and ministry of Jesus to contemporary historical events. The second chapter opens with the following words: "Now it came to pass in those days, there went out a decree from Caesar Augustus that all the world should be enrolled. This was the first enrolment made when Quirinius was governor of Syria. And all went to enrol themselves, every one to his own city. And Joseph also went up from Galilee, out of the city of Nazareth, into Judaea, to the city of David, which is called Bethlehem, because he was of the house and family of David" (vv. 1-4). The third chapter begins with an even more detailed historical statement: "Now in the fifteenth year of the reign of Tiberius Caesar, Pontius Pilate, being governor of Judaea, and Herod being tetrarch of Galilee, and his brother Philip tetrarch of the region of Ituraea and Trachonitis, and Lysanias tetrarch of Abilene, in the high priesthood of Annas and Caiaphas, the word of God came unto John the son of Zacharias in the wilderness" (vv. 1, 2). The Book of Acts is nothing else but history. Not only are the Pauline Epistles interpenetrated with historical references, but so also is the Apocalypse, as we shall soon see.

Professor G. Ernest Wright has issued an over due pronouncement on the relationship of Biblical theology to Biblical history:

"In considering Biblical faith, it seems to me that the point at which we must begin is not with the history of its evolving ideas but with history in another sense. It is history as the arena of God's activity. Biblical theology is first and foremost a theology of recital, in which Biblical man confesses his faith by reciting the formative events of his history as the redemptive handiwork of God. The realism of the Bible consists in its close attention to the facts of history and of tradition because these facts are the facts of God . . . At the centre of Israelite faith lay the great proclamation that the God of the fathers had heard the cry of a weak, oppressed people in Egypt. They had been slaves, but then freed by mighty acts which demonstrated God's power to the Egyptians and to the world. As slaves for whom the justice of the world made no provision, they were delivered by a most extraordinary exhibition of Divine grace. This was a sign, a wonder, not to be explained by fortune or

15

irrational chance, but solely by the assumption of a personal Power greater than all the powers of this world. This was a God who could make the forces of nature serve him as well as the recalcitrance of the heart of Pharaoh. He was one who for some reason had set his love on a defenceless people and had chosen them for his own. The Israelite eye was thus trained to take human events seriously, because in them was to be learned more clearly than anywhere else what God willed and what he was about. Consequently, in all that happened subsequently the Israelite simply interpreted the meaning of events by recognizing and acknowledging in them the God who had formed the nation by the remarkable events at the Exodus and in the wilderness . . .

"Since God is known by what he has done, the Bible exists as a confessional recital of his acts, together with the teaching accompanying these acts, or inferred from them in the light of specific situations which the faithful confronted. To confess God is to tell a story and then to expound its meaning. Is Biblical theology solely concerned with abstractions of the meaning, or must it be as primarily concerned with the story as were the Biblical writers? Obviously, it must be both at the same time, for the abstractions cannot be separated from the history. They are inferences from the history and are always subject to deepening and correction in the light of the history." [5]

Now, one cannot have history without also having chronology and geography. It is the latter of these that requires our attention here. The Bible is the only volume of the literature of a major world religion that in modern times is continually bound with extensive geographical helps and

16

maps. So elaborate is this geographical theme in the Scriptures that the *Westminster Atlas of the Bible*, for example, is compelled to list over two thousand different geographical sites for the accurate interpretation of these sacred records! So significant and so far-reaching in consequences were the events occurring in some of these sites that the very place names have entered into the linguistic lore and the literature of almost all European nations; and in our own English language, what deep meanings are called up by such words as Eden, Canaan, Sodom, Bethel, Egypt, the Jordan, Jerusalem, Babylon, Gethsemane, and Armageddon.

Not only are the historical events of the Old and New Testaments placed in chronological and geographical frameworks, but the provenance of most of the events of Scripture is recognized by everyone as the most important single geographical area of our day—Palestine. Significant as were the peninsulas of Greece and Italy in the history of 700 B.C. to A.D. 400, it was nevertheless in this Biblical territory between the Tigris River and the Mediterranean, from the Lebanon Mountains to Sinai, that the human race began its course, where the earliest civilizations and empires flourished two millennia before the age of Pericles and Plato. Here was the home of the chosen people of God, the place where the supreme revelations of God were given, and where that marvelous group of prophets ministered, the like of which the world has not seen since. Here was our redemption worked out in the Birth and Life, the Death and Resurrection, of our Lord. Here the early Church originated, with the descent of the Holy Spirit. Here was the goal of the Crusades, and here the last great battle of this age will be fought.

EGYPT IN BIBLICAL PROPHECY

So full of interest, so widely studied by millions, we may safely say, is the geography of the Scriptures, that more elaborate maps and atlases have been published of this particular area, so far removed from most western nations, than of any other area of this earth of similar size, ancient or modern. One can find many more elaborately illustrated and beautifully printed atlases of Bible lands than he can of the United States or Great Britain for any given decade.

In spite of the extensive, and ever-increasing literature of Biblical geography, one particular aspect of this subject has been strangely ignored, namely, *the geography of the fulfilled and unfulfilled prophecies of the Bible.* A few elementary maps have been constructed which attempt to set forth the boundaries of a Roman Empire according to Daniel 2 and 7.[6] There are some charts—for the most part in literature seldom seen—of the realignment of the tribes of Israel according to Ezekiel 48:1-9; and of course we often see photographs and drawings of the Valley of Jezreel, the Plain of Megiddo.[7] But, as far as I am aware, no complete investigation has ever been undertaken of the geography of the prophecies of the Old and New Testaments which are identified with specific sites. Here is an opportunity for a work that could prove of inestimable help to Bible students. Several years ago a student in my seminary class in English Bible, a graduate of a well-known technological institution, submitted as a term paper, at my suggestion, a map covering only the geographical prophecies of Isaiah. He was able to locate ninety-eight sites in this one study excluding the many prophecies relating to Israel, Judah, and Jerusalem. Actually, fifteen different nations are the recipients of predictions concerning their future in the three great collections of nation prophecies in Isaiah, Jeremiah and Ezekiel—a subject that will occupy us in the next chapter.

Apparently there is not in existence a book which adequately and thoroughly discusses the prophecies of the Old and New Testaments regarding the city of Jerusalem, as numerous and as significant as they are. One could almost say that the debate over Jerusalem in the United Nations was hardly more than a confirmation of the words of Zechariah that at the end of this age the Lord "will make Jerusalem a cup of reeling unto all the peoples round about . . . a burdensome stone for all the peoples" (12:2, 3).[8] Not only is Jerusalem central in the major prophecy of Daniel 9, but it forms the principal theme in the utterances of our Lord on more than one occasion. He not only clearly and specifically foretold the fall of the holy city under Titus, to occur some forty years after His death, but He also depicted the shameful subjection of this city to the Gentiles until the end of this age: "Jerusalem shall be trodden down of the Gentiles until the times of the Gentiles be fulfilled" (Luke 21:24).

It is not relevant to the purpose of this book to enter into any discussion of the geographical data of great predictive statements of the Scriptures, such as that of the northern confederacy of Ezekiel 38:5, 6, etc., but I cannot bring this brief survey to a close without directing attention to a fact which is generally ignored in literature on the Book of Revelation, that even in this book geographical factors are numerous and important.[9] The first three chapters of Revelation contain specific references to the island of Patmos and to the seven cities of Asia, which in turn carry us back into the

epistles of Paul and the Book of Acts, where the ministry of
the apostles in these cities is mentioned. In Revelation 11 the
description of future events in Jerusalem takes us back into
the Gospels, "where the Lord was crucified" (v. 8). In Chapter
9 and again in Chapter 16, the Euphrates River is spoken of,
and Chapters 17 and 18 are devoted to the subject of Babylon,
in a phraseology taken for the most part from Jeremiah 50 and
51.

It is not my intention here to discuss the very difficult subject of the identification of Babylon, but I cannot refrain from
quoting an amazing statement from Toynbee's *Christianity
on Trial,* whether or not one thinks it has any bearing upon
this subject. "We hear and feel the moving of three-quarters
of the population of the world awakening now for the first
time: India, China, Indo-China, Indonesia, Islam and eastern
Europe. Now their gravitational pull will draw the center
of gravitation away from the islands of the sea, and locate
it some place equidistant from the western pole of the
world's population in Europe and North Africa, and the
eastern pole of the world's population in China and India.
This new location of the gravitational center of humanity
would indicate a site in the neighborhood of ancient Babylon." [10] The battle at Megiddo turns our minds back to the
first chapter of Judges, where we read that this city's stubborn
resistance to Israel made it impossible for her to capture it
in those early days.

Whatever might be one's convictions in the realm of
eschatology, whatever type of interpretation one chooses to
place upon the geographical prophecies of the Old Testament
and the Apocalypse, one indisputable fact stands out, namely,

that the area embracing the nations and cities constantly referred to in these ancient prophecies is the focal point of world history today; and those very nations which students at the beginning of the twentieth century thought were forever dead and buried are now alive again, vigorously acting out their self-appointed parts—according to the counsels of God, though they know it not—on the trembling stage of world history.

Notes

CHAPTER 1

1. See for a brief introduction the edition *The Ramayana* and *The Mahabharata* by R. C. Dutt. London, 1910. pp. 154-169. Professor G. Ernest Wright has said: "It has often been pointed out that the pagan religions have no sense of history. Polytheistic men, borne on the rhythmic cycle of nature, has no primary concern with history; instead his focus of attention is upon the yearly cycle in which life is re-created each spring and the blessing of order re-established. He is 'bound in the bundle of life' with nature, which is the kingdom of the gods, and his existence moves with the natural rhythm. Biblical man was 'bound in the bundle of life' with God who was not an immanence in nature but the Creator of nature, and who revealed himself by means of historical acts in which there were also historical promises." (*The God Who Acts*. London, 1952. p. 24)

2. The paucity of geographical references in the Koran is in sharp contrast to the vast amount of geographical data in the Old and New Testaments. This deserves some careful examination. From a fairly close reading of the Koran I have discovered that it not only has comparatively few geographical references, but many of these references are expressed in non-geographical terms. For example, the city mentioned most frequently is Mecca, but only once do I find it actually named, and there it is called Becca (III. 96); elsewhere it is designated as "this town" (IV. 75); "the mother of villages" (VI. 93); "the city" (XVIII. 22; XC. 1, 2); "the mother town" (XLII. 7). The Kaabah is referred to as "the secret house" (V. 2); "thy holy house" (XIV. 37); "the ancient house" (XXII. 29); and "a sure sanctuary" (XXVIII. 57).

The battle of Badr is mentioned frequently in the Koran, but the name of the place is never given (III. 12; VIII. 7; XXII. 25, etc.) Medina

EGYPT IN BIBLICAL PROPHECY

is referred to by name only once (IX. 120). Once we have the phrase, "the two towns," meaning Mecca and Ta'if (XLIII. 31). All other allusions to Arabia concern obscure places, as the two mountains of Safa and Marwah near Mecca (II. 158); Hijr (XV. 80) near the northern boundary of Arabia. Sinai is named but once (XCV. 2) and is elsewhere called "the mount" (II. 93; VII. 171). Some commentators interpret Tasnim (LXXXIII. 27) not as a town but as a word meaning "water coming upon them from above," so also some Mohammedan scholars make Rass (XXV. 38; L. 12) refer to the well into which Joseph was cast. Sheba or Seba is referred to once (XXXIV. 15). The ark is said to have rested upon Al-judi (XI. 44). In the frequent references to the lives of Joseph and Moses, Egypt is spoken of four times (VII. 105; X. 88; XII. 21, 99), but Jerusalem is never named (II. 259; XVII. 5). To summarize, we can say that apart from Mohammed's references to events recorded in Genesis and Exodus of our Bible, he never mentions by name any place located more than sixty miles from the city of Mecca; in other words, his references are most provincial. In spite of the fact that he has scores of references to Old Testament events and the life of Jesus, and was writing as late as the seventh century A.D., there is no mention of the city of Rome, or Athens, or Alexandria, or Cairo, or even of Damascus, and particularly, no reference to Jerusalem by name; actually, he never speaks of the Red Sea, the Dead Sea, or the Mediterranean, the Nile, the Jordan, or the Euphrates Rivers. No battles of history, outside of local ones in which he was engaged, are recorded, and he does not even name Palestine or Canaan. Some translations of the Koran assert that Mohammed could neither read nor write, and this may account for the indefiniteness of his geographical data.

The single tenth chapter of Genesis has five times more geographical data of importance than the whole of the Koran. Apart from those battles in which Mohammed was engaged, no world event is set forth in the Koran, except those copied from the ancient history of the Old Testament.

3. W. F. Albright in *The Lutheran Commentary on the Old Testament*. Philadelphia, 1948 p. 138.
4. *Cambridge Ancient History*. Vol. III. London, 1925. pp. 815-821.
5. G. Ernest Wright: *The God Who Speaks*. Chicago, 1952. p. 38. quoted with the kind permission of the publishers, the Henry Regnery Co.
6. Among those who have attempted to draw maps depicting boundaries of the last great empire was W. E. Vine, in *The Roman Empire in the Light of Prophecy*. London, 1916. See also the "Map of the Ten Kingdoms of the Roman Empire," by B. W. Newton.
7. For maps of the future battle of Armageddon, see e.g., C. H. Titterton: *Armageddon and the Last War*. London, 1916. Vitringa, in emphasizing

the importance of geography in a study of the Scriptures, quotes an older commentator, Gaussenus, as follows: "That because mention is frequently made by the prophets, not only of the places of Palestine, but also of the regions bordering upon it, the nations of which were in continual hostility with Israel, insomuch that they sometimes formed the awful *'burden'* of their denunciations; it especially behoves the student of these things to have his maps continually at hand. For in the first place they serve to assist his memory; in the second place they afford him a clearer idea of the matter before him; and thirdly they will in some measure relieve his mind when wearied with intense study." In *The Temple of Ezekiel's Prophecy* by Henry Sully (London, 1929) a large map illustrates "the resettlement of Israel according to Ezekiel's Prophecy" (p. 148), and an elaborate drawing depicts the relationship of this Temple to the present topography of Jerusalem (p. 65). The strange volume by R. C. Shimeall, *Political Economy of Prophecy* (New York, 1866) contains a large folding "Map of Canaan Enlarged Adapted to the Book of Ezekiel" (at p. 181). There are also prophetic maps in *The True Boundaries of the Holy Land,* by Samuel H. Isaacs. The title of the work by Robert B. Seeley, *The Atlas of Prophecy, Being the Prophecies of Daniel and St. John with a Simple Exposition and Series of Maps and Charts* (London, 1849) is misleading, for the maps are almost worthless. B. W. Newton published *A Prophetic Map of the World* (1846).

8. David Baron: *The Visions and Prophecies of Zechariah.* 3d ed., London, 1919. pp. 421-432.

9. One excellent exception is a chapter on "The Geography of the Revelation" in Emil G. Kraeling: *Rand McNally Bible Atlas.* Chicago, 1956. pp. 465-474.

10. Arnold J. Toynbee: *Civilization on Trial.* New York: Oxford, 1948. p. 93.

2

THE THREE GREAT COLLECTIONS OF
PROPHECIES REGARDING THE NATIONS

The three most extended major prophetic passages relating to Egypt, some fulfilled centuries ago and some yet to be fulfilled, are found in the three great collections of prophecies pertaining to the nations of the Biblical world of ancient times: in the eighth century B.C. in Isaiah's prophecy; in Jeremiah, who wrote, for the most part, toward the end of the seventh, and the beginning of the sixth century B.C.; and in Ezekiel's writings, of the sixth century B.C. These collections are contained in eleven successive chapters of Isaiah, 13-23, in six successive chapters of Jeremiah, 46-51, and in eight successive chapters of Ezekiel, 25-32: a total of 680 verses. It will hardly be disputed by any careful student of the literature bearing upon Biblical prophecy that these sections have been amazingly ignored, generally, in books devoted to the interpretation of Biblical predictions, though they form the very center of the prophetic work of Isaiah, bring to a conclusion the prophecies of Jeremiah, and form the bridge in the Book of Ezekiel between the ethical exhortations of the earlier chapters and the famous, though difficult, prophecies regarding Gog and Magog, and the millennial temple, which terminate that book.[1]

An adequate comprehension of those prophecies about

Egypt, which form the main theme of study in this book, is only possible if we have a general understanding of the character and basic factors of these three groups of nation prophecies. For the most part, I have had to plow new ground here.

The Context of These Three Collections of Prophecy

The eleven-chapter section in Isaiah is surrounded by some of the most wondrous passages regarding the future of this earth, and the ultimate establishment of the kingdom of God, to be found in all the Bible. The two chapters immediately preceding this section begin with the familiar Messianic statement: "And there shall come forth a shoot out of the stock of Jesse, and a branch out of his roots shall bear fruit. And the Spirit of Jehovah shall rest upon him, the spirit of wisdom and understanding, the spirit of counsel and might, the spirit of knowledge and of the fear of Jehovah. And his delight shall be in the fear of Jehovah; and he shall not judge after the sight of his eyes, neither decide after the hearing of his ears; but with righteousness shall he judge the poor, and decide with equity for the meek of the earth; and he shall smite the earth with the rod of his mouth; and with the breath of his lips shall he slay the wicked" (Isa. 11:1-4). A phrase in verse 9 is often used in the nation prophecies of Ezekiel, "The earth shall be full of the knowledge of Jehovah, as the waters cover the sea." Chapter 12 gives us a promise of that day when all Israel shall with joy draw water out of the wells of salvation, declaring the work of God among the peoples of the earth, and exalting His holy name. Now it is immediately following this promise, which still awaits fulfilment, that we have the

25

series of prophecies regarding *ten nations* of the earth then in existence and located in what we now call the Near East.[2]

Throughout the Scriptures, the kingdoms of this world are everywhere found to be in opposition to the kingdom of God, and both the Old and New Testaments declare that these antagonistic governments must be overcome before the kingdom of God is established. This is the major theme of the Book of Revelation, down to the battle of Armageddon, when the kings of the earth come out against the King of Kings.

Immediately following this Isaianic collection of nation prophecies, the prediction is made that "In this mountain will Jehovah of hosts make unto all peoples a feast of fat things, a feast of wines on the lees, of fat things full of marrow, of wines on the lees well refined . . . He hath swallowed up death forever; and the Lord Jehovah will wipe away tears from off all faces; and the reproach of his people will he take away from off all the earth: for Jehovah hath spoken it" (25:6, 8). Chapter 27 closes with a promise of the ultimate establishment of holiness: "And it shall come to pass in that day, that a great trumpet shall be blown; and they shall come that were ready to perish in the land of Assyria, and they that were outcasts in the land of Egypt; and they shall worship Jehovah in the holy mountain at Jerusalem."

Between these two predictions of the ultimate establishment of the kingdom of God, of righteousness and holiness on this earth, Isaiah places his predictions of God's judgment upon the nations round about Israel. Many of these prophecies as we have said before, have been fulfilled, and some remain to be fulfilled, but God's judgment upon the nations of the past only adumbrates the final judgment on the nations of the whole earth which must take place before the establishment of the everlasting kingdom of God.

The appropriateness of the location of these nation prophecies in Isaiah reappears in the parallel prophecies in the Book of Ezekiel. In the chapters that precede the section we are to study, we have first of all a survey of God's dealings with Israel through the centuries, which concludes with the promise, "As a sweet savor will I accept you, when I bring you out from the peoples, and gather you out of the countries wherein ye have been scattered; and I will be sanctified in you in the sight of the nations. And ye shall know that I am Jehovah, when I shall bring you into the land of Israel, into the country which I sware to give unto your fathers" (20:41, 42). Chapters 21 to 24 describe God's punishment of Jerusalem because of her sins.

The section on the nations (Chs. 25-32) is followed by the promise of Israel's restoration to the land, one of the most beautiful passages in all the Scriptures: "For thus saith the Lord Jehovah: Behold, I myself, even I, will search for my sheep, and will seek them out. As a shepherd seeketh out his flock in the day that he is among his sheep that are scattered abroad, so will I seek out my sheep; and I will deliver them out of all places whither they have been scattered in the cloudy and dark day. And I will bring them out from the peoples, and gather them from the countries, and will bring them into their own land; and I will feed them upon the mountains of Israel, by the watercourses, and in all the inhabited places of the country. I will feed them with good pasture; and upon the mountains of the height of Israel shall their fold be: there shall they lie down in a good fold; and on fat pasture shall they feed upon the mountains of Israel. I myself will be the shepherd of my sheep, and I will cause them to lie down, saith the Lord Jehovah. I will seek that which was lost, and will bring back that which was driven away, and will bind up that which was broken, and will strengthen that which was sick: but the fat and the strong I will destroy; I will feed them in justice . . . And I will set up one shepherd over them, and he shall feed them, even my servant David; he shall feed them and he shall be their shepherd. And I, Jehovah, will be their God, and my servant David prince among them; I, Jehovah have spoken it . . . And they shall no more be a prey to the nations, neither shall the beasts of the earth devour them, but they shall dwell securely, and none shall make them afraid" (34:11-16, 23, 24, 28).

The vision of dry bones (Ch. 37), referring to the ultimate resurrection of Israel, coming up from among the nations of the earth, is followed by the conspiracy of Gog and Magog, the destruction of this northern confederation, and the millennial chapters. So Ezekiel's collection of nationalistic prophecies, as Isaiah's, falls between two sections depicting in vivid language the ultimate redemption of his people, which will not be accomplished until these nations are judged.

The nation prophecies of Jeremiah are found near the end of that book, but they are not embraced by predictions of the coming kingdom of God; rather, they are immediately preceded by chapters describing the impending destruction of Jerusalem, first unfolded in Chapter 39, and repeated in Chapter 52.

EGYPT IN BIBLICAL PROPHECY

The Nations Enumerated in These Prophecies

It is not without significance that in the fundamental collection of Isaiah, ten nations are listed. This inevitably reminds one of another grouping of ten nations, represented by the ten toes of Daniel 2 and the ten horns of Daniel 7, as well as Revelation 12:3; 13:1; 17:3, 7, 12, 16. The ten nations of Isaiah's group are not to be entirely identified with the ten nations forming the Roman Empire, but the fact that both should consist of *ten* separate units is interesting.[3] The ten nations and cities (some of these are cities, but for convenience I am using the general designation "nations") appear in the following order: Babylon—59 verses of text, the longest of any separate prophecy here—Philistia, Moab, Damascus, Ethiopia, Egypt, Dumah (which is Edom), Arabia, the Valley of Vision, and the city of Tyre. The Jeremiah passages contains eight instead of ten specific nation prophecies. Six of these are found also in the Isaiah collection, but two of them are new: the prophecy against the Ammonites (49:1-6, also Ezek. 25:1-7), and the brief prediction concerning Kedar and Hazor (49:28-31). Strange to say, while the Isaiah section opens with an extended statement concerning Babylon, and the Jeremiah account concludes with an even longer prophecy on this area, the name is not even mentioned in the Ezekiel section.

The collection of prophecies in Ezekiel concerns but seven different geographical areas. Four of these are set forth in both Isaiah and Jeremiah, namely, the prophecies against Edom, Egypt, Moab and Philistia; one in Jeremiah, pertaining to the Ammonites; one in Isaiah, regarding Tyre (26:1-28:19); while one is unique in Ezekiel, that relating to Zidon (28:20-24). Taking the sequence of the prophecies in Isaiah as basic, the order in which the cities and nations appear in the groupings of Jeremiah and Ezekiel in relation to it is as follows:

Isaiah	1	2	3	4	5	6	7	8	9	10
Jeremiah	9	2	3	6	7	1	5	0	0	0
Ezekiel	0	4	2	0	0	7	3	0	0	5

Israel Frequently Referred to in the Midst of These Prophecies Concerning Gentile Nations

In this chapter I am not attempting even a summary interpretation of this vast body of prophetic material, but only the listing of some fundamental factors, pervading the entire corpus. It should be remembered that the viewpoint here, as throughout the whole of the Old Testament, is of God's election relationship to Israel. None of these nations would be the subject of predictions by any of the prophets of Israel and Judah unless it had some bearing upon God's purposes toward Israel and, eventually, His purposes through Israel for the whole world. For this reason, as one follows a prophecy regarding Babylon, Moab, Edom, Egypt, or some other near-by country, he invariably comes upon a phrase bearing directly upon the future and redemption of Israel. Thus, e.g., in the midst of the prophecy on Babylon, we read, "For Jehovah will have compassion on Jacob, and will yet choose Israel, and set them in their own land: and the sojourner shall join himself with them, and they shall cleave to the house of Jacob. And the peoples shall take them, and

30

bring them to their place; and the house of Israel shall possess them in the land of Jehovah for servants and for handmaids: and they shall take them captive whose captives they were; and they shall rule over their oppressors" (Isa. 14:1, 2). In the great oracle concerning Egypt is this enigmatical statement: "And the land of Judah shall become a terror unto Egypt; every one to whom mention is made thereof shall be afraid, because of the purpose of Jehovah of hosts, which he purposeth against it" (Isa. 19:17). This same chapter concludes with one of the most familiar announcements relative to Egypt in all of Scripture, and it, also, is made to include Israel: "In that day shall Israel be the third with Egypt and with Assyria, a blessing in the midst of the earth; for that Jehovah of hosts hath blessed them, saying, Blessed be Egypt my people, and Assyria the work of my hands, and Israel mine inheritance" (19:24, 25).

Turning to the Book of Jeremiah, written just before and immediately after the downfall of Judah at the hands of Babylon, we come upon a comforting promise to the children of God in the prophecy regarding Egypt: "But fear not thou, O Jacob my servant, neither be dismayed, O Israel: for lo, I will save thee from afar, and thy seed from the land of their captivity; and Jacob shall return, and shall be quiet and at ease, and none shall make him afraid. Fear not thou, O Jacob my servant, saith Jehovah, for I am with thee: for I will make a full end of all the nations whither I have driven thee, but I will correct thee in measure, and will in no wise leave thee unpunished" (46:27, 28). The lengthy prophecy on Babylon is interrupted by this as-yet-unfulfilled promise to Israel: "And I will bring Israel again to his pasture, and he shall feed on Carmel and Bashan, and his soul shall be satisfied upon the hills of Ephraim and in Gilead. In those days, and in that time, saith Jehovah, the iniquity of Israel shall be sought for, and there shall be none; and the sins of Judah, and they shall not be found: for I will pardon them whom I leave as a remnant" (50:19, 20). In the same Babylonian prediction we read, "For Israel is not forsaken, nor Judah, of his God, of Jehovah, of hosts; though their land is full of guilt against the Holy One of Israel . . . The portion of Jacob is not like these; for he is the former of all things; and Israel is the tribe of his inheritance: Jehovah of hosts is his name" (51:5, 19).

References to Israel in Ezekiel's nation prophecies are few. At the conclusion of the brief statement on Zidon we have what might be called a summarizing preliminary announcement of all that will be unfolded later in Chapter 33-37: "Thus saith the Lord Jehovah: When I shall have gathered the house of Israel from the peoples among whom they are scattered, and shall be sanctified in them in the sight of the nations, then shall they dwell in their own land which I gave to my servant Jacob. And they shall dwell securely therein; yea, they shall build houses, and plant vineyards, and shall dwell securely, when I have executed judgments upon all those that do them despite round about them; and they shall know that I am Jehovah their God" (28:25, 26; see also 29:16).

A Word About the Prophecies Already Fulfilled

When one seriously attempts to ascertain what prophecies of this group of fourteen nations have been fulfilled, and what remain to be fulfilled, he is confronted with a number of problems. To begin with, as a modern commentator reminds us, a number of geographical references in these verses cannot be definitely identified. As an illustration, in Isaiah's prophecy regarding Moab, that country which lay east of the Jordan between the Arnon and Jabbok Rivers, there are twenty-two different geographical designations. In the indispensable *Westminster Atlas of the Bible,* one of these, Jazer, is not even listed in the index, and eight of them are marked as unknown or uncertain—Dimon, Horonaim, Lukith, Sibmah, Beer-elim, Eglaim, Jahaz, Kir. If we do not even know where some of these places are, it is not possible to look for evidence confirming the fulfillment of a particular prophecy about that area. Problems in history also loom here. Aside from these difficulties a large number of the predictions are related to historical personages who appeared on the stage of history during the sixth and fifth centuries b.c. and who fulfilled the foreannouncements of God of their activities and ultimate destruction, as revealed through these prophets. This is preeminently true of the remarkable character Nebuchadnezzar, whose position in the Word of God is far greater than generally comprehended by most readers of the Bible. We shall devote an entire chapter to him later.

Some Prophecies Concerning the Nations That Are Confessedly Unfulfilled

Various passages in these three collections of nation prophecies have conferredly not seen fulfillment—predictions relative to Babylon, to Moab, to Israel, to the end of this age, to certain conditions prevailing throughout the world. Thus, while it is true that Babylon did fall, as foretold in Isaiah 13 and 14, and the Babylonian empire did come to an end when the Medes captured the city in October, 539 B.C., during the reign of Darius, there are certain elements of this prophetic utterance which were not fulfilled then and which, if the prophecy is to be interpreted literally, await fulfillment. The physical phenomena described in 13:10, the stars of the heavens not giving light, and the sun and moon being darkened, were not observed at that time, as far as we know. The Lord did not then visit Jacob with rest (14:1-3), the Assyrian was not then trodden under foot in Palestine (14:25), and God's entire purpose was not then accomplished on *the whole earth* (14:26).

Unfulfilled prophecies are also evident in the almost totally ignored, though extensive prophecy against Moab in Jeremiah 48. Certainly the concluding prediction, "Yet will I bring back the captivity of Moab in the latter days, saith the Lord" (48:47) has not come to pass; likewise the words concerning Ammon, "But afterward I will bring back the captivity of the children of Ammon, saith Jehovah" (49:6). It is, however, in carefully examining the prophecies involving Israel that we are compelled to acknowledge that many of these utterances still await fulfilment, unless the prophecies are to be cancelled, as some suggest. A good example is in the opening verses of Isaiah 14: surely the condition described here has never been witnessed by mankind: "For Jehovah will have compassion on Jacob, and will yet choose Israel, and set them in their own land: and the sojourner shall join himself with them, and they shall cleave to the house of Jacob. And the peoples shall take them, and bring them to their place; and the house of Israel shall possess them in the land of

Jehovah for servants and for handmaids: and they shall take
them captive whose captives they were; and they shall rule
over their oppressors. And it shall come to pass in the day
that Jehovah shall give thee rest from thy sorrow, and from
thy trouble, and from the hard service wherein thou wast
made to serve."

At no time in history could one say that the promise of
Jeremiah 50:20 had been carried through, and not yet has
Israel enjoyed the blessings outlined in Ezekiel 28:25, 26:
"Thus saith the Lord Jehovah: When I shall have gathered
the house of Israel from the peoples among whom they are
scattered, and shall be sanctified in them in the sight of the
nations, then shall they dwell in their own land which I gave
to my servant Jacob. And they shall dwell securely therein;
yea, they shall build houses, and plant vineyards, and shall
dwell securely, when I have executed judgments upon all
those that do them despite round about them; and they shall
know that I am Jehovah their God."

In addition to these prophecies involving specific nations,
many of the *predictions embracing the entire world,* especially those of Isaiah, have not yet come to pass. When has it
been true, for instance, that "the whole earth is at rest, and is
quiet: they break forth into singing" (Isa. 14:7)? In the same
prophetic passage we are told that God will punish the world
for its wickedness (13:11); but since then the world has not experienced a universal chastening (see also 18:3 and 20:19, 20).
The concluding words of this prophecy could never be identified with any particular era of history: "And it shall come to
pass in that day, that Jehovah will punish the host of the
high ones on high, and the kings of the earth upon the earth"

(24:21). Finally, a constantly-repeated phrase in the writings of Ezekiel reveals that the nation Israel shall know that the Lord is God (28:24, 25; 29:6, 9; 30:8, 19, 26), of which more will be said in another chapter, since many of these predictions concern Egypt at the end of this age.

The Reappearance of Persons and Places of the Book of Genesis in These Nation Prophecies

I become increasingly amazed at the peculiar phenomenon, as it were, of the reappearance in Old Testament prophecies delivered during the eighth, seventh, and sixth centuries B.C. of the names of men who became founders of tribes and nations, and of actual geographical loci first mentioned in the Book of Genesis, in the record of patriarchal and pre-patriarchal times. How unique that the Garden of Eden should be so frequently mentioned in these prophecies which have to do with the nations of the Near East and the end of this age! We have in Ezekiel not only a reference to a garden of God (38:8, 9) but a number of occurrences of the actual name of the garden, Eden (27:13, 23, 28; 31:18). Practically all of the geographical terms used in relation to this Garden (Gen. 2:13, 14) reappear in one or the other of these three collections: Ethiopia (Isa. 18:1 ff. and 20:3; Ezek. 29:10 and 30:4); the Euphrates River (Jer. 46:2, 6); the great area even then called Assyria (Isa. 19:24 ff); and Cush, son of Ham, who strangely appears in this account of man's first habitation (Isa. 18:1). The only reference to Mount Ararat in the Old Testament after the account of the flood is here in the Jeremiah collection (Gen. 8:4; Jer. 51:27).

It is however in the reintroduction of a number of names

from the genealogical and ethnological data of Genesis 10 that we get our greatest surprise. The basic names of Javan, Tubal and Meshech found in the opening verses of this famous genealogical table become prominent both in the nation prophecies of Ezekiel (27:13, 19; 32:20, 26), and in the Gog and Magog passage (38:2, 3). In this same 27th chapter of Ezekiel we also find Togarmah, Tarshish, Cush, Sheba, Dedan, Arvad (v. 8), Ludim (v. 21). In the central prophecies of Isaiah there are pronouncements concerning Cush (Ch. 18), Mizraim (Ch. 29), Canaan (23:11), Dedan (21:13), the Jebusites (22:10, 21, and elsewhere), Elam (21:2; 22:6) and Ophir (13:12). I do not recall seeing in any work on Old Testament history a discussion of the reappearance of these ancient names for the peoples of the Near East in the prophetic literature of hundreds of years later, and the phenomenon warrants a far more minute examination than can be given it here.

The later use of the geographical nomenclature in later chapters of Genesis is more or less incidental (with the exception of Chapter 25). In Isaiah 15:5 there is a reference to Zoar, the town to which Lot wished to flee (Gen. 14:2, 8), and in Jeremiah 48:13, a reference to Bethel (Gen. 12:8; 13:3). The major prophecies relative to Damascus found in all three of our collections have to do with the city mentioned as early as Genesis 14:15 and 15:2; two other cities of the same chapter, Seir (Gen. 14:6 and 32:3) and Elam (14:1, 9) are introduced again by both Isaiah and Ezekiel (Isa. 21:2, 11; 22:6; and Ezek. 25:8), and the prediction regarding the Ammonites takes us back to Genesis 19:38.

From one verse, Genesis 25:13, three geographical terms

are used by Israel's later prophets—Kedar, Dedan, and Tema (Teman) (Ezek. 27:21; Isa. 21:16, 17, 14), and in 25:30 we have the first occurrence of the word Edom, concerning which both Jeremiah and Ezekiel uttered extended predictions. (The land of Teman is referred to also in Genesis 36:34, reappearing in Jeremiah 49:20.) Moab, found in all three of the prophets we are studying, appears originally in Genesis 36:35; Gilead, in Jeremiah 46:11, originally in Genesis 37:25; and Ephraim, in Isaiah 17:3, a name for Judah, originally in Genesis 14:52, and later.

The Basic Theme of Judgment

The basic theme dominating these three collections of nation prophecies is *judgment,* a judgment executed in terms of desolation and destruction, the result of the wrath and anger of God toward those people who have resisted His will, who boast of their might and wisdom, and who attempt to exalt themselves to heaven. Often throughout these chapters, particularly in relation to Babylon and in the prophecies of Isaiah, the idea of universality is presented. This judgment theme is vividly set forth at the very beginning of the series, in the 13th chapter of Isaiah:

The noise of a multitude in the mountains, as of a great people! the noise of a tummult of the kingdoms of the nations gathered together! Jehovah of hosts is mustering the host for the battle. They come from a far country, from the uttermost part of heaven, even Jehovah, and the weapons of his indignation, to destroy the whole land. Wail ye; for the day of Jehovah is at hand; as destruction from the Almighty shall it come. Therefore shall all hands be feeble, and every heart of man shall melt: and they shall be dismayed; pangs and sorrows shall take hold of them; they shall be in pain as a woman in travail: they shall look in amazement one at another; their faces shall be faces of flame. Behold, the day of Jehovah cometh, cruel, with wrath and fierce anger; to make the land a desolation, and to destroy the sinners thereof out of it. For the stars of heaven and the constellations thereof shall not give their light; the sun shall be darkened in its going forth, and the moon shall not cause its light to shine. And I will punish the world for their evil, and the wicked for their iniquity; and I will cause the arrogancy of the proud to cease, and will lay low the haughtiness of the terrible, (vv. 4-11).

Of the reasons given by the prophets for the judgment that is to fall upon these nations, fundamentally there is the spirit of pride. Even of Moab it is said, "We have heard of the pride of Moab, that he is very proud; even of his arrogancy, and his pride, and his wrath; his boastings are nought. Therefore . . ." (Isa. 16:6). Regarding Tyre, Ezekiel brings the accusation, "Because thy heart is lifted up, and thou hast said, I am a god, I sit in the seat of God, in the midst of the seas; yet thou art man, and not God, though thou didst set thy heart as the heart of God; therefore . . ." (Ezek. 28:2). It is against the city and nation of Babylon, and all that Babylon stands for, however, that the charge of pride is so frequently leveled: "She hath been proud against Jehovah, against the Holy One of Israel" (Jer. 50:29). "Behold, I am against thee, O thou proud one, saith the Lord, Jehovah of hosts" (Jer. 50:31). Her princes are called "boasters" (v. 36). This subject of pride among the nations of the earth leads the prophets eventually to speak of the supreme manifestation of pride, the person of Satan himself: "And thou saidst in thy heart, I will ascend into heaven, I will exalt my throne above the stars of God:

39

and I will sit upon the mount of congregation, in the uttermost parts of the north" (Isa. 14:13, 14). The nations addressed by the prophets are not only proud of their power, their military might, their conquests of other nations, but their wise men are particularly arrogant, chiefly those in the courts of Pharaoh, and in Babylon and Tyre (for Babylon see Jer. 50:35, 36 and 51:15, 57; for Tyre see Ezek. 28:4, 5, 7, 12, 17). "Jehovah of hosts hath purposed it, to stain the pride of all glory, to bring into contempt all the honorable of the earth" (Isa. 23:9).

Not alone because of their boastfulness in regard to military might, and wisdom in the things of this world, are the nations judged, but also because of their oppression of Israel, their destruction of the land of Canaan, and the spirit of derision which characterized their attitude toward the people of God. Though the Lord had used Babylon in punishing Judah, Babylon is to be judged for her bitter cruelty toward the children of God. "As Babylon hath caused the slain of Israel to fall, so at Babylon shall fall the slain of all the land" (Jer. 51:49). Even the comparatively small country of Moab comes under this condemnation. "For was not Israel a derision unto thee? was he found among thieves? for as often as thou speakest of him, thou waggest the head (Jer. 48:27). The charge is likewise made against Edom, relative to events occurring centuries before the prophet spoke: "For thus saith Jehovah, the God of Israel, unto me: Take this cup of the wine of wrath at my hand, and cause all the nations to whom I send thee, to drink it" (25:15); also against Tyre (Ezek. 26:2, 3).

The one word which appears with greatest frequency throughout these chapters to indicate the nature of these

40

judgments is *destruction* (and its verbal forms). In the Septuagint version of these nation prophecies, we find the word *apolluein*—generally translated *perish* or *destroy* in the New Testament—57 times: 15 times in the Isaiah collection, 14 times in the Jeremiah passages, and 28 times in the chapters from Ezekiel; in addition, *erēmoō* (*make desolate or destroy*) is used 19 times, making a total of 76 occurrences of the two words meaning *destruction* in these nation prophecies. *Apōleia* (destruction) and its verbal form *apollymi* are the words so continuously used in the New Testament for the condition of a lost soul, as in John 3:16. The noun form *apōleia* is often used for *hell*, being generally translated *perdition* in our versions, e.g., Revelation 17:8, 11.

The destructions referred to by the prophets in relation to the nations of the earth take the form of judgment. Here the Septuagint uses the familiar New Testament terms *krisis* (judgment), *krima* (judicial decision), or *ekdikein* (exact vengeance from). An important clue to the deeper meanings of these prophecies is here uncovered: while they frequently relate to nations that existed in the eighth, seventh and sixth centuries B.C., and suffered judgments in a historical period many centuries ago, they are also warnings of those greater and final judgments to which the Apocalypse so continually refers.

The Septuagint translates the word for *wrath* in Jeremiah 25:15, *hēmah*, with the familiar Greek New Testament words *orgē* (anger) 33 times and *thymos* (wrath) 79 times—the very words continually used in that final apocalyptic work, the Book of Revelation, where we find the kings of the earth, the princes, and the chief captains crying out to the

41

mountains, "Fall on us and hide us from the face of him that sitteth on the throne, and from the wrath of the Lamb: for the great day of their wrath is come, and who is able to stand?" (6:16, 17). Of the beast it is said, "He also shall drink of the wine of the wrath of God, which is prepared unmixed in the cup of his anger; and he shall be tormented with fire and brimstone in the presence of the holy angels, and in the presence of the Lamb" (14:10). This same chapter concludes with the terrible announcement that "the angel cast his sickle into the earth, and gathered the vintage of the earth, and cast it into the winepress, the great winepress of the wrath of God" (v. 19). The account of the judgments of the seven vials begins, "And I heard a great voice out of the temple, saying to the seven angels, Go ye, and pour out the seven bowls of the wrath of God into the earth" (Rev. 16:1). In the vivid portrayal of the battle of Armageddon we read, "And out of his mouth proceedeth a sharp sword, that with it he should smite the nations: and he shall rule them with a rod of iron: and he treadeth the winepress of the fierceness of the wrath of God, the Almighty" (Rev. 19:15).

Still another element of these nation prophecies renders them types and foretokens of the world-wide judgment to come, namely, the frequently-found expressions which might be summed up in the term *universality*, primarily in the prophecies of Isaiah, and in the 51st chapter of Jeremiah. In this 13th chapter of Isaiah we read: "The noise of a multitude in the mountains, as of a great people! the noise of a tumult of the kingdoms of the nations gathered together! Jehovah of hosts is mustering the host for the battle" (v. 4).

Even more is this evident in the subsequent clause, "He will punish *the world* for their evil" (v. 11). In his prediction regarding Babylon, Isaiah's thought embraces the whole world in such phrases as "the whole world is at rest" (14:7); "all the kings of the nations" (14:8); and "this is the purpose that is purposed upon *the whole earth,* and this is the hand that is stretched out on *all the nations*" (14:26). In the difficult prophecy regarding Ethiopia, Isaiah addresses "all ye inhabitants of the world and ye dwellers on the earth" (18:3), and at the conclusion of the series, he declares, "The earth mourneth and fadeth away, the world languisheth and fadeth away, the lofty people of the earth do languish."

The place of Babylon in history has attached to it the sense of universality: surely the entire ancient world is included in such characterizations as "the hammer of the whole earth" (Jer. 50:23) and "the destroying mountain which destroyeth all the earth" (51:25). In the Book of Revelation, individual nations almost drop out of sight, and all the judgments, with the exception of those upon Jerusalem and Babylon—whatever Babylon might here mean—involve all mankind. To those who overcome, our Lord says he will "give authority over the nations" (2:26). Before the opening of the seven-sealed book, the four and twenty elders in heaven declare of Christ, "Worthy art thou to take the book, and to open the seals thereof: for thou wast slain, and didst purchase unto God with thy blood men of every tribe, and tongue, and people, and nation" (Rev. 5:9). Of one of the angels of Revelation 14 we read, "And I saw another angel flying in mid heaven, having eternal good tidings to proclaim unto them that dwell on the earth, and

EGYPT IN BIBLICAL PROPHECY

unto every nation and tribe and tongue and people" (v. 6). The book sets forth this promise concerning the nations of the earth: "Who shall not fear, O Lord, and glorify thy name? for thou only art holy; for all the nations shall come and worship before thee; for thy righteous acts have been made manifest" (15:4). The waters upon which the harlot is said to be seated are identified as "peoples, and multitudes, and nations, and tongues" (17:15).

Notes

1. It is surprising to note how even the most conservative students of prophecy pass by these large sections of prophecies regarding the nations. In the *Scofield Reference Bible,* for the six chapters in Jeremiah there are only five lines of notes; for the eight chapters in Ezekiel, only one note, apart from that on the King of Tyre as a type of Satan; and for the last six chapters in the section in Isaiah, two notes totaling five lines. Some pages of Leviticus in the *Scofield Reference Bible* have as many notes for a single chapter as this Bible assigns for the 680 verses of these nation prophecies. In his generally commendable work, *What Do the Prophets Say?* (1918), Dr. Scofield ignores the subject of nation prophecies, and Dr. Biederwolf, in his *Millennial Bible* (1924) seems interested exclusively in those sections of these prophecies that relate to Israel's future. In his *Systematic Theology,* Dr. Lewis Sperry Chafer has no comment on the prophecies of Egypt in Isaiah, Jeremiah and Ezekiel, with the exception of Ezekiel 28:1-19, where all of his ten references relate to the teaching of this passage regarding Satan. Even such a writer as G. H. Pember in *The Great Prophecies of the Centuries Concerning Israel and the Gentiles* (rev. ed., 1895) discusses the Ammonites, Edomites, Kennites and the Moabites in relation to prophecy, to the last of which he devotes eight pages of text—but he has absolutely nothing to say about Egypt in prophecy. The same strange ignoring of these large areas of Old Testament prophetic writings is noted in the more exhaustive modern works on prophecy. For example, in the four thousand lines of index of subjects in *The Theocratic Kingdom of the Lord Jesus Christ,* Peters has not a single reference to Philistia, Moab, Damascus, Ethiopia, Arabia, Tyre, Sidon, or Ammonites, and the one reference to Egypt in these three massive volumes relates to Matthew 2:15. The same phenomenon is found in the most comprehensive survey of prophetic literature that has appeared in our language, *The Prophetic Faith of Our Fathers,* by Dr. LeRoy Froom. I would estimate that the elaborate indexes

44

to subjects in these four volumes contain not less than twenty thousand references, to hundreds of different subjects, but here again *not one of these nations is mentioned.* Of course there are scores of references to Babylon, but it is spiritual Babylon, for Froom does not believe that literal Babylon has any future at all. In the conservative and generally excellent work, ed. by Dr. W. J. Purkiser (Kansas City, 1955), *Exploring the Old Testament,* seventeen lines of text are all that are assigned for the interpretation of these twenty-four chapters—the Jeremiah and Ezekiel sections are dismissed each with a single line. J. N. Darby, in his voluminous writings, wholly passed up these large policies of the Old Testament. Is it not strange that while the prophetic literature of the nineteenth century is saturated with articles and books on the Ottoman Empire and Turkey in prophecy, though neither of these two words appears in the Old or New Testaments, a real confrontation of the geographical areas prophetically discussed in the Scriptures is rarely attempted.

I know of only four major works that attempt a discussion of these prophecies concerning the nations, the last of which was written eighty years ago. The first to exercise wide influence was *Dissertations on the Prophets* by Bishop Thomas Newton (1704-1782); originally published 1754-1758, it reached an 8th edition by 1789 and an 18th edition by 1834. A century later, Alexander Keith published his famous work, *Evidence of the Truth of the Christian Religion Derived from the Literal Fulfillment of Prophecy* (London, 1861). Of this work Thomas Chalmers once wrote, "It is recognized in our halls of theology as holding a high place in sacred literature, and it is found in almost every home and known as a household work throughout the land." In our own country, the outstanding volume was by a distinguished Presbyterian scholar, E. H. Gillett, *Ancient Cities and Empires: Their Prophetic Doom* (Philadelphia: Presbyterian Board of Publication, 1867). (Why is it that no large denominational publishing house has attempted to issue such a work in our generation?) The last volume, greatly indebted to the earlier volumes by Newton and Keith, is John Urquhart's *The Wonders of Prophecy,* which attained an amazing circulation during the decades immediately following its publication (3rd ed., rev., 1906). (In over eighty years of the International Sunday School lesson series these chapters have never been assigned for study.) Among volumes in which appear *brief* discussions of the fulfillment of these prophecies of gentile nations from an apologetic viewpoint, one might mention Floyd Hamilton: *The Basis of Christian Faith,* 3rd ed., New York. 1946 pp. 298-317.

2. In my opinion, one of the most regrettable paragraphs ever written by the brilliant, liberal Old Testament scholar George Adam Smith introduces his discussion of these prophecies of the nations in the Book of Isaiah. "With the exhilaration of one who traverses plain roads and beholds vast pros-

pects, he (the conscientious reader of the Bible) has passed through the opening chapters of the book as far as the end of the twelfth . . . but here he loses himself among a series of prophecies obscure in themselves and without obvious relation to one another . . . The names and allusions are foreign, some of them the names of tribes long since extinct, and of places which are no more possible to identify. It is a very jungle of prophecy in which without much gospel or geographical light we have to grope our way, thankful for an occasional gleam of the picturesque, a sandstorm in the desert, the forsaken ruins of Babylon haunted by wild beasts, etc." (*Book of Isaiah.* 1903. Vol. I, pp. 271-272).

3. Delitzsch reminds us that in ancient times "ten was regarded as the number of completeness and the signature of the finished whole." (F. Delitzsch: *Commentary on Genesis,* Vol. I, p. 59). It is not without significance that in the most detailed of the divine announcements to Abraham specifying the boundaries of the promised land, there are exactly ten tribes, or nations, identified as then occupying the land that would someday be possessed by Israel; see Genesis 15:19.

3

EGYPT IN THE HISTORY
OF THE HEBREW PEOPLE

Egypt, though actually embracing only the northeast corner of the African continent, has been for five thousand years the most important geographical area of that immense portion of this earth's surface. It is here that Asia and Africa meet. From this soil arose the greatest civilization of the ancient world up to the time of the flowering of Greek civilization. Egypt represented the only mighty empire that would ever confront the kingdoms of the Mesopotamian world, until the time of the Persians. Strictly speaking, Egypt is the land of the Nile, though the Nile extends far beyond Egypt. From its source in Lake Victoria Nynaza to the Mediterranean is a distance of 3,760 miles, though because of its winding, twisting course, the Nile is 4,000 miles in length. At Khartum, above the Sixth Cataract, the Blue Nile and the White Nile join, and flow on to enrich the narrow valley from which, for millennia, millions of people have been fed.

In ancient times, Egypt proper extended from the First Cataract to the Mediterranean, and was generally divided into two unequal areas, the larger and southern part being called Upper Egypt, and the northern area, around the Delta, being designated as Lower Egypt. From time to time these kingdoms had separate rulers, but in the eras of Egypt's greatest strength, in the Old Kingdom, Middle Kingdom, and New Kingdom, they were united under one reigning pharaoh. From the First Cataract south is the country known as Cush in the Old Testament, and as Ethiopia in modern times. The Nile Valley proper, which made possible the famous Egyptian civilization, is 550 miles in length, and about 12 miles wide; thus, the cultivatable area of the empire was not quite 13,000 square miles. It was the seasonal rise of the Nile, fed by the snows of the Lake Victoria region, from June through October—often reaching a height of forty feet at Assuan and twenty-five feet at Cairo—which made possible the rich agricultural life of Egypt.

"No people of the earth," wrote Delitzsch, "was so closely interwoven with the history of the kingdom of God from the patriarchal time as Egypt." [1]

The first reference to Egypt in our Bible would not be immediately detected by a casual reader. The genealogical table of Genesis 10 lists four sons of Ham: *Cush,* who settled in Ethiopia; *Put,* who gave the name to the country of Punt, and who settled in the region along the south end of the Red Sea; *Canaan,* who settled along the eastern shore of the Mediterranean; and *Mizraim* (vv. 6, 13; I Chron. 1:8, 11). *Mizraim* is a Hebrew form of the early Canaanitic name for Egypt, *Misri,* meaning district region. The name has come down to us in modern times, for the Arabic name for Egypt is *Misr.* The Egyptians themselves call the land *Kemet,* meaning "the black land," a name no doubt derived from the rich, black soil of the Nile Valley. Among the Greeks, even in the days of Homer, this part of the Near East was known as *Aegyptos,*

48

and philologists have developed arguments to show that the word may be derived from one of the capitals of Egypt, Memphis. In more recent times, the first letter and the last two letters have been dropped, giving us the designation Egypt. The early Egyptians, then, according to this ancient genealogical record, were descendants of Ham, a fact poetically set forth by the Psalmist, when he speaks of Egypt as "the land of Ham" (105:23).[2]

The First Prophecy Concerning Egypt in the Bible

The first Biblical *prophecy* about Egypt actually does not contain the word *Egypt,* or any synonym for it, but no one doubts but that the passage, whatever else its problems might be, does refer, at least in part, to the sojourn of the descendants of Abraham, particularly the house of Jacob, in this land immediately south of the territory which had been promised to them. The chapter in which this prophetic utterance occurs, Genesis 15, is outstanding for at least six different reasons. First we have here that great declaration which forms a cornerstone in the Pauline doctrine of justification by faith: Abraham "believed in the Lord and He counted it to him for righteousness" (vs. 16; quoted in Romans 4:3). Secondly, the chapter contains the initial delineation of the boundaries of the kingdom of Israel to be established nearly a millennium later: "In that day Jehovah made a convenant with Abram, saying, Unto thy seed have I given this land, from the river of Egypt unto the great river, the river Euphrates" (v. 18). While a few commentators, such as Hengstenberg and Kurtz, insist that this "river of Egypt" is the Nile, it is generally taken to be the Wady el-Arish, which formed the northern boundary of Egypt and the southern boundary of Palestine. Thirdly, here is the first enumeration of the ten nations which, surrounding Israel at one time or another, will be referred to scores of times in the subsequent historical records of the Israelites. Most cetainly in this chapter geographical data is assigned a prominent place. Fourthly, these verses contain the first of many declarations that although Abraham did not up to this time have an heir, the children of Israel to proceed from his loins would some day be as numerous as the stars of heaven. Fifthly, as has often been said by Old Testament commentators, the burning lamp that passed before Abraham (v. 17) represents the first appearance of the Shekinah glory of the Lord. Finally, this 15th chapter of Genesis embraces the first chronological prophecy found in the Scriptures, and the chronological data of Biblical prophecy has always been considered of the greatest importance, in spite of the fact that many such tables have been constructed which were neither Biblical nor sensible. (I am assuming here that the 120 years of Genesis 6:3, while probably indicating the length of time that Noah would live until the flood, could not be specifically called a chronological prophecy.)

In the midst of this significant passage, we have the fourth promise of God to Abraham concerning his seed (the three preceding references are 12:1-3; 13:14-17; 15:4-7). The text reads as follows: "And he said unto Abram, Know of a surety that thy seed shall be sojourners in a land that is not theirs, and shall serve them; and they shall afflict them four hundred years; and also that nation, whom they shall serve, will I judge: and afterward shall they come out with great substance" (vv. 13, 14). To begin with, this prophecy concerns the *seed* of Abraham, and contains a definite time period, four hundred years, during which the children of Abraham "shall be sojourners in a land that is not theirs," a sojourn which will terminate in servitude and affliction, followed by deliverance. One question must be faced immediately—what period is covered by these four hundred years? There are two major interpretations, and it makes considerable difference which one is adopted. The four hundred years certainly conclude with a deliverance from affliction; therefore, all agree that the end of this prophetic period must be the exodus from Egypt. But when did the four hundred years *begin?* Did the sojourn of the children of Israel in Egypt last four centuries; or does that period include some of the time spent sojourning in Palestine? I am assuming the latter, and will argue for it, without attempting to propose anything new or irrevocable in regard to this disputed subject. I have always agreed with those who have placed the time of the Exodus at about 1440 B.C., as against 1280 B.C. set forth by many. If the Exodus took place in 1440 or even 1400 B.C., there is no possibility of reckoning four hundred years for an Egyptian bondage, for the descendants of Abraham were not even in Egypt in 1840 B.C.

St. Paul's statement in the Epistle to the Galatians sheds some light on this question: "Now this I say: A covenant confirmed beforehand by God, the law, which came four hundred and thirty years after, doth not disannul, so as to make the promise of none effect" (3:17). Here the Apostle speaks of the covenant of Sinai being confirmed 430 years after the covenant made with Abraham. This, of course, refers to a period when Abraham was still in Palestine, for there was no covenant made with Abraham on either of his two unfortunate and brief visits to Egypt, and at the time Jacob and his descendants went down into that land as a body, Abraham was dead. In the stirring address which led to his martyrdom, St. Stephen alludes to this very passage in Genesis: "And God spake on this wise, that his seed should sojourn in a strange land, and that they should bring them into bondage, and treat them ill, four hundred years. And the nation to which they shall be in bondage will I judge, said God: and after that shall they come forth, and serve me in this place" (Acts 7:6, 7). It would seem clear from these words of God to Abraham that the four-hundred-year period could not begin until there was a seed to be a stranger in some land, and the earliest date at which that could be placed would be the year of Isaac's birth, or, as some prefer, of the weaning of Isaac, an event which had not taken place when this prophecy was given to Abraham (Gen 21:1-8). The passage will then mean that this period of four centuries embraces the period of time extending from the birth of Isaac, which occurred in Palestine, down to the Exodus. The last part of this prediction, relating to *servitude and affliction,* is not necessarily to be thought of as continuing for four hundred years. There will be four hundred years of sojourning in a strange land, Palestine and Egypt, the latter of which will witness a time of increasing severity.

This interpretation, significantly, is supported by the Septuagint text of Exodus 12:40, 41, "And the sojourning of the children of Israel while they sojourned in the land of Egypt and the land of Canaan was four hundred and thirty years." The Samaritan text reads: "And the sojourning of the sons of Israel and of their fathers who sojourned in the land of Kenaan and in the land of Mizraim was four hundred and thirty years." Josephus himself on one occasion accepted such an interpretation, though elsewhere he contradicts this: "They left Egypt in the month Xanthicus, on the fifteenth day of the lunar month: four hundred and thirty years after our forefather Abraham came into Canaan, but two hundred and fifteen years only after Jacob removed into Egypt." Personally, I take the position that the original pronouncement involves the period from the birth or weaning of Abraham's *seed* in Canaan down to the time of the Exodus, and that, therefore, the text should be read as follows: "Thy seed shall be sojourners in a land that is not theirs four hundred years," with only one clause, "and shall serve them and they shall afflict them" referring to the latter part of that sojourn which was to be in that nation "whom they shall serve." More than once the Bible speaks of the patriarchs as *sojourning* in the land of Palestine (Gen. 21:23, 34; 36:7; 37:1; Ex. 6:4; Heb. 11:9). The words of Murphy here are well worth quoting: "Now Isaac was born when Abraham was a hundred years old, and therefore thirty years after he was called. The Exodus, therefore, was four hundred years after the birth of Isaac. But Isaac was sixty years old when Jacob was born, and Jacob was one hundred and thirty years old when he came into Egypt (Gen. 25:26; 47:9). Hence the sojourn in Egypt lasted 210 (400 − (60 + 130)) years. Again, from Ex. 6:16-20, we learn that Moses was the grandson of Levi by the mother's side, and the great-grandson by the father's side. As Moses was

53

EGYPT IN BIBLICAL PROPHECY

eighty at the Exodus, if Jokebed was born when Levi was one hundred years old, and therefore, sixty-six years after the immigration, she must have been sixty-four at the birth of Moses (66 + 64 + 80 = 210). It is manifest that we cannot add two hundred and twenty years to this period without presuming with some expositors that several generations are omitted. The writer, however, plainly gives us all the links of the genealogical chain, and not the slightest hint of any omission. He is precise not only in names, but in relationships and other circumstances. We have no more right to insert new and unknown links here than in the genealogies before and after Noah. And lastly, the Apostle Paul (Gal. 3:17) affirms that the law was four hundred and thirty years after the covenant with Abraham. Any one of these arguments is sufficient to confirm what we hold to be the fair interpretation of the text." [3]

The Hebrew word here translated "stranger," *ger,* is from the same root as the Hebrew word frequently rendered "sojourn," *gur,* a term often used of Abraham's sojourning in various areas of Palestine, as in 20:1; 21:23, 24, as well as of the brief period that he sojourned in Egypt, recorded in Genesis 12:10. Actually, at the time that Abraham discussed with the sons of Heth the matter of a burying place at Machpelah, he himself confessed, "I am a stranger and a sojourner with you: give me a possession of a burying-place with you" (Gen. 23:4). Is this not an excellent illustration of the fact that this land did not legally belong to Abraham at that time, though it was his through a covenant promise, and he was a stranger in a land not his own, as were also his immediate descendants?

Two subsequent factors are involved in this prophecy, namely, the prediction of judgment upon Egypt, which refers to the ten plagues, and the promise that the children of Israel would come out of the land "with great substance." Leupold directs attention to the interesting fact that the word here translated "substance," *rekhush,* means "moveable possessions," for Israel was not to be rich in real estate, but in *rekhus.* He also asks a question which I have not seen in any other commentary, "Why is Egypt not specifically named here?" and suggests that perhaps it was "lest Abraham's descendants conceive an undue prejudice against this land." [4]

The basic factor in this first announcement of Israel's relationship with Egypt will dominate the scores of future references to this same relationship from the time of the exodus to the prophecy of the king of the south, who will invade the holy land at the end of the age: at the hands of Egypt and while in Egypt, Israel will suffer. Egypt stands for the world, and has nothing to commend it as an abiding place for the children of God. To this statement there is one exception—for a short while it did shelter the holy family when Herod the Great, in his final spasm of jealousy and cruelty, sought the young child to destroy him—of which we will have more to say in a later chapter.

Abraham's Visit to Egypt

In the *history* of the chosen people, the first contact with Egypt occurred early in the life of Abraham (Gen. 12:1—13:1), when the father of the faithful was compelled—at least so he thought—to seek relief from the famine conditions of southern Canaan by going down into Egypt, until the famine should terminate. It was here in Egypt that Abraham deliberately lied regarding his relationship to Sarah, for which he was rebuked by Pharaoh, who in this case was acting according to a higher ethic than was Abraham himself. The time of Abraham's visit to Egypt has been placed generally at about 1935 B.C., during what has been termed Egypt's Middle Kingdom. Egypt had possessed for many centuries before this a notable culture, and a continuity of kings; in fact, the period of 3000 B.C. has been called "the first great epoch of international commerce." There appeared at this time "an advanced technique and style in the erection of recessed brick buildings, evidently based upon knowledge of architectural achievements in Mesopotamia." [5] It was during the IVth Dynasty of what has been termed the Old Kingdom, about 2700 B.C., that the greatest of all the pyramids was erected by Khufu at Gizeh, outside the city of Cairo. Resting upon a base of thirteen acres, 2,300,000 blocks of yellow limestone, each averaging two and one-half tons in weight, were piled up in pyramidal form to a height of 481 feet, the stone work being so exquisitely accurate that some of the huge blocks are separated by no more than one ten-thousandth of an inch! Breasted has called this, "the earliest and most impressive witness surviving from the ancient world to the final emergence of organized society from prehistoric chaos and local conflict, thus coming for the first time completely under the power of a far-reaching and comprehensive civilization effected by one controlling mind." [6] Khafre, who succeeded Khufu on the throne of Egypt, built the second pyramid at Gizeh—it is he whose face is carved on the head of the Sphinx, east of the pyramid which he had erected. During the Fifth and Sixth Dynasties of the Old Kingdom, many inscriptions of what have been called the Pyramid Texts were made on the inner passages and rooms of these monumental erections. Literature began to flourish and imposing cities, such as Memphis and Thebes, arose. There were large estates in Egypt at the time of Abraham's first visit. Jewelry of unsurpassed beauty adorned the women of Pharaoh's court, and then, as now, a vast chasm separated the rich from the poor.

The first occurrence of the word Egypt in the Scriptures assigns to that country the characteristics that will appear again and again in its subsequent relationship to Israel. Egypt represents the world and the pull of the world, a magnetism from which Israel was never fully loosened. "This country bordering on the land of promise held out the temptation of riches, of worldly culture and wisdom, thus forming a type of the kingdoms of this world in their power and glory. Egypt was to the chosen race, as it were, like the tree of the knowledge of good and evil. The same wants brought Abraham and Israel to Egypt, the same danger threatens them, and the same mighty arm delivers and brings them power." [7] Israel is not in the wilderness long before she expresses regret at leaving Egypt, calling up the days when "we sat by the flesh-pots, when we did eat bread to the full" (Ex. 16:3). As there was a judgment upon this house of Pharaoh now, and a much more pronounced series of judgments upon the whole nation subsequently, so Egypt also symbolically represents divine judgment. "And Jehovah will take away from thee all sickness; and none of the evil diseases of Egypt, which thou knowest, will he put upon thee, but will lay them upon all them that hate thee" (Deut. 7:15; see also 28:16).

Later References to Egypt in Patriarchal History

Between the account of the return of Abraham from Egypt and the sale of Joseph to merchants enroute to Egypt, there are three statements bearing upon the relationship of Israel to this ancient empire, two of which concern marriage. When Sarah, Abraham's wife, had come to the conclusion that she was to remain barren, we are told, in the well-known, tragic narrative of Genesis 16, that she "took Hagar the Egyptian, her handmaid, after Abram had dwelt ten years in the land of Canaan, and gave her to Abram her husband to be his wife" (v. 3). In the later narratives, she is invariably called "Hagar the Egyptian" (21:9; 25:12). From Hagar was born Ishmael, and from Ishmael descended all those Arabian tribes which have been a thorn in the flesh to modern Israel since the establishment of that nation in Palestine. He himself being one-half Egyptian, Ishmael, at the instigation of his mother "took him a wife out of the land of Egypt," the children of which relationship would be three-fourths Egyptian (for Ishmael's descendants, see Gen. 25:12-18).

When a second famine struck lower Palestine and Abraham was contemplating another journey into Egypt, in spite of the unfortunate experiences of the first journey, he had a direct command from God forbidding him to go: "Go not down into Egypt; dwell in the land which I shall tell thee of: sojourn in this land, and I will be with thee, and will bless thee" (Gen. 26:2, 3).

EGYPT IN BIBLICAL PROPHECY

Joseph "Lord of All Egypt"

The next historic action on the part of the chosen people in relation to Egypt involved the entire family of Jacob, from which ultimately came the twelve tribes of Israel. Abraham went down into Egypt of his own free will, to escape the famine, but Joseph, next to the youngest son of the patriarch Jacob, was brought into Egypt as a slave, bought by the Midianites from his envious brothers and sold by them to Potiphar, the captain of Pharaoh's guard. When for the third time in the patriarchal age, famine strikes southern Palestine, Jacob is forced to send his sons into Egypt to buy wheat, an errand which ultimately brings them into the presence of the brother whom they had sold, now the prime minister of this powerful country in a time of crisis ("the lord of all Egypt," Gen. 45:9). It would be out of place here to enter into the details of the familiar and moving story of Joseph and his brethren. Vested with great authority, wealthy, and in favor with the ruling Pharaoh, Joseph persuades his brothers to bring their father Jacob and all the family, numbering seventy souls, down into Egypt to dwell (Gen. 46; Deut. 26:5; Josh. 24:4; Ps. 105:23; Acts 7:12-17). It may well have been, though it is not so indicated in the text, that conditions in Canaan made Jacob glad to leave that land at a time when its grossness stamped it as one of the most sensualistic cultures of the ancient world. The family of Jacob settled in that part of Egypt nearest to Palestine, called in the Bible the land of *Goshen,* or the land of Rameses (Gen. 47:11; 46:26). The valley of Goshen extended for forty miles, from Timsah on the east to the Nile River on the west, with the two great cities of Pithom and Succoth on the southern edge, and the famous temple city of On in the southwest. This was an exceedingly fertile area of the African coast, but a region somewhat avoided by the Egyptians themselves because of its distance from the irrigation system of their land. This area later became known as the Wadi-Tumilat, of which we shall have more to say later.

The Egyptian Oppression

The descendants of Jacob lived, flourished and multiplied in a land not their own until the time came that the pharaohs, who had forgotten all that Joseph had done for that nation in a time of need, began to enslave these hated foreigners, making them toil in the brick kilns of the hot African climate and labor under taskmasters in the erection of some of the structures which were Egypt's glory. Israel never forgot what she suffered in that land: "We were Pharaoh's bondmen," is the cry often heard in later Pentateuchal literature, with the added note of remembrance, "strangers in the land of Egypt." God himself declared to Moses, "I have seen the affliction of my people that are in Egypt, and have heard their cry by reason of their taskmasters; for I know their sorrows" (Ex. 3:7). Later Old Testament records certainly imply that during the oppression, for the most part under Thotmes III of the XVIIIth Dynasty (-1450 B.C.).

In his final charge to Israel (Josh. 24:14) after their return to Canaan, Joshua exhorted them to put away the gods which their fathers had served not only in Mesopotamia before the call of Abraham, but also in Egypt, a practice easily accounted for when one realizes that these Israelites had no written

Scriptures in their hands, no tabernacle in their midst, and, for the most part, no priesthood, while day by day, year by year, they worked at the construction of massive temples and images of the world-famous Egyptian gods and goddesses. But through a divine overruling, a Hebrew is being prepared, in Egypt, to lead his people out of that land into the land which God promised Abraham, Isaac and Jacob would be theirs, forever. Brought up in the court of Pharaoh, Moses moved in the highest official circles for forty years.

As the late Professor Peet has said, while it is true that "Egyptian records contain no reference to the sojourn, the fact does not in the least affect the problem; for, in the first place, our Egyptian records are far from complete, in the second, the sojourn may well have been on so small a scale that the Egyptians never thought it worthy of recording, and in the third place, the Delta, which was the scene of the events, is still almost a closed book to us in early times, at least nine-tenths of our records coming from and referring to Upper Egypt." [8]

It is of course not necessary in a work on Egypt in prophecy to discuss the many thorny problems of the route of the exodus, but one aspect of the event must be considered here, namely, the place at which Israel actually passed out of Egypt into Asia, for it is very close to the area of which Israel's later prophets will be speaking in connection with events to take place at the end of this age. For over two thousand years the name of this place has been wrongly interpreted. We read that "God led the people about by the way of the wilderness by the Red Sea: and the children of Israel went up armed out of the land of Egypt" (Ex. 13:18;

15:4, 22). All the principal English versions down to the twentieth century, and even the Revised Standard Version, render the geographical term here "the Red Sea." Jerome did the same, *mare Rubrum.* The Septuagint reads, "ten eruthran thalassan." The Hebrew word here for reed is *sūph* = "sea of sedge or reed" which, by the Greek translators, Jerome, and our English translators, was invariably but incorrectly made to mean the *Red* Sea. Actually sūph is used of reeds or rushes growing along the Nile River, as in Ex. 2:3; Isa. 19:6; Jonah 2:6. As Driver has well said, "Reeds or rushes do not grow in the salt water of the Red Sea, though clumps of them have been found on spots south of Suez, where fresh water mixes with the salt; but they abound in Lake Timsah. If it is true that there was once a shallow extension of the Gulf of Suez reaching to Lake Timsah, it is possible that it was called by the Hebrews, from these growths, the 'Sea of reeds'; and that afterwards the name was extended to the 'Red Sea' generally." [9] Furthermore, as Wright and Filson remind us, "If the Red Sea were meant, then the Hebrews would have been forced to cross a long expanse of desert in order to get to it. On the contrary, however, the verses imply that the Reed Sea was not far from Succoth. Since the Suez Canal was dug, the topography of this region has changed somewhat and at least one lake, Lake Baalah, has disappeared. In the days of the Old Testament, the region around Lake Timsah between Lake Baalah and the Bitter Lakes may well have been more marshy than it is at present." [10] If, then, the crossing was at Lake Timsah, the distance from Succoth was less than twenty miles. As soon as they reached the eastern bank of this body of water, they apparently traveled straight down along the shores of the Bitter Lakes, and then near the shores of the Gulf of Suez, before turning inward toward the Wilderness of Sin, three-fourths of the way down the Sinaitic Peninsula. Only Moffatt, of all the modern translators, interprets this geographical identification as "the Reed Sea."

Israel never forgot her terrible experiences during the Egyptian oppression. Moses frequently reminded them that they had been strangers in the land of Egypt (Exodus 22:21; 23:9; Lev. 19:34; Deut. 10:19). In the Book of Deuteronomy there is the constant reminder, "We were Pharaoh's bondmen" (6:21; 7:8; 15:15; 16:12; 24:18, 22).

While in the land, Israel must have lived in gross sin: centuries later, Ezekiel brought this indictment against the same nation Israel, now thinking she might improve her situation by going down into Egypt: "And they played the harlot in Egypt; they played the harlot in their youth; there were their breasts pressed, and there was handled the bosom of their virginity" (Ezek. 23:3; see also 23:8, 19, 27). One bright aspect of this sojourn was in the thorough preparation for his task received by Moses, enabling St. Stephen to say that he was "learned in all the wisdom of the Egyptians" (Acts 7:22).

In a work of this kind, there is no need for a detailed study of the plagues sent of God upon Egypt. These judgments, above all other acts of God in the Old Testament, are referred to as "signs and wonders" (see Deut. 7:22; 11:3; 34:11; I Sam. 4:8; Neh. 9:10; Ps. 105:27, etc.; Jer. 32:20, 21). Murphy has well said in speaking of these miracles being directed against the deities of Egypt, "Now for the first time since the dispersion of mankind, the opposition between the children of God and the children of disobedience is coming out into broad daylight. Egypt has become the avowed antagonist of God. It is the controversy between light and darkness in which the God of heaven and earth manifests His presence and power on behalf of His people and against the defiant nation. This nation is for the time being the representative of all heathendom, which is the kingdom of the prince of darkness, and the battle now fought is the model and type of all future warfare between the seed of the woman and the seed of the serpent." [11]

No one in contemporary literature has more vividly described the display of omnipotent power at that time than Professor Phythian-Adams. "No god in heaven or earth had ever stretched out his hand to work such marvels as these. But that was not all. To turn the greatest river in the world to blood and cover the mightiest kingdom on earth with darkness; to call back the heaving masses of the sea and release them in one terrific avalanche upon the enemy; to set up in the sky His towering beacon of cloud and flame; to descend upon His Holy Mountain in raging torrents of fire and lift up to His Chosen Leader the awful thunder of His Voice;—it was not merely that no god had done these things, it was much more that no god hitherto believed in and worshipped by Israel or its neighbours had been conceived of as possessing either the power or the will to do them. From that day, in one small corner of the earth the very word God received, however, unconsciously, a new meaning; for from that day out of the womb of awe and wonder and gratitude true Monotheism was destined to be born." [12]

The Exodus

The Exodus from Egypt forms one of the supreme events in God's redemptive program for His people: emancipating them from this wretched bondage, enabling them to conquer and occupy the only piece of land which He has ever, and forever, assigned to any one nation on this earth, His land, Immanuel's land, the land of promise. This is not the place to examine the various aspects of the Exodus, except to point out the fact that no historical event in all the Old Testament is so constantly referred to as this time of divine deliverance, through faith in shed blood and by the exercise of God's omnipotence. There are over ninety different references in Old Testament literature to God's bringing Israel out of this land, right down to the minor prophets (Amos 3:10; Micah 6:4; Haggai 2:5), and even in the New Testament (Heb. 8:9, Jude 8). Indeed, one of the most beautiful utterances in all the Old Testament relates to this event and is used by Matthew as a prophecy of another visit to, and exodus from Egypt, that of our Lord as a babe with the holy family: "When Israel was a child then I loved him, and called my son out of Egypt" (Hosea 11:1; Matt. 2:15).

There has been for many decades now a radical difference of opinion among Biblical scholars as to the exact date of this event. Those who hold to a late date place it about 1290 B.C., while others, supporting an earlier date, locate it about 1446 B.C. As previously remarked, I am assuming the earlier date here without presenting the argument for it, which can be found in many books on Biblical history and commentaries on the Book of Exodus.[13]

The deeper aspects of this move from Africa into Asia are vividly set forth by Dean Stanley in his well-known *History of the Jewish Church,* and I take the liberty of quoting his comment in full: "They had passed in that night from Africa to Asia; they have crossed one of the great boundaries which divide the quarters of the world; a thought always thrilling, how much more when we reflect on what a transition it involved to them.

"Further, this change of local situation was at once a change of moral condition. From slaves they had become free; from an oppressed tribe they had become an independent nation. It is their deliverance from slavery. It is the earliest recorded instance of a great national emancipation. In later times religion has been so often and so exclusively associated with ideas of order, of obedience, of submission to authority, that it is well to be occasionally reminded that it has had other aspects also. This, the first epoch of our religious history, is, in its original historical significance, the sanctification, the glorification of national independence and freedom. Whatever else was to succeed to it, this was the first stage of the progress of the Chosen People. And when in the Christian Scriptures and in the Christian Church we find the passage of the Red Sea taken as the likeness of the moral deliverance from sin and death—when we read in the Apocalypse of the vision of those who stand victorious on the shores of 'the glassy sea, mingled with fire, having the harps of God, and singing the song of Moses the servant of God, and the song of the Lamb,'—these are so many sacred testimonies to the importance, to the sanctity of freedom, to the wrong and the misery of injustice, oppression, and tyranny. The word 'Redemption,' which has now a sense far holier and higher, first entered into the circle of religious ideas at the time when God 'redeemed His people from the house of bondage.'

"But another and still more abiding impression was that this deliverance—the first and greatest in their history—was effected, not by their own power, but by the power of God. There are moments in the life both of men and of nations, both of the world and of the Church, when vast blessings are gained, vast dangers averted, through their own exertions —by the sword of the conqueror, by the genius of the statesman, by the holiness of the saint. Such, in Jewish history, was the conquest of Palestine by Joshua, the deliverances wrought by Gideon, by Samson, and by David. Such, in Christian history, were the revolutions effected by Clovis, by Charlemagne, by Alfred, by Joan of Arc, and by Luther. But there are moments of still higher interest, of still more solemn feeling, when deliverence is brought about not by any human energy, but by causes beyond our own control. Such, in Christian history, are the raising of the siege of Leyden, and the overthrow of the Armada; and such, above all, was the Passage of the Red Sea." [14] From the time of this destruction of the Egyptian host, to the reign of Solomon, a period of over four hundred years, no historical contact of Israel with Egypt is recorded in the Old Testament.

EGYPT IN BIBLICAL PROPHECY

Egypt in Israel's Kingdom Age

Not long after Solomon began his reign (965-926 B.C.), he "made affinity with Pharaoh king of Egypt, and took Pharaoh's daughter, and brought her into the city of David, until he had made an end of building his own house, and the house of Jehovah, and the wall of Jerusalem round about" (Kings 3:1). The pharaoh contemporary with Solomon was Sheshonk I (945-924 B.C.) first king of the XXIInd Dynasty. Solomon, with his great love for display, for wealth, and for all that went with oriental splendour, was responsible for a heavy traffic between Israel and Egypt in things that would magnify his royal glory. "And the horses which Solomon had were brought out of Egypt; and the king's merchants received them in droves, each drove at a price. And a chariot came up and went out of Egypt for six hundred shekels of silver, and a horse for a hundred and fifty; and so for all the kings of the Hittites, and for the kings of Syria, did they bring them out by their means" (I Kings 10:28, 29). The Chronicler tells us that during his reign Solomon "ruled over all the kings from the River (that is, the Euphrates) even unto the land of the Philistines, and to the border of Egypt" (II Chron. 9:26).

During this period of Israel's greatest glory, when her fame was known from the Euphrates to the Nile, Egypt also served as a place of refuge for Jeroboam, the son of Nebat, who was sought by Solomon upon the occasion of the rebellion which he, Jeroboam, had initiated in an attempt to seize the throne; here he remained until the death of Solomon (I Kings 11:40; 12:2; II Chron. 10:2). Shishak was ruler in

Egypt at this time. Another enemy of Israel's ruling family, Hadad, prince of Edom, also found protection from Solomon's wrath in this southern empire, and while there, married the sister of Tahpenes the queen (985 B.C.). Petrie says that he must have been in Egypt from twenty to thirty years.

For over five hundred years following the overwhelming defeat of the pursuing Egyptian host by a divine miracle at Pihahiroth, the Israelites had not been troubled by any invading army from Egypt, nor even the threat of such. However, immediately upon the division of the kingdom, the larger and more powerful section being separated from Judah under Jeroboam, the Egyptian king Shishak, aware of Judah's weakness, marched into the southern part of Palestine about the year 921 B.C. and destroyed numerous cities, not only in Judah but in Israel and Edom as well (I Kings 14:25-28).

There is scarcely a more pitiful statement in the whole of Judah's recorded history, from her entrance into Palestine to the time of Nebuchadnezzar's invasion, than that which depicts the spoiling of Solomon's Temple by Shishak, who in the Egyptian records is called Sheshonk I, and all this within five years of Solomon's death: "And he took away the treasures of the house of Jehovah, and the treasures of the king's house; he even took away all: and he took away all the shields of gold which Solomon had made. And king Rehoboam made in their stead shields of brass, and committed them to the hands of the captains of the guard, who kept the door of the king's house" (I Kings 14:26, 27).

After the invasion of Shishak, Egypt is not mentioned again in the Biblical record until we come to the difficult question of the invasion of Judah, in the reign of Asa, by Zerah the Ethiopian (II Chron. 14:9-15) who led an army of 100,000 foot soldiers and 300 chariots into the tiny kingdom of Judah, but was defeated by king Asa at Mareshah, in the south, known during the Greek period as Marissa. This probably occurred during the reign of Osorkon I, successor to Shishak.

Toward the end of the eighth century b.c., Assyria was threatening the Northern Kingdom in such an ominous manner that king Hoshea (730-722 b.c.) sent an embassy to So, generally identified with Sib'e the tartan of Egypt, to request assistance in meeting what he thought was an impending invasion by the Assyrian power (II Kings 17:4-7). Apparently the assistance was not forthcoming, and Hoshea became tributary to Assyria.

The next major event bringing Judah into contact with Egypt proved disastrous for the Southern Kingdom. When Pharaoh-necho, second rule of the XXVIth Dynasty (609-593 b.c.) came to the throne of Egypt, he had every reason to believe that nothing would prevent his re-establishment of the Egyptian empire in Asia. With the fall of Nineveh, Assyria "was in such a state of collapse that Necho immediately began the realization of his father's imperial designs in Asia. He built a war fleet both in the Mediterranean and the Red Sea, and in his first year invaded Philistia. Gaza and Ashkelon, which offered resistance, were taken and punished (Jer. 47:1, 5) and with a great army Necho then pushed northward. As Judah had been delivered from Sennacherib nearly a century before, they fondly believed that they might now face Egypt with the same assurance of deliverance. On

the historical plain of Megiddo, where Egypt had first won
the supremacy of Asia nearly nine hundred years before, the
young king Josiah (631-608 B.C.) recklessly threw himself
upon Necho's great army. His pitiful force was quickly
routed and he himself, fatally wounded, retired to die at
Jerusalem. Necho pressed on, but failing to find an Assyrian
army and persuaded that he was not strong enough to advance
against Nineveh, he returned southward, having gained all
Syria and at one stroke recovered the whole of the old
Egyptian conquests of the empire." (II Chron. 35:20; II
Kings 23:29).[15]

Retribution was not long in coming for Judah's unsuccess-
ful attempt to thwart Egypt's purposes toward Assyria. After
a brief reign of three months as king of Judah, Jehoahaz was
captured by Pharaoh-necho and taken to Egypt, where he died
(II Kings 23:34; II Chron. 36:3, 47). "At a single stroke Necho
had recovered the Egyptian empire in Asia to its fullest extent, from the borders of Egypt through Palestine, Syria
proper and Naharina to the upper waters of the Euphrates." [16]
There stood up in Judah at this time the prophet Uriah, who,
because he dared to predict that Judah would soon fall, was
forced to flee to Egypt to escape the wrath of Jehoiakim II,
but was apprehended, brought back to Jerusalem and slain
(Jer. 26:20-23). At the same time, Jehoiakim (608-597 B.C.)
was compelled by Necho to pay a heavy tribute to powerful
Egypt. "He taxed the land to give the money according to the
commandment of Pharaoh: he exacted the silver and the gold
of the people of the land, of every one according to his taxa-
tion, to give it unto Pharaoh-necoh" (II Kings 23:34, 35).

A ruler now appears on the horizon who will bring an end

to this growing Egyptian empire—Nebuchadnezzar. Hearing of the approach of Nebuchadnezzar's army, Pharaoh-necoh determined to meet his enemy in what he knew would be a final battle on the northern frontier of Syria at Carchemish on the Euphrates River, in 605 B.C. His army was no match for the well-drilled host of Nebuchadnezzar, and so completely was he routed that, as the Scriptures say, Necho was never again able to stand against the Assyrians, or even to threaten the little kingdom of Judah: "And the king of Egypt came all that pertained to the king of Egypt" (II Kings 24:7; Jer. 46:2). In one of the early sieges of Jerusalem by the Babylonian forces, an army from Egypt marred the initial plans for taking the city, but later was compelled to retreat to Egypt (Jer. 37:5-8, 11).

The fall of Jerusalem is now not far off. All in Judah who had any discernment of world events knew that the hour could not be far distant when Babylon would come down to destroy their holy city. The panic created by this threat persuaded many in Judah to flee into Egypt, a decision against which Jeremiah gave repeated warnings.

Thus saith Jehovah, the God of Israel, unto whom ye sent me to present your supplication before him: If ye will still abide in this land, then will I build you, and not pull you down, and I will plant you, and not pluck you up; for I repent me of the evil that I have done unto you. Be not afraid of the King of Babylon of whom ye are afraid; be not afraid of him, saith Jehovah: for I am with you to save you, and to deliver you from his hand. And I will grant you mercy, that he may have mercy upon you, and cause you to return to your own land. But if ye say, We will not dwell in this land; so that ye obey

not the voice of Jehovah your God, saying, No; but we will go
into the land of Egypt, where we shall see no war, nor hear the
sound of the trumpet, nor have hunger of bread; and there will
we dwell: now therefore hear ye the word of Jehovah, O remnant
of Judah: Thus saith Jehovah of hosts, the God of Israel, if
ye indeed set your faces to enter into Egypt, and go to sojourn
there; then it shall come to pass, that the sword which ye fear,
shall overtake you there in the land of Egypt; and the famine,
whereof ye are afraid, shall follow hard after you there in
Egypt; and there ye shall die. So shall it be with all the men
that set their faces to go into Egypt to sojourn there: they shall
die by the sword, by the famine, and by the pestilence; and none
of them shall remain or escape from the evil that I will bring
upon them . . . Jehovah hath spoken concerning you, O
remnant of Judah, Go ye not into Egypt: know certainly that
I have testified unto you this day, (42:9-17, 19)

The warning availed nothing. It would seem that those in
power in Mizpah immediately determined to act contrary
to the will of God:

And it came to pass that, when Jeremiah had made an end
to speaking unto all the people all the words of Jehovah their
God, wherewith Jehovah their God had sent him to them,
even all these words, then spake Azariah and son of Hoshaiah,
and Johanan the son of Kareah, and all the proud men, saying
unto Jeremiah, Thou speakest falsely: Jehovah our God hath
not sent thee to say, Ye shall not go into Egypt to sojourn
there; but Baruch the son of Neriah setteth thee on against us,
to deliver us into the hand of the Chaldeans, that they may put
us to death, and carry us away captive to Babylon. So Johanan
the son of Kareah, and all the captains of the forces, and
all the people, obeyed not the voice of Jehovah to dwell in the
land of Judah. But Johanan the son of Kareah, and all the

EGYPT IN BIBLICAL PROPHECY

captains of the forces, took all the remnant of Judah, that were returned from all the nations whither they had been driven, to sojourn in the land of Judah: the men, and the women, and the children, and the king's daughters, and every person that Nebuzaradan the captain of the guard had left with Gedaliah the son of Ahikam, the son of Shaphan; and Jeremiah the prophet, and Baruch the son of Neriah. And they came into the land of Egypt; for they obeyed not the voice of Jehovah, (43:1-7).

Among those taken was Jeremiah who, at a date unknown, died in that land concerning which he had delivered such a solemn warning. Before being carried into Egypt, however, Jeremiah sent a message to the Jews living in Egypt who had refused to heed his warning, a message expressed in words more solemn than any that had proceeded from his lips regarding a Gentile nation; for already the Jews were provoking God to anger by "burning incense unto other gods in the land of Egypt":

Therefore thus saith Jehovah of hosts, the God of Israel: Behold, I will set my face against you for evil, even to cut off all Judah. And I will take the remnant of Judah, that have set their faces to go into the land of Egypt to sojourn there, and they shall all be consumed; in the land of Egypt shall they fall; they shall be consumed by the sword, and by the famine; they shall die, from the least even unto the greatest, by the sword and by the famine; and they shall be an execration, and an astonishment, and a curse, and a reproach. For I will punish them that dwell in the land of Egypt, as I have punished Jerusalem by the sword, by the famine, and by the pestilence; so that none of the remnant of Judah, that are gone into the land of Egypt to sojourn there, shall escape or be left, to return into the land of Judah, to which they have a desire to return to dwell there: for none shall return save such as shall escape. (44:11-14)

There is only one more historical event involving the Jews and Egypt in the Old Testament. In the midst of the book of Ezekiel, we read that Zedekiah rebelled against Nebuchadnezzar "in sending his ambassadors into Egypt that they might give him horses and much people. Shall he prosper? shall he escape that doeth such things? shall he break the covenant and yet escape? As I live, saith Jehovah, surely in the place where the king dwelleth that made him king, whose oath he despised and whose covenant he brake, even with him in the midst of Babylon he shall die. Neither shall Pharaoh with his mighty army and great company help him in the war, when they cast up mounds and build forts, to cut off many persons" (17:15-17). This occurred in the year of the accession of Apries (Hophra in Jer. 44:30). Of the details of this campaign, we know nothing from the Biblical record. In the following year, Jerusalem fell and was destroyed. Zedekiah was brought before the Assyrian king at his headquarters at Riblah in northern Syria, and after seeing his sons slain before him, was blinded and carried away to Babylon.

Notes

1. Franz Delitzsch: *Biblical Commentary on the Prophecies of Isaiah.* 4th ed., Edinburgh, 1890. Vol. I, p. 357.
2. For the origin and meaning of the names Mizraim, Egypt, etc., see George Rawlinson: *History of Ancient Egypt,* p. 2, note 2. There are three names in the Old Testament which must also be connected with this geographical area: the Naphtuhim, an Egyptian tribe living near Memphis in the Delta (Gen. 10:13; I Chron. 1:11); Pathros, a name for Upper Egypt (Isa. 11:11; Ezek. 29:14, etc.) and the Pathrusim, descendants of Mizraim, living in Pathros (Gen. 10:14; I Chron. 1:12).
3. J. G. Murphy: *Commentary on the Book of Exodus.* Andover. 1868. p. 38.

EGYPT IN BIBLICAL PROPHECY

4. H. C. Leupold: *Exposition of Genesis.* Columbus, Ohio, 1942. pp. 484-485. It is interesting to note that Ruskin was unusually drawn to this chapter. "Read the fifteenth chapter with extreme care. If you have a good memory, learn it by heart from beginning to end; it is one of the most sublime and pregnant passages in the entire compass of ancient literature." "Fors Clavigea" LXIV.

5. James H. Breasted: *The History of Egypt.* 2nd ed. New York, 1909 p. 422.

6. Breasted, *op cit.,* p. 440.

7. J. H. Kurtz: *History of the Old Covenant.* Vol. I, p. 213.

8. T. Eric Peet: *Egypt and the Old Testament.* London, 1923. p. 21.

9. S. R. Driver: *The Book of Exodus,* in *The Cambridge Bible for Schools and Colleges.* Cambridge, 1911. pp. 111-112.

10. *The Westminster Historical Atlas to the Bible,* edited by G. Ernest Wright and F. V. Filson. Philadelphia, 1945. p. 38.

11. J. G. Murphy: *Critical and Exegetical Commentary on the Book of Exodus.* Andover, 1868. p. 78.

12. Phythian-Adams, *op. cit.,* pp. 171, 172.

13. On the date of the Exodus, the most recent scholarly treatment is that by H. H. Rowley, "Israel's Sojourn in Egypt," in *The Bulletin of the John Rylands Library,* Vol. XXII (1938) pp. 243-290. The date I have adopted here is defended in Merrill F. Unger: *Archaeology and the Old Testament.* Grand Rapids, 1954. p. 140-152. The following statement is from one of the distinguished Old Testament scholars of a former decade: "Today it is become more and more probable that . . . the Exodus took place in the reign of Amenhotep II, about 1440 B.C." W. J. Phythian-Adams: *The Call of Israel.* London, 1934. p. 47.

14. A. P. Stanley: *History of the Jewish Church,* Vol. I, pp. 113-114. On the significance of the Exodus, see also H. H. Rowley: *The Biblical Doctrine of Election.* London, 1950. pp. 36-44, and the same author's article, "The Eisodus and the Exodus," in *The Expository Times,* Vol. 50, 1938-1939, pp. 503-508.

15. Breasted, *op. cit.,* p. 582.

16. T. Eric Peet: *Egypt and the Old Testament.* 1923. p. 183.

4

THE BURDEN OF EGYPT

The 19th chapter of the Book of Isaiah contains the most important prophetic utterance concerning Egypt in all of the Old Testament. There is no basic theme of the predictions about Egypt that is not to be found here. The 46th chapter of Jeremiah and the long passage in Ezekiel (Chs. 29-32) only set forth developments of the cardinal thoughts of this pronouncement. Delitzsch says that Chapters 18, 19 and 20 form a trilogy, and that all three prophecies refer to the same kingdom, the Egypto-Ethiopian kingdom. "The first treats of Ethiopia in language of the sublimest pathos. The second treats of Egypt in language of calmer description. The third treats of Egypt and Ethiopia in a setting of plain historical prose." Here, however, we shall confine ourselves to the 19th chapter. While it is true that Ethiopia was contiguous to Egypt, the actual word Egypt does not occur in the 18th chapter, and because the chapter itself involves so many difficulties and has been given so many interpretations, I have not felt compelled to discuss it here. The 20th chapter, predicting an invasion of Assyria, will be dealt with when we come to the subject of Nebuchadnezzar's invasion of Egypt.

Regardless of the view taken of the general application of this prophecy, all would agree that the chapter divides into two parts: the first, and longer section, verses 1-16, refers to various aspects of God's judgment upon Egypt, while the remaining nine verses foretell a time of healing and blessing for Egypt, for herself and in relation to other nations. The chapter may be outlined as follows:

I. God's Judgment Upon Egypt, 19:1-16
   1. A summary and introductory statement, v. 1
   2. A judgment upon the government of Egypt, vv. 2-4
   3. Economic distress, vv. 5-10
   4. Intellectual confusion, vv. 11-15
   5. A concluding summary, v. 16

II. Jehovah's Ultimate Healing of Egypt, 19:17-28
   1. Egypt in relation to the land of Judah, vv. 17, 18
   2. Egypt's ultimate recognition and worship of Jehovah, vv. 19-22
   3. Egypt and Assyria, v. 23
   4. The three-fold blessing upon Israel, Egypt and Assyria, vv. 24, 25

Various Schemes of Interpretation

Anyone attempting a prolonged study of this chapter, in an effort to ascertain the exact meaning of these predictions must ultimately come to some conclusion as to the general idea which the prophet is here endeavoring to set forth. This being true, in the history of the interpretation of the passage, we find ourselves confronted with what may be called a confusion of basic concepts. This should not, however, prevent us from arriving at some conclusion of our own.

Let us consider the symbolical, or mystical, or figurative types of interpretation first. The early church fathers, Eusebius, Cyril, Jerome and, during the Reformation, Calvin, believed that the chapter fundamentally depicts, in various figures of speech, the conversion of Egypt to Christianity. This is the position of many modern commentators. Cocceius (1603-1669) understood Egypt to mean Rome or the Roman Empire, and took the chapter as a synopsis of church history from the conversion of Constantine to the end of this age. Martin Luther held the very opposite view: that Egypt here stands for the idolatry, superstition and priest-craft of the Roman Church. Commenting on verses 11 and 12 he says, "Downfall is certain for the papacy which now triumphs in all security and against all threatenings, all admonitions, all pleading. The closer they are to catastrophe, the more obstinate they are. They point to their wisdom and antiquity. By these two things, the conceit of wisdom and pride in antiquity, the hearts of the godless are inflated." He goes so far as to attack Erasmus himself: "The diatribe of Erasmus is no different from what is stated here: I am the son of the ancients. For he appeals to the authority of the church fathers. The prophets fought against such pride and today we withstand it as well."

Many consider this prophecy only a reference to Egypt's final downfall as a nation, an event which certainly must be placed between the time of Isaiah in the eighth century B.C. and the advent of Alexander the Great four centuries later. Egypt was already a nation declining in power. One can hardly overlook the significance of the geographical references in this chapter, to specific places in Egypt as a whole and in her cities, and to events that would occur there. But the later part of the chapter, which tells of Egypt's ultimate turning to God, cannot be located in any particular historical period, even after the advent of Christ. This forces commentators to take two different views of verses 17-25. Some believe that these verses simply portray the spread of Christianity, which will include Egypt. Others assign the ultimate fulfilment of these verses to the end of the age, a position which I am taking here. Alexander, the greatest of all American commentators on Isaiah, and one of the finest the Church has produced in modern times, says, "The prophet, wishing to announce to the Jews the decline and fall of that great heathen power in which they were so constantly disposed to trust (30:1; 31:1) describes the event under figures borrowed from the actual condition of Egypt . . . Whether particular parts of the description were intended to have a more specific application is a question not affecting the truth of the hypothesis, that the first part is a metaphorical description of the downfall of the great Egyptian monarchy. So too in the second part, the introduction of the true religion, and its effect as well on the internal state as on the international relations of the different countries, is expressed by figures drawn from the civil and religious institutions of the old economy." Later Alexander admits that, "The chapter is a prophecy not of a single event but of a great progressive change to be wrought in the condition of Egypt by the introduction of the true religion . . . in the highest sense, by Christ himself . . . And who shall say what is yet to be witnessed and experienced in Egypt under the influence of the same gospel." [1] In all fairness to Alexander, it must be pointed out that he does not place the fulfilment of any of these prophecies at what we call the end of the age, or at the time of our Lord's return, but he does clearly affirm that they can refer to a period in the history of the kingdom of God subsequent to the one in which he was living. One phrase in the passage we have quoted is significant: "the international relations of the different countries." At the time this work was published, in 1846, there was no reason for speaking of international relations between Assyria, Egypt and Israel. All three of them are amazingly active today—Iraq, Israel and Egypt. I like the words of William Kelly that "enough was then accomplished for a stay to the faithful; but it was no more than an earnest of that perpetual and full payment which God will yet render . . . Egypt has its part to play in the tremendous convulsions which precede Jehovah's appearing; and to this our chapter looks onward; with which compare Daniel 11:40-43." [2] Kelly also wrote nearly a hundred years ago.

A Summary and Introductory Statement

The first verse of this chapter may be understood as a summary of both of the prophetic themes of the passage—the coming of the Lord to Egypt first to smite her and then to heal: "The burden of Egypt. Behold, Jehovah rideth upon a swift cloud, and cometh unto Egypt: and the idols of Egypt shall tremble at his presence; and the heart of Egypt shall melt in the midst of it." The concept of God coming in clouds when He is about to manifest himself to men is found often in the divine epiphanies of the Scriptures.

It is significant that the first statement made regarding God's judgment upon Egypt involves her idols, a theme that will appear again and again in the prophecies we shall be considering in this volume—as far as I recall, there is no judgment pronounced upon any of the gods of any one nation in the Old Testament, except those of Egypt.

A Judgment Upon the Government of Egypt

Isaiah's picture of God's judgment upon Egypt embraces four major aspects of Egyptian life and power in the ancient world—her government, her religion, her wealth, and her wisdom. It will not be possible in this chapter to examine every phrase of this rich pronouncement. Our chief concern is with the general drift of the chapter. It is interesting that in the Septuagint, the word translated kingdom is the Greek word *nomē*, a technical term for the major geographical and governmental divisions of Egypt, the Nomes, of which there were forty-two. "And I will stir up the Egyptians against the Egyptians: and they shall fight every one against his brother, and every one against his neighbor; city against city, and kingdom against kingdom" (v. 2). The fulfilment of this verse could be seen in many episodes of Egyptian history. One such episode referred to by Diodorus Siculus is almost an echo of Isaiah's words: "After the abdication of Sabacon (supposed to be the So who joined with Hosea, king of Israel) there was anarchy in Egypt for two years; but the people falling into broils and tummults and slaughter one of another, twelve of the chief nobility took upon them the regal power and authority. Psammetichus I, one of the kings, whose province was upon the sea coast, being envied by the others on account of the wealth which he derived from commerce, made war upon him; but he, having hired soldiers from Arabia, gained a victory over them. Some of the kings were slain, and the rest fled into Africa; and Psammetichus I gained possession of the whole kingdom." [3]

In almost every one of the rich prophecies of Isaiah, while

the message is generally one of judgment and destruction for the nation, there is a word of comfort and hope for Israel. Thus, in the midst of the prophecy on Babylon we read,

For Jehovah will have compassion on Jacob, and will yet choose Israel, and set them in their own land: and the sojourner shall join himself with them, and they shall cleave to the house of Jacob. And the peoples shall take them, and bring them to their place; and the house of Israel shall possess them in the land of Jehovah for servants and for handmaids: and they shall take them captive whose captives they were; and they shall rule over their oppression (Isa. 14:1-3).

This theme is repeated, though with brevity, in six of the subsequent burdens of this familiar passage: 14:32; 16:5; 17:4; 18:7; 19:24, 25; 22:22, 23. The same is true, though not with such frequency, in the nation prophecies of Jeremiah, as, e.g., at the end of the prophecy regarding Egypt:

But fear not thou, O Jacob my servant, neither be dismayed, O Israel: for, lo, I will save thee from afar, and thy seed from the land of their captivity; and Jacob shall return, and shall be quiet and at ease, and none shall make him afraid. Fear not thou, O Jacob my servant, saith Jehovah; for I am with thee: for I will make a full end of all the nations whither I have driven thee; but I will not make a full end of thee, but I will correct thee in measure, and will in no wise leave thee unpunished (Jer. 46:27, 28; see also 50:5; 51:10, 24).

One factor in the Jeremiah prophecies is not found in Isaiah in regard to certain of these nations—Moab, Ammon and Elam—when the Lord says, "I will bring again the captivity of Moab in the later days (48:47; 49:6; 49:35). This peculiar phrase reappears in Ezekiel in relation to Egypt (29:14) and in the later prophetic writings in relation to

Jacob or Judah (Ezek. 39:5; Joel 3:1; Amos 9:14; Zeph. 2:7). As the prophecies of Jeremiah are marked by the frequent recurrence of the phrase, "bring again the captivity of . . ." the nation prophecies of Ezekiel bear the constantly repeated pronouncement, "they shall know that I am the Lord." For example, in the prophecy against the Ammonites we read, "Therefore, behold, I have stretched out my hand upon thee, and will deliver thee for a spoil to the nations; and I will cut thee off from the peoples, and I will cause thee to perish out of the countries: I will destroy thee; and thou shalt know that I am Jehovah" (25:7; see also 25:11, 14, 17; 28:24, 26; 29:21; 30:19, 26). Indeed, these three collections of nation prophecies bear witness to three fundamental truths throughout: First, God will ultimately be known to the peoples of the earth, an assertion which Isaiah made shortly before these nation prophecies were uttered, "They shall not hurt nor destroy in all my holy mountain; for the earth shall be full of the knowledge of Jehovah, as the waters cover the sea" (11:9), and which Habbakuk re-echoed (2:14). Secondly, though God destroys the other nations of the earth He will preserve Israel. Finally, Zion, Jerusalem, will become what it was intended to be at the time of its establishment as Israel's capital and site of the temple of Jehovah, the center of a great revival of obedience to the law of the Lord, with a resultant joy to take the place of the sorrow and shame that disobedience to God always brings.

Do we not have in this first paragraph one of those revelations, which occur here and there in the Scriptures, linking the activity and doom of the gods of a nation with the governmental doom of that nation? In a statement in the

Olivet Discourse, our Lord brings together the convulsions that will mark the distress of nations at the end of this age and the shaking of the powers of the heavens, with signs in the sun, moon and stars (Luke 21:25-28), a truth later reiterated by the Apostle Paul when he speaks of "principalities, the powers, the world rulers of this darkness" (Eph. 6:12). Over and over again in the Old Testament these idols of Egypt are condemned, as in Exodus 12:12; Numbers 33:4; Jeremiah 46:25. Literally, the Hebrew word means *nonentities*, as in Isaiah 2:8. In no nation of the ancient world was the activity of people and government so dominated by the gods as in Egypt. There was Amon-ra the sky god of solar deity; Osiris, god of the underworld; his sister-wife the cow-headed Isis, goddess of fertility; their son, Horus, the hawk-headed god of light; and Anubis, who with Thoth, was assigned the task of conducting souls to the underworld. Egypt was filled with temples to these gods, and their various priesthoods exercised the most powerful influence over that land during many periods of its history, and were exercising such influence in the days of Isaiah. But they are all gone: no one worships these gods today, the ordinary Egyptian would not even recognize the names, and there is no priest of any of these deities on the Nile River today. No one has more dramatically set forth the doom that the advent of Christ brought to this pantheon of gods than John Milton, in his inimitable "On the Morning of Christ's Nativity":

"And sullen Moloch fled
Hath left in shadows dread
　His burning idol all of blackest hue;
In vain with cymbals' ring

They call the grisly king,
  In dismal dance about the furnace blue;
The brutish gods of Nile as fast,
Isis and Orus, and the dog Anubis, haste.

Nor is Osiris seen
In Memphian grove or green,
  Trampling the unshowered grass with lowings loud:
Nor can he be at rest
Within his sacred chest,
  Nought but profoundest Hell can be his shroud,
In vain with timbrelled anthems dark
The sable-stoled sorcerers bear his worshipped ark.

He feels from Juda's land
The dreaded Infant's hand,
  The rays of Bethlehem blind his dusky eyn;
Nor all the gods beside,
Longer dare abide,
  Not Typhon huge ending in snaky twine:
Our Babe, to show His Godhead true,
Can in His swaddling bands control the damned crew."

Isaiah even includes in this prophecy of judgment the failure of the famous wise men of Egypt, "charmers and them that have familiar spirits, and wizards." The Egyptians in their perplexity will turn in vain to the spirits of the dead.

There is here also a very strange pronouncement, that the Lord would stir up the Egyptians against the Egyptians, so that they would fight every one against his brother. This is nothing less than civil war, internal strife, and anarchy in general. This may refer to a number of different periods of Egyptian history, for in that rich Mediterranean land there has often been rebellion against the ruling class, and, later, rebellion against those who overthrew the ruling powers.

Who the "cruel lord and fierce king" of verse 4 is, we are not quite sure. Driver takes this to be Sargon; W. R. Smith identifies the phrase with Sennacherib, and Delitzsch and Breasted say it is a prophecy of Psammetichos (663-609 B.C.), a position defended at length by Boutflower. It may be that the writer did not have some definite individual in his mind. "Any conqueror would *ipso facto* be mighty: any foreign ruler as the imposer of hard, that is, foreign, service, would from the point of view of the conquered, especially in expectation, be a hard lord." [4]

A Prediction of Coming Economic Distress (19:5-10)

The Nile River has always been the life stream of this nation Egypt. Were it not for the Nile, Egypt would be nothing more than the eastern end of the Sahara Desert; in fact, much of the country is still desert. Isaiah now turns his attention to this aspect of Egypt's life and predicts that the time will come when the streams of Egypt will be dried up, the sown fields become barren, the fishers will fail in their tasks, and those working in flax will be confounded. A careful study of the prophecies regarding Egypt in Isaiah, Jeremiah and Ezekiel reveal that no one factor of Egyptian life is so continually emphasized as that of the rivers and streams. If my listing is correct, in these prophecies of Egypt the words *sea, rivers, water, streams, the deep, channels, water courses,* and the *Nile* are found forty-five times.[5] Herodotus himself often spoke of the commercial items here mentioned: "With a considerable part of this people, fish constitutes the principal article of food; they dry it in the sun and eat it without further preparation . . . Each person has a net with which they fish by day and with which they cover their beds by night to protect them from the gnats." [6] Pliny says, "The flax of Egypt, though the least strong of all as a tissue is that from which the greatest profits are derived. There is no tissue known that is superior to those made from the thread of the Egyptian xylon, either for whiteness, softness, or dressing: the most esteemed vestments worn by the priests of Egypt are made of it." [7] I think there is no contemporary record left to us that acknowledges such an overwhelming, disastrous judgment upon the Nile as is here depicted; which means, if the prophecy is to have a fulfilment, that hour has not yet come.

Intellectual Confusion (19:11-15)

According to Isaiah's prophecy, Egypt's gods are doomed to oblivion, those claiming to communicate with the dead will fail to help, the land will suffer a staggering blow economically, and now we are told that "the counsel of the wisest counsellors of Pharaoh" will be brought to nought; so that the prophet can taunt them with the question, "Where then are thy wise men? and let them tell thee now; and let them know what Jehovah of hosts hath purposed concerning Egypt" (v. 12). This condemnation of the wise men of Egypt is especially significant because Egypt was noted for its superior wisdom. Zoan is another name for the city of Tanis, one of the Egyptian towns nearest to Palestine, situated on one of the eastern arms of the Nile River near its mouth (Num. 13:2; Ps. 78:12, 43). As Poole has said, "A great seat of land traffic should stand as near as possible to the eastern border; it should have a harbor secure from war and storms. Tanis was almost the first town to fall under the rule of a conquering race." [8] Zoan was a city of importance as early as 2500 B.C. and a residence of Egyptian kings in the thirteenth century. While the city was prominent in the days of Isaiah, from that time on "her decline was certain. Pelusium first and Alexandria later usurped her place." [9] At the beginning of our era, Strabo referred to Zoan as "a great city"; today it is but a small fishing hamlet. Memphis was the center of the Memphite dynasties, and here was located the most powerful priesthood Egypt has ever known. Poole says, "The foundation of Memphis is the first event in Egypt's history, the one large historical incident in the reign of the first king." Yet, as the same writer tells us, "Memphis was a great mass of huge temples. Even in the XXth Dynasty, the temple of Ptah was the largest in the country but two. Even down into the thirteenth century of our own era, many temples could still be seen standing. No one of the great cities of the old world has so utterly disappeared as Memphis. There is neither sacred building nor palace nor a trace of common house. All are gone but the broken Colossus." [10] The doom of these two cities, with others, is described in more detail in Ezekiel's prophecies about Egypt.

The second half of this chapter is devoted to the subject of God's ultimate healing of Egypt, especially as the history of that land is interwoven with that of Judah. One section of this latter portion of the chapter (vv. 18-20) has probably had more different interpretations than any other passage in the book of Isaiah.

EGYPT IN BIBLICAL PROPHECY

Egypt in Relation to the Land of Judah 19:17, 18

"And the land of Judah shall become a terror unto Egypt;
every one to whom mention is made thereof shall be afraid,
because of the purpose of Jehovah of hosts, which he purposeth against it" (v. 17). Here indeed is a strange statement,
that Egypt should be afraid of "the land of Judah." One
thing is certain—for over two thousand years Egypt did not
have to be afraid of Judah, for Judah was not an independent
kingdom. Have we not seen, however, a preliminary fulfillment of this in the events of the last two years, when Egypt
had to cry to the great powers to be delivered from the army
of the land of Israel? But probably an even more comprehensive thought is compressed into this verse. "It is not the people
of Israel but the land of Judah that is the cause of terror to
Egypt. The land of Judah is the seat of Jehovah's kingdom,
which will comprise all nations. Jehovah's plan concerning
the land of Judah is to make it the seat of a universal kingdom." [11]

If there is any one sentence in all the multitudinous prophetic passages relative to Egypt about which I would not
dare be dogmatic, it is this 18th verse: "In that day there shall
be five cities in the land of Egypt that speak the language of
Canaan, and swear to Jehovah of hosts; one shall be called
The city of destruction." The very thought that Egypt will
"speak the language of Canaan" has given rise to many interesting interpretations. Some of the older commentators believe that this prediction alluded to the restoration of the
Hebrew language in that part of the world. The words of
Vitringa sound almost contemporary:

"The Hebrew word for language here is Saphah, the same term as is used in Zephaniah 3:9: 'Then shall I turn unto the peoples a pure language,' that is, the doctrine of the true religion. But it would be entirely outside of the scope of the prophet's purpose to assert something which would be quite absurd, that the Egyptians would exchange their language for that of the Jews, for such a change of language would by no means render them more blessed; yet it is clear from what the prophet says in the following, that they will sware unto the Jehovah of hosts, the Lord. What he means to say is that the Egyptians will not only have respect unto the God of Israel and worship Him as the ruler of mankind and the avenger of falsehood, but also that by taking oath they will bring themselves under obligation and obedience to Him, as to Venerate Him and to render Him all the worship of religion . . .

"Indeed, since Saphah signifies not merely conversation but a certain manner and form of enunciation, which depends upon the moving and bending of the lips and of the tongue, this phrase advises us that a school of true wisdom and of the heavenly sanctuary has its own special and appropriate way of speaking, its own diction, which passes on divine matters and the mysteries of the faith, and which greatly differs from the phrases and modes of speech and even the words with which men set forth their opinions concerning the world and these same matters. The school of God has its own mode of speech, its own dialect, its own phrases, everywhere significant and suited to set forth spiritual matters, and these have been used by the patriarchs, prophets, Jesus Christ himself, and His apostles." [12]

Two centuries ago Adam Clarke declared that this pointed "to the flourishing state of Judaism in that country in consequence of the great favor shown to the Jews by the Ptolemies," [13] and others have followed him in assigning the fulfillment of this prediction to historical events of the long distant past. While Clarke saw this as having been fulfilled during the days of the Ptolemies, Kay found the fulfilment in "the first four centuries of our era, when Christian theology had one of her chief seats in Egypt," [14] actually in Alexandria. Of course Egypt was not then speaking the language of Canaan, if by that is meant Hebrew; so Kay has to make the passage refer to Hellenistic Greek which, he says, "was practically the language of Canaan." Kay goes into more detail on this point than any other writer I know of when he asserts that "the language that had once been that of the debased Canaanites but which had been rescued out of its corruption and sanctified by being employed as the vehicle for God's purposes to mankind . . . was no doubt largely spoken in Egypt by numerous Jewish settlers; and there it transfused its spirit into the Greek forms of speech." [15]

Professor Wade expressed still another view in casting the fulfilment of this prophecy into the future, where it certainly belongs: "The conversion of Egypt will begin with the adoption of the Hebrew faith and language of a few cities." [16] The situation today in regard to the language of Canaan is different from what it has been for hundreds of years; for if by "the language of Canaan" Hebrew is meant, the nation contiguous to Egypt on the north is at present, for the first time in hundreds of years, speaking the Hebrew language.

Still another problem is presented in this 18th verse, in the enigmatical phrase, "the city of destruction." In the Hebrew text, the word is *ir-ha-heres*, meaning literally, as the ordinary English text reads, "city of destruction." Moreover, as Delitzsch reminds us, *haras* is the word commonly used to signify the throwing down of heathen altars (Judges 6:25; I Kings 18:30; and 19:10, 14). In some manuscripts, however, the

Hebrew *ir-ha-cheres* is used, which means not "the city of destruction," but "the city of the sun." The Septuagint goes even further and translates this *polis asedek,* meaning "the city of righteousness." These three concepts, of course, have resulted in confusion. The actual sun city of Egypt was Heliopolis, that is, "the city of the sun god," situated northeast of Memphis and in the Old Testament called On. Nothing of this city remains standing, out of all its monuments, but one granite obelisk. So, Delitzsch concludes—and I find his comment here the most satisfying—the meaning of the prophecy may be "that the city which had been called the chief city of sun worship would become the city of the destruction of idolatry, as Jeremiah prophesies, 'Jehovah will break in pieces the obelisks of the sun temple in the land of Egypt.' "[17]

Egypt's Ultimate Recognition and Worship of Jehovah (19:19-22)

Here again, in regard to the erection of a pillar at the border of Egypt, interpretations vary, and, personally, I am not sure to what the text refers. Kay, a sound exegete, understood it to be first the Jewish synagogue and later the Christian Church at Alexandria, which, he says, "stood like a lofty obelisk, with the name of the Lord inscribed upon it, at the entrance of Egypt." The difficulty with this interpretation is that the border of Egypt in this passage must be the boundary toward Palestine, and Alexandria is not on that border. As we observed in the preceding chapter, this prophecy was taken by the Jews of the century before Christ as having been fulfilled in the building of the temple at Elephantine by Onias IV.

Writing in the *International Critical Commentary,* Gray gives this interpretation: "According to Genesis 31:45, a *massebah* marked the boundary between the Aramaeans and Hebrews in Gilead, so according to this passage a *massebah* is to mark or already marks the boundary of Egypt . . . The altar most readily understood is the altar at Leontopolis, north of Memphis." Alexander rightly says that we are not quite sure whether this was an altar for sacrifice or a memorial altar, and concludes that this is just another way of expressing the general truth of the latter part of the chapter, of "the prevalence of the true religion and the practice of its rites. As we might now speak of a missionary 'pitching his tent' at Hebron or at Shechem, without intending to describe the precise form of his habitation, so the Prophet represents the converts to the true faith as erecting an altar and a pillar to the Lord in Egypt, as Abraham and Jacob did of old in Canaan." [18]

The chapter concludes with a glorious promise of a final redemption for Egypt. "And Jehovah shall be known to Egypt, and the Egyptians shall know Jehovah in that day; yea, they shall worship with sacrifice and oblation, and shall vow a vow unto Jehovah, and shall perform it. And Jehovah will smite Egypt, smiting and healing; and they shall return unto Jehovah, and he will be entreated of them, and will heal them" (vv. 21, 22). It must be admitted that such a promise has not yet been fulfilled. The conditions described here are to be permanent, and certainly will not allow, e.g., of any conquest of Egypt by the religion of the false prophet, and the false religion holding sway over Egypt for hundreds of years. The three great empires flourishing during Israel's kingdom age are here brought back upon the stage of history, and this time not in war, jealousy, or in an attempt to destroy one another, but in peace, in a unified worship, in a universal recognition of Israel's God as the true God, displayed before the nations of the earth.

Israel, Egypt and Assyria will each be a third of a trinity of nations receiving a special benediction from the Lord. Such interpretations as that of Boutflower, in which this prophecy is said to have been fulfilled in the conquest of Assyria and Egypt by Darius, accompanied by the restoration of the Jews to Palestine, or that of Hengstenberg, who says this was "gloriously fulfilled" at the time that "there existed a flourishing church in Egypt," are surely in error. Hengstenberg does add, however, "Although the candlestick of that church be now removed from its place, yet we are confident of and hope for a future in which this prophecy shall anew powerfully manifest itself." Writing a century ago, Hengstenberg did not foresee such a time of bitterness and strife as we now behold in the Near East; thus, he optimistically wrote, "The broken bow of the Mohammedan delusion opens up the prospect that the time in which this hope is to be realized is drawing near." [19] This hope is further away from being realized today than it was when Hengstenberg wrote—but it will be realized. Incidentally, Nagelsbach calls attention to the interesting fact that Egypt is called "my people," as Israel is sometimes called (Isa. 3:12; 10:2, 24) and Assyria is called "the work of my hands," a phrase also used of Israel (Isa. 60: 21; 64:7), "but Israel retains the name of honor, 'mine inheritance,' for thereby it is characterized as the actual son of the house and head of the family." [20]

Although I do not follow his interpretations of the prophecies of this chapter, Boutflower's graphic summary of the burden of Egypt forms a fitting conclusion to our investigation of this passage.

"Taken as a whole the Burden of Egypt may be described as a peep down the long-drawn vista of the future, and the seer to whom this peep is granted may be likened to a traveller standing on the summit of some mountain pass commanding a prospect down the far-receding valley in front of him. At first he can see nothing, for a thunderstorm which is raging in the foreground blots out the landscape. This is a picture of Jehovah's judgment poured out on idolatrous Egypt. But instead of swollen brooks and raging torrents, the sequel of the storm, so peculiar are the conditions of that country that the effect of those judgments on Egypt must needs be described in the Burden by the very opposite figure, viz. the drying up of the Nile. As the storm passes our traveller begins to see down the valley, and in mid distance catches sight of a mountain range, one bold peak of which more especially arrests his attention. This is the form of the 'cruel lord' and the 'fierce king'—or as I would prefer to render the adjectives the 'hard lord' and the 'strong king'—into whose hand Jehovah will deliver the Egyptians. But the prospect opens out further as the storm recedes, and in the distance the traveller sees another mountain range, on a grander and loftier scale than the former, and also distinguished by a commanding peak of very noble outline. Over this range storm and sunshine play alternately, until finally the latter gains the victory and the far distance is all bathed in light. This second range is another and greater power which is to dominate over the former, and the commanding peak of noble outline is the 'saviour' and 'defender,' whom, in answer to their cry, Jehovah will send to deliver the Egyptians; but as this deliverance is not to come all at once, the storm and sunshine playing upon

EGYPT IN BIBLICAL PROPHECY

it are figures of the 'smiting and healing,' by which under this second power He will heal the Egyptians." [21]

Notes

1. Joseph Addison Alexander: *Commentary on the Prophecies of Isaiah.* New York, 1846. Vol. I, p. 349. For the opinions of earlier commentators used here, I am indebted to Alexander's preceding pages.
2. William Kelly: *An Exposition of the Book of Isaiah.* New ed., 1947. p. 189.
3. Diodorus Siculus. Book I. Chap. 66.
4. Alexander takes the same position, in saying it refers in a general way to the political vicissitudes of Egypt.
5. The Nile is referred to in Isa. 19:7, 8; Jer. 46:7, 8; and Zech. 10:11; the deep and channels in Ezek. 31:4; watercourses in Ezek. 31:12; 32:6; streams in Isa. 19:6; the sea in Isa. 11:15; 19:5; and Ezek. 32:2; the river in Isa. 19:5, 6; Jer. 46:7, 8, and frequently in Ezek. 29-32; waters in Isa. 19:5, 8; Jer. 46:7, 8; and Ezek. 31 and 32.

For an elaborate consideration of these verses on the drying up of the streams, see Albert Barnes: *Notes Critical, Explanatory and Practical on the Book of the Prophet Isaiah.* New ed., New York, 1857. Vol. I, pp. 352-354. A contemporary authority on Egypt has said, "If the Nile were by some chance cut off, that soil would dry to dust and blow away. The land of Egypt would become a vast dry wadi of the great north African desert." John A. Wilson: *The Burden of Egypt.* Chicago, 1951. p. 8. A famous classicist has made a comment on the relation of the gods to the Nile that should be considered: "The Nile puts the Egyptian on a level with the gods with respect to the tilling of his soil; for whereas to all other people rains and droughts are dispensed by Zeus, every Egyptian can control both these matters for himself." (F. M. Cornford: *Plato's Cosmology.* London, 1937. p. 366).

6. Herodotus: *History.* Book II, Chaps. 92, 95.
7. Pliny: *Natural History.* XIX. 2.
8. Reginald Stewart Poole: *The Cities of Egypt.* London, 1882. p. 79.
9. Poole, *ibid.,* p. 79.
10. Poole, *ibid.,* pp. 17, 18, 24.
11. Edward J. Kissane: *The Book of Isaiah.* Dublin, 1941. Vol. I, p. 218.
12. Campegii Vitringa: *Commentarius in Librum Prophetiarum Iesaiae.* 1720. Vol. I, pp. 762, 763. We might here note the comment of the famous Hebraist, Hengstenberg: "When viewed more deeply, the language of Canaan is spoken by all those who are converted to the true God. Upon

the Greek language, e.g., the character of the language of Canaan has been impressed in the New Testament. That language which, from primeval times, has been developed in the service of the Spirit, imparts its character to the languages of the world, and changes their character in their deepest foundation." E. W. Hengstenberg: *Christology of the Old Testament.* Vol. II, p. 143. Edinburgh. 1871.

13. Adam Clarke: *The Holy Bible . . . with Commentary.* London, 1837. Vol. IV, p. 2721.
14. W. Kay in *The Bible Commentary (Anglican Commentary)* ed. by F. C. Cook. New York, 1890. Vol. V, p. 138.
15. Kay, *ibid.,* p. 139.
16. G. W. Wade: *The Book of the Prophet Isaiah.* London, n.d. p. 138. For a helpful note on this much-disputed passage, see Kissane, *op. cit.,* p. 218.
17. F. Delitzsch: *Biblical Commentary on the Prophecies of Isaiah.* Edinburgh, 1879. Vol. I, p. 364.
18. G. B. Gray: *Critical and Exegetical Commentary on the Book of Isaiah* (in *International Critical Commentary*). Edinburgh, 1912. p. 338.
19. E. W. Hengstenberg: *The Prophecies of the Prophet Ezekiel Elucidated.* Edinburgh, 1869. pp. 256, 261.
20. Carl W. E. Nagelsbach: *The Prophet Isaiah.* p. 230.
21. Charles Boutflower: *The Book of Isaiah, I-XXXIX.* London, 1930. pp. 312, 313.

5

OTHER PROPHECIES OF EGYPT'S HUMILIATION

If Joel was the first of the writing prophets, as many believe, then we have in nucleus toward the end of his book, so apocalyptic in style, themes that continue to be reiterated and enlarged upon by that great body of prophets of Israel and Judah in the subsequent generation. Consequently, Pusey can rightly say that in Joel we find "the first prophecy of the humiliation of Egypt." [1] This concluding chapter brings on to the stage of history four of those nations—Tyre, Sidon, Philistia, and Egypt—found clustered in the nation prophecies of Isaiah, Jeremiah and Ezekiel. Joel waits to the very end of his book to mention the name of Egypt: "Egypt shall be a desolation, and Edom shall be a desolate wilderness, for the violence done to the children of Judah, because they had shed innocent blood in their land. But Judah shall abide for ever, and Jerusalem from generation to generation. And I will cleanse their blood, that I have not cleansed: for Jehovah dwelleth in Zion" (3:19-21). The events prophesied in this chapter will occur at the end of this age, when all the nations are judged before Jehovah, when "the harvest is ripe . . . the winepress is full, the vats overflow . . . the sun and the moon are darkened . . . and the heavens and the earth shall shake . . . then shall Jerusalem be holy, and there shall no stranger pass through her any more" (3:13-17). These factors have never been found combined in any event of history. Thus the prediction concerning the desolation of Egypt must also be fulfilled at the end of the age, at a time when God will judge the nations of the earth.

There is nothing particularly new here in the fact that "Egypt shall be a desolation," for this theme was considered in our study of Isaiah 19. In this passage, however, Egypt is set in contrast to Judah, which nation, God promises, should abide forever. We should remember, as Pusey has pointed out, "When Joel thus threatened Egypt there were no human symptoms of decay; and instruments of its successive over-throws were as yet wild hordes (as the Persians and Mace-donians) to be consolidated thereafter into powerful empires, or, as Rome, had not the beginnings of being." [2] It is true that Egypt has supported millions of people without interruption down through the centuries, but what misery attends the larger part of that population. Perhaps nowhere else in the world are there so many millions of impoverished people crowded together in so small an area as in the pitiful mud villages scattered along the Nile River. This ancient land may have been at one time the granary of the world and famous for its cotton, later a winter resort for the rich and a paradise for archaeologists, but the condition of the poor in Egypt is more tragic than anything prevailing in all the Near East.

Taking the prophecies concerning Egypt in chronological order, the next forecast of Egypt's desolation would be that of Isaiah 11:11-16, a passage we shall examine thoroughly in Chapter VIII. In the seventh century, we have Jeremiah's extensive prophecy of the conquests of Nebuchadnezzar, which will be the subject of the next chapter. This leaves us the single paragraph from that inexhaustible chapter on world conditions, Jeremiah 25:15-29. Once again the nations included in the collection of nation prophecies appear. The prophet Joel named four of them. In this one paragraph there are seven: Philistia, Edom, Moab, Ammon, Tyre, Sidon, and Egypt. The reference to Egypt is brief and only incidental—"Pharaoh king of Egypt, and his servants and his princes, and all his people"—and needs no special consideration.

Ezekiel's prophecy of the invasion of Egypt by Nebuchadnezzar is treated with some detail in Chapter VI, but there are two additional themes in this section (Chaps. 29-32) which demand attention. One of the most familiar phrases in all Biblical predictions concerning Egypt is found in 29:15: "It shall be the basest of the kingdoms; neither shall it any more lift itself up above the nations: and I will diminish them, that they shall no more rule over the nations." This prophecy has truly been fulfilled. Egypt became entirely subject to the Persians 350 years before Christ. It was then overrun by the Macedonians, governed by the Ptolemies for nearly three hundred years, and about thirty years before the coming of Christ, became a province of the Roman Empire. From subjection to Rome, it came under the rule of Constantinople, and in A.D. 641, was transferred to the dominion of the Saracens. In 1250 the Mamelukes deposed their rulers and introduced one of the cruelest and most exhausting periods of Egypt's history. As another has said, "Each successive ruler was raised to supreme authority from being a stranger and a slave; no son of the former ruler, no native of Egypt succeeded to the sovereignty; but a chief was chosen from among a new race of imported slaves. When Egypt became tributary to the Turks in 1517, the Mamelukes retained much of their power and every pasha was an oppressor and a stranger. During all these ages, every attempt to emancipate the country or to create a prince of the land of Egypt has proved aborted, and has often been fatal to the aspirant." A parallel to this prediction is the declaration in the following chapter, "There shall be no more a prince from the land of Egypt" (30:13). As Urquhart said many years ago, "Again and again has Egypt changed masters, but among them all no son of hers is numbered." [3]

The grandfather of Farouk I, king of Egypt, was the Khedive Ismail, deposed by the Turkish Sultan and exiled to Italy. The rule of his son Tewfik was only nominal, the British ruling in Egypt from 1882. The sixth son of Ismail Ahmed Fuad, the father of King Farouk, died April 28, 1936. Farouk himself had no qualities of kingship and his licentiousness and extravagance are too notorious to need mention here. The present ruler of Egypt, Gamel Abder Nasser, leader of the military junta since the bloodless *coup d'état* of July 23, 1952, and premier of Egypt since April, 1954, is the oldest of four sons of an upper Egypt middle-class family. His father was of Arabian stock, and thus Nasser is not even a pure Egyptian—if there is such a thing as a pure Egyptian. A man of severe self-discipline who can endure hardness and who commands the respect of all who are under him, Nasser is the very opposite of Farouk in character. He may be the ruler of Egypt, but he is not what the prophets meant by "a prince of Egypt"; there is no royal blood in his veins.

One of the most unique passages in the prophetic literature of the Old Testament, not found in any other of these remarkable writings, is the long lamentation, or dirge, over Pharaoh's death and descent into Hades (Ezek. 31:14-18; 32:16-32). This is not strictly a prediction of any event to take place on this earth, and no particular Pharaoh is referred to; but it seems almost certain that the reason Ezekiel devotes so much space to this peculiar theme is that Egypt, in her architecture, her religion, and her priestly rites, puts more emphasis upon the provision for death, and life after death, than any other nation of the ancient world. The pyramids bear witness to this, as do all the tombs of the kings with their vast treasures. The greatest single body of literature that has come to us from Egypt is the *Book of the Dead.* Most of Egypt's gods were in one way or another related to this matter of death, judgment, and eternal life. When, then, Ezekiel so graphically depicts the certainty of the Pharaoh's descent to the underworld, where all the other kings of antiquity have assembled previously, it is a rebuke to the whole scheme of Egyptian thought and the aristocratic idea that the Pharaohs would live forever under the propitious favor of the gods to whom they had offered extravagant sacrifices.

Let me conclude this brief chapter with a word from an older work on prophecy, because its author saw more deeply into some of the prophetic movements of the Old Testament Scriptures than most modern writers, and what he wrote nearly a century ago regarding Egypt's humiliation still accurately summarizes what we have been trying to say in these two chapters.

"Why should the same not have been predicted of Egypt (as of Tyre)? Why only a perpetual depression in the one case, and a total subversion in the other? Egypt was not, according to the delineations of prophecy, to become so thoroughly extinct in its national power and resources as Tyre or Babylon. It was not to be made perpetual desolations, but to be brought down from its supremacy, to lose its ancient prestige, to be humbled, and made to serve, and rendered base among the nations—which, indeed, as compared with what Egypt from of old had claimed to be, and still in a great degree was when the prophet wrote, indicated an entire revolution and change in the relative position of the earthly kingdoms. We need scarcely say that this also has happened. The land of the Pharaohs has never lost its fertility; its natural capacities, to this day, are great, though but imperfectly developed; yet from the period of the Persian conquest it has never regained its independence as a nation. Degradation and servility have been stamped upon its condition for more than twenty centuries; and, beyond all doubt, its ancient assumption of the highest place of honour, and pretentious rivalry with the kingdom of God, have irrevocably gone." [4]

Notes

1. E. B. Pusey: *The Minor Prophets*. New York, 1885. Vol. I, p. 215.
2. Pusey, *ibid.*, p. 215.
3. John Urquhart: *The Wonders of Prophecy*. 5th ed., rev. New York, n.d. p. 42.
4. Patrick Fairbairn: *Prophecy Viewed in Respect to Its Distinctive Nature, Its Special Function and Proper Interpretation*. 2nd ed., Edinburgh, 1865. pp. 213, 214.

6

THE PREDICTIONS OF NEBUCHADNEZZAR'S INVASION OF EGYPT

The prophecies of Jeremiah and Ezekiel regarding the invasion of Egypt by Nebuchadnezzar represent one of the most baffling problems of Old Testament interpretation, for in the narratives of the ancient Greek historians, no invasion of Egypt by Nebuchadnezzar is recorded. It was not until the actual cuneiform records of the Mesopotamian Valley began to be read, toward the latter part of the nineteenth century, with other records since, that we had any confirmation of an event to which the Old Testament gives considerable space. For a proper understanding of these prophecies, we must go back a century in our survey of the empires of the Near East. Under Sennacherib (705-681 B.C.) the Assyrian empire rose to new heights of power and influence. All of his efforts to settle difficulties in Babylon having failed, and his own son having been murdered by the Elamites, Sennacherib sacked the city, massacred its inhabitants, and, he thought, destroyed it forever. He reduced the city of Tyre, captured the Philistine cities, and forced Hezekiah, king of Judah, to accept a humiliating peace. His attempt to invade Egypt, however, ended disastrously, when most of his army was destroyed by bubonic plague. Moving the capital of his empire to Nineveh, the Assyrian king adorned the city with a great palace and a library, and made it one of the wonders of his age. His son Esarhaddon (681-669 B.C.) rebuilt the city of Babylon and engaged in a temporarily successful invasion of the Nile Valley. On the way back to Asia to quell a rising revolt, he fell sick and died, but the army continued southward and succeeded in forcing Egypt into submission.

"Soon after Esarhaddon's death the Assyrian Empire reached the greatest extent which it was ever to attain. The whole Fertile Crescent, including Egypt, was under effective control, and an ill-defined 'sphere of influence' had been established in the adjacent mountainous areas of the north and east. Although most of this wide domain was administered by Assyrian governors, some states, such as Judah were ruled by vassal princes. The population was a motley array of tongues, kindreds, and peoples, with no bond of unity except common subjection to the Assyrian king. In spite of the fact that his rule was strong and reasonably just except in cases of revolt, few of his subjects had any affection for him. Every misfortune was certain to be followed by a wave of revolts, and foreign agents found receptive hearers when they attempted to incite the subjects to rebellion." [1]

Under Ashur-bani-apal (669-625 B.C.) after a series of rebellions in Egypt, one by the name of Psamtik was set up as ruler in that land, but by 650, the Assyrian garrisons had been driven from the land and Egypt was once again independent. Psamtik, generally referred to as Psammetichus I (663-609) became the founder of the Twenty-sixth Dynasty of Egypt, under which reign Egypt had a temporary but vigorous revival. Rebellion rapidly spread through various centers of the great Assyrian empire, and toward the end of Ashur-bani-apal's reign, "Assyria was nearing exhaustion. Her manpower was so depleted that the ranks of the army were filled with conscripts drawn from the conquered peoples. Most of her free commoners had either sunk into tenancy or left their bones on foreign battlefields. Only a vigorous foreign power was needed in her neighborhood to give her the death-blow." [2] This blow came when Cyaxares and Nabopolassar united forces to take the city of Nineveh (612 B.C.); for with the destruction of that city, the Assyrian power collapsed. A new empire soon arose to take its place. For over fifty years a measure of peace reigned among the numerous kingdoms existing side by side, at a time when no strong man was able to unite them. The four principal powers at this time were the new Babylonian empire, the Medes, Egypt and Lydia.

There now arose one who has rightly been called "the ablest Mesopotamian ruler for a period of 1100 years," Nebuchadnezzar II (604-562 B.C.). The new king rebuilt Babylon on a vast scale. Its walls may be traced today as a square over two miles long. Herodotus says that the fortified area was fifty-six miles in circumference. Near the royal palace stood the famous hanging gardens, one of the seven wonders of the world. More attention is given to this monarch in the Old Testament historical records than to any other ruler, apart from the kings of Judah. Bible students are prone to forget that God gave to Nebuchadnezzar a power and a greatness of kingdom such as that assigned to no other ruler in all the Biblical writings. "Behold, I will send and take all the families of the north, saith Jehovah, and I will send unto Nebuchadnezzar the king of Babylon, my servant, and will bring them against this land, and against the inhabitants thereof, and against all these nations round about; and I will utterly destroy them, and make them an astonishment, and a hissing, and perpetual desolations" (Jer. 25:9). "And all the nations shall serve him, and his son, and his son's son, until the time of his own land come: and then many nations and great kings shall make him their bondman" (Jer. 27:7). This is the king who conquered Jerusalem in 597, and utterly destroyed it in 586 B.C., and who, in the great image of Daniel 2, was called the head of gold, representing the beginning of the period of Gentile supremacy in the divine program of redemption.

Many Bible students are, I believe, unaware that there are more verses in the Old Testament prophetic writings devoted to Nebuchadnezzar's invasion of Egypt than are found in the prophecies relating to his conquest of Jerusalem! His conquest of Jerusalem is recorded in almost all of the ancient historical writings which cover that period, but, as we have noted before, his invasion of Egypt is wholly ignored.

Chronologically, the first prediction of Egypt's fall before Nebuchadnezzar, is found in Jeremiah 46, a prophecy uttered perhaps in 605 B.C. Not only is Nebuchadnezzar mentioned by name (v. 13), but we also have the name of the pharaoh who will be defeated, Pharaoh-neco II (609-593 B.C.). This is the pharaoh who invaded Palestine and Syria shortly after the fall of Nineveh in 608 B.C. Josiah, king of Judah, a vassal of Assyria, foolishly attempted to disrupt the pharaoh's advancing army and was slain at Megiddo in 608 B.C. (see II Kings 23:29, 30). Syria was subdued, but in the great battle of Carchemish in 604 B.C., Pharaoh-neco was defeated by Nebuchadnezzar.

We must now turn to the prophecy of Nebuchadnezzar's invasion of Egypt. It will not be necessary to examine this long passage of Jeremiah 46 verse by verse. Verses 7-9 no doubt refer to Pharaoh-neco's attempted advance to the Euphrates River, all of which was to be "in vain." Three geographical terms relative to Egypt are contained in verse 14. The exact location of Migdol is not known, though from the prophecy on Egypt in Ezekiel 29:10 and 30:6, we learn that it was somewhere on the northern boundary of Egypt. The best-known city of this name was twelve miles south of Pelusium. Noph was the city of Memphis, also mentioned in Ezekiel 30:13, 16, situated on the west bank of the Nile, twelve miles south of the modern Cairo. We shall return to this in our study of Ezekiel's prophecy. Tahpanhes, the city to which Jeremiah and many of the Jews had fled after the murder of Gedeliah (Jer. 43:7 ff.), was located on a branch of the Nile River, five miles southeast of the city of Tanis (this is also mentioned in Ezekiel 30:18). Perhaps Canon Payne Smith was correct in saying that this prophecy was "probably spoken in Egypt to warn the Jews there that the country they were so obstinately determined to make their refuge would share the fate of their native land." [3] In verse 25 we have a fourth geographical identification, the city of No, none other than the mighty city of Thebes, the capital of Egypt as early as the Eleventh Dynasty, which had been captured at least three different times by Assyrian rulers. In the days of Jeremiah and Ezekiel it was still known as a populous center. Under the Ptolemies it lost all significance. Today it consists of a group of small, unimportant villages. Binns has well remarked on the phrase "her hired men" in verse 21, "It is a strange paradox that Egypt of all nations should have been compelled to trust to foreign mercenaries for her safety; in the earlier history of the nation her people were noted for their dislike of foreigners." [4] On Nebuchadnezzar's actual invasion of Egypt we shall have more to say after the prophecies of Ezekiel have also been considered.

Nearly twenty years later, after the destruction of Jerusalem in 586 b.c., Jeremiah, while in Egypt, has a second, briefer revelation concerning this same invasion, in which Tahpanhes is again mentioned and also Beth-shemesh—not the Beth-shemesh of Palestine where the ark once rested (I Sam. 6:9 ff), but a city of Egypt, probably the great city of On, also called Heliopolis. One factor in this particular prophecy will be emphasized by Ezekiel also, that is, the destruction of the gods of Egypt. "And I will kindle a fire in the houses of the gods of Egypt; and he shall burn them, and carry them away captive: and he shall array himself with the land of Egypt, as a shepherd putteth on his garment; and he shall go forth from thence in peace. He shall also break the pillars of Beth-shemesh, that is in the land of Egypt; and the houses of the gods of Egypt shall he burn with fire" (43:12, 13).

Ezekiel's Prophecy Concerning Egypt

We often hear people say—and they are right in saying it—that they believe the Bible from cover to cover, that it is all inspired, that God can speak to us from every page, etc. But how many, many pages of the Word of God are practically unknown to multitudes, even loyal believers. An illustration of this is the long section in the Book of Ezekiel on Egypt. How few Christians could write even a brief paragraph, if so requested, on the subject of Egypt in the prophecies of Ezekiel. Yet, in these four chapters (29-32) we have ninety-seven verses, more than are contained in the First Epistle of Peter, more than in Paul's Second Epistle to Timothy, and more than in the Epistle to the Colossians.

These chapters, one paragraph excepted, were written during the years 587 to 585 B.C.—Ezekiel himself tells us that the prophecy concerning Nebuchadnezzar was written in what we now call 571 B.C. Davidson well reminds us that "Each of the four chapters is formed in the main upon the same model, containing first, a general threat of destruction upon Egypt, represented by the Pharaoh, under some allegorical designation; secondly, a more particular detail of the instrument whom Jehovah shall use (the king of Babylon), the destruction of the country and the dispersion of its inhabitants; to which, thirdly, in several of the chapters a description is added of the effect on the nations and all creation which these terrible convulsions shall produce." [5]

The first of these seven prophecies against Egypt (29:1-16) was made in January, 587 B.C., and emphasizes particularly the pride of Egypt, and the desolation which God will bring upon her for her arrogance. The nature of this pride is vividly expressed in verse 3: "Thus saith the Lord Jehovah: Behold, I am against thee, Pharaoh king of Egypt, the great monster that lieth in the midst of his rivers, that hath said, My river is mine own, and I have made it for myself." "Pharaoh calls himself the creator of the Nile because he regards himself as the creator of the greatness of Egypt. God will draw the crocodile, Pharaoh, out of his Nile with hooks and cast him upon the dry land, where he and the fishes that have been drawn out along with him upon his scales will not be gathered but devoured by the wild beasts and birds of prey. The fishes which hang upon the scales of the monster are the inhabitants of Egypt, for the Nile represents the land." [6] As in other prophecies regarding the nations, so here, the history of Israel is introduced as it bears upon the Egyptian empire to the south. When Israel turned to Egypt for help instead of to God, Egypt became nothing but a broken reed to her, as the prophet Isaiah had warned more than a century before: "Behold, thou trustest upon the staff of this bruised reed, even upon Egypt, whereon if a man lean, it will go into his hand, and pierce it: so is Pharaoh king of Egypt to all that trust on him" (36:6). "The tall reed of the Nile, more especially the papyrus, is furnished with hollow sword-shaped leaves at the lower part of the stalk. When it cracks, the reed-staff pierces the shoulder of the man who has grasped it, and tears it; and if a man lean upon it, it breaks in pieces and causes all the loins to tremble." [7]

The prophecy of verse 13 has given rise to a number of different interpretations. "For thus saith the Lord Jehovah: At the end of forty years will I gather the Egyptians from the peoples whither they were scattered." Some believe that this forty-year period refers to a definite historical epoch; for example, Redpath reminds us, "It is noticeable that the first occupation by the Persians, which began under Cambyses lasted close upon forty years, 525-487 B.C., and many cruelties from which the Egyptians suffered are attributed to him by Herodotus." [8] Hengstenberg says, "The period of time here, as most of the periods in the Book of Judges, is a round number which in general better suits the nature of prophecy." Then he adds what he could not prove, "The end of the forty years at all events coincides with that of the seventy years." [9] If by this he means the seventy years of Daniel 9, he is projecting the fulfilment of this prophecy to the end of the age, for which interpretation there seems little support. Keil is perhaps more accurate in assuming, "The number forty is neither a round number nor a very long time, but is a symbolical term denoting a period appointed by God for punishment and penitence which is not to be understood in a chronological sense or capable of being calculated." [10]

Though Egypt will be greatly weakened during the days of this conflict, she will be brought back again; however, from this time on she will be "the basest of kingdoms." She will be so stripped of her former greatness and power that she will never again rule over other nations. How true this has been of that once-mighty empire. In 332 B.C., Egypt was invaded by Alexander, and for nearly thirty years, 332-305 B.C., was under the control of the Macedonians. This was followed at once by three centuries of Ptolemaic rule, 305-30 B.C. Then followed four centuries of Roman domination, 30 B.C.-A.D. 394, and the Byzantine period of power, 394-638, at which time she was conquered by the Arabs. Thus down to 1922, Egypt remained a nation under the sovereignty of some foreign power.

The second prophecy, occupying the remainder of this

113

29th chapter, is the latest dated portion of the entire book of Ezekiel, having been written in 571 B.C. Here for the first time Nebuchadnezzar is introduced as the one who will lead the invasion of Egypt and subdue her to the Babylonian empire. Once again Israel is brought into the record in an interesting way: "In that day will I cause a horn to bud forth unto the house of Israel, and I will give thee the opening of the mouth in the midst of them; and they shall know that I am Jehovah" (v. 21). I must here again depend upon the excellent commentary of Professor Keil. After referring to such passages as Psalm 132:17, Jeremiah 48:25, and I Samuel 2:1, he interprets the horn as neither Zerubbabel nor the Messiah, but "the Messianic salvation. In the might of Egypt the world-power is shattered, and the overthrow of the world-power is the dawn of the unfolding of the might of the kingdom of God. Then also will the Lord give to His prophet an opening of the mouth in the midst of Israel. These words are unquestionably connected with the promise of God in 24:26, 27, that after the fall of Jerusalem the mouth of Ezekiel should be opened, and also with the fulfillment of that promise in 33:22; but they have a much more comprehensive meaning; namely, that with the dawn of salvation in Israel, that is, in the church of the Lord, the word of prophecy would sound forth in the richest measure." [11]

The third prediction is found in 30:1-19, without any indication of the time it was uttered, though it is commonly understood that all of these prophecies, except the second, followed closely one upon the other between 587 and 585 B.C. Here the area is extended beyond Egypt, to include

Ethiopia, Libya, Lydia and Chub. Most commentators join Keil in his insistence that "the land of the covenant" (v. 5) is, not the holy land, but "a definite region, though one unknown to us, in the vicinity of Egypt, which was inhabited by a tribe that was independent of the Egyptians, yet bound to render help in time of war." [12] Once again the invasion of Nebuchadnezzar is referred to, and as in the prophecy of Jeremiah, the destruction of the idols of Egypt is foretold, (v. 13). The temples of Egypt and the elaborate carvings and drawings of her gods and goddesses are still the wonder of modern students; but her gods are gone. No temple to an Egyptian god or goddess has a priest in attendance today; no offering is presented to any of these once powerful deities representing the sun, the stellar bodies, the river Nile, and the underworld; no one bows the knee to any of these ancient images.

The geographical delimitation "from the tower of Seveneh, even unto the borders of Ethiopia," (29:10) means from lower Egypt, that is toward the Delta, to the southern border of upper Egypt. Normally the phrase, "from the tower" is translated "from Migdol," twelve miles south of Pelusium. The phraseology of verse 18 is amazingly similar to that found in the great prophetic chapter at the end of the Book of Leviticus: "I am Jehovah your God, who brought you out of the land of Egypt, that ye should not be their bondmen; and I have broken the bars of your yoke, and made you go upright" (26:13).

The fourth prophecy, which can be dated April, 587 B.C., has one dominating theme; namely, that God will break the arms of Pharaoh and strengthen the arms of the king of

Babylon, by which is meant, of course, the military might of these two empires. It is with the arm that the sword is wielded, and when the arm is broken, the warrior is helpless. The great military victories of Egypt are over.

The fifth prophetic utterance occupies all of Chapter 31, and is dated February, 585 B.C. The first of these prophecies against Egypt was expressed in terms of that land's principal geographical feature, the Nile Valley. While the waters of Egypt are mentioned here, the primary figure of speech is a large tree. The prophet introduces the concept by recalling that the Assyrian was once as a cedar in Lebanon (see Ezek. 17:23, 24; and Dan. 4:4-37) a tree exalted above all the other trees of the field, in the branches of which the fowls of heaven made their nests—certainly the origin of our Lord's words in Matthew 13:32—but as this tree ultimately fell, in the downfall of the Assyrian empire, so also will the great empire of Egypt fall, "his boughs broken by all the rivers of the land." Many nations began to take on new life when Assyria collapsed, and in a like manner will Egypt "be brought down with the trees of Eden unto the nether parts of the earth." The reference to Eden is interesting. This ancient paradise is mentioned in 28:13 and again in 36:35, but here the reference is three-fold—verses 9, 16, 18.

The 32nd chapter of Ezekiel, containing the sixth and seventh prophecies against Egypt, is unique in Biblical literature, for here we have a lamentation over Pharaoh, as he goes down, as at death, into the underworld, where the mighty kings of other empires are already imprisoned.

"Asshur is there and all her company, her graves are round about her; all of them slain, fallen by the sword; whose graves are set in the uttermost parts of the pit, and her company is round about her grave; all of them slain, fallen by the sword, who caused terror in the land of the living. There is Elam and all her multitude round about her grave; all of them slain, fallen by the sword, who are gone down uncircumcised into the nether parts of the earth, who caused their terror in the land of the living, and have borne their shame with them that go down to the pit. They have set her a bed in the midst of the slain with all her multitude; her graves are round about her; all of them uncircumcised, slain by the sword; for their terror was caused in the land of the living, and they have borne their shame with them that go down to the pit; he is put in the midst of them that are slain. There is Meshech, Tubal and all their multitude; their graves are round about them; all of them uncircumcised, slain by the sword; for they caused their terror in the land of the living" (32:22-26).

The pharaohs of Egypt will come to disgrace, not only through defeat in battle by armies sent by God, but in the fact that they "shall be laid in the midst of the uncircumcised." This nation which put such strong emphasis upon the burial of her kings, with provision for most elaborate entombment, such as that for Tutankhamen, the wonders of which still amaze this satiated twentieth century; this nation which developed embalming to such a remarkable degree of perfection; this nation whose rulers made every conceivable provision for an abundant life in the after-world, and whose theology was more concerned with the life to come than with life on this earth—cannot prevent her pharaohs being brought down in shame to the pit, at the hands of God.

As noted previously, Ezekiel was uttering these prophecies about the time that Jerusalem fell, 586 B.C. Before that century closed, all had come to pass. The final page of

117

EGYPT IN BIBLICAL PROPHECY

Breasted's monumental *History of Ancient Egypt* is nothing less than a witness by one of the foremost Egyptologists of modern times to the fulfilment of Ezekiel's words: "The fall of Egypt and the close of her characteristic history, were already an irrevocable fact long before the relentless Cambyses knocked at the doors of Pelusium. The Saitic state was a creation of rulers who looked into the future, who belonged to it, and had little or no connection with the past. They were as essentially non-Egyptian as the Ptolemies who followed the Persians. The Persian conquest in 525 B.C., which deprived Psamtik III, the son of Amasis of his throne and kingdom, was but a change of rulers, a purely external fact. And if a feeble burst of national feeling enabled this or that Egyptian to thrust off the Persian yoke for a brief period, the movement may be likened to the convulsive contractions which sometimes lend momentary motion to limbs from which conscious life has long departed. With the fall of Psamtik III, Egypt belonged to a new world, toward the development of which she had contributed much, but in which she could no longer play an active part. Her great work was done, and unable, like Nineveh and Babylon, to disappear from the scene, she lived on her artificial life for a time under the Persians and the Ptolemies, ever sinking, till she became merely the granary of Rome, to be visited as a land of ancient marvels by wealthy Greeks and Romans, who have left their names scratched here and there upon her hoary monuments, just as the modern tourists, admiring the same marvels, still continue to do. But her unwarlike people, still making Egypt a garden of the world,

118

show no signs of an awakening and the words of the Hebrew seer, 'There shall be no more a prince out of the land of Egypt,' have been literally fulfilled." [13]

The Question of an Actual Invasion of Egypt by Nebuchadnezzar

Most of the more important commentaries on Jeremiah and Ezekiel written since the close of the nineteenth century insist that these prophecies of an invasion of Egypt by Nebuchadnezzar were never fulfilled. Writing in 1881, Cheyne mentions a fact which at that time one could not deny; namely, that "no monumental evidence has as yet been found of anything approaching to an invasion of Egypt by Nebuchadnezzar." [14] More than forty years later, H. R. Hall, then Keeper of Egyptian and Assyrian Antiquities in the British Museum, developed this position in the *Cambridge Ancient History:* "Jeremiah's prophecy of an immediate invasion of Egypt by Nebuchadnezzar was not fulfilled, for in Palestine the prince heard of the death of his father, Nabopolassar, and returned hastily to Babylon to assume his crown." In reference to Nebuchadnezzar, he adds, "We have no warrant to suppose that the Babylon king, who was now growing old, ever carried out great warlike operations against Amasis, far less that he conquered or even entered Egypt either personally or by proxy. It does not seem probable that Jeremiah's prophecy that he should pitch his royal tent before the entry of Pharaoh's house at Tahpanhes, a prophecy made in the excitement of the year 605, was ever fulfilled, probable though such an event must necessarily have appeared at the time, judging by Assyrian precedents." [15]

Archaeology has since presented us with evidence more than ample for confirming the accuracy of the prophetic statements of Jeremiah. Before looking at the archaeological data, it would not be out of place to enter here the testimony of Josephus in his *Antiquities of the Jews,* a statement which was generally repudiated by most nineteenth century historians, who asserted that Josephus wrote it not from any historical information he might have had, but only as an attempt to support the accuracy of the statements which he found in the Book of Daniel: "Johanan took those whom he had rescued out of the hands of Ishmael, and the eunuchs, and their wives and children, and came to a certain place called Mandara, and there they abode that day, for they had determined to remove from thence and go into Egypt, out of fear lest the Babylonians should slay them, in case they continued in the country, and that out of anger at the slaughter of Gedaliah, who had been by then set over it for governor . . .

"So when the prophet had informed Johanan and the people that God had foretold these things, he was not believed, when he said that God commanded them to continue in that country . . . And when they were there God signified to the prophet that the king of Babylon was about making an expedition against the Egyptians and commanded him to foretell to the people that Egypt should be taken, and the king of Babylon should slay some of them, and should take others captive, and bring them to Babylon; which things came to pass accordingly; for on the fifth year after the destruction of Jerusalem, which was the 23d of the reign of Nebuchadnezzar, he made an expedition against Cele-Syria; and when he had possessed himself of it, he made war against the Ammonites and Moabites; and when he had brought all those nations under subjection, he fell upon Egypt, in order to overthrow it, and he slew the king that then reigned, and set up another: and he took those Jews that were there captives, and led them away to Babylon; and such was the end of the nation of the Hebrews." [16]

Passing over the many centuries between the days of Josephus and this twentieth century, let us turn again to the *Cambridge Ancient History*. We have noted that in this volume Mr. Hall denied that Nebuchadnezzar ever entered Egypt. In this same work, however, Dr. R. Campbell Thompson of Oxford, in the chapter on "The New Babylonian Empire," makes an equally positive assertion that Nebuchadnezzar did enter Egypt: "The great campaign of Nebuchadnezzar's later years was directed against Egypt in retaliation for the trouble caused by Hophra . . . The small fragment of a Babylonian chronicle first published by Pinches shows that Nebuchadnezzar launched an expedition against Egypt in his thirty-seventh year, that is about 567 B.C. Whether he marched against Egypt with any aim other than conquest, we cannot say; the very distance to which he penetrated is a matter of dispute. We might almost assume from the tradition that certain Babylonian deserters built a Babylon in Egypt near the pyramids which appears to have existed as an important fort in the time of Augustus, and that his army at all events left some mark there." [17]

In the latter part of the nineteenth century, an historical

text was discovered in the vast collection of Babylonian tablets in the British Museum which actually states that Nebuchadnezzar did invade Egypt. The text is somewhat mutilated, but according to the restoration by scholars, it reads in part as follows: "In the thirty-seventh year, Nebuchadnezzar, king of Babylon marched against Egypt (the name of the land here is Mi-sir) to deliver a battle." [18]

I am not an authority on archaeology and cannot speak on the subject of Nebuchadnezzar's invasion of Egypt from intimate acquaintance with the sources; but I would like to conclude this study with a statement from one of the most distinguished critical Old Testament scholars of the early part of our century, the late Professor S. R. Driver, Regius Professor of Hebrew at the University of Oxford, who could not be called a conservative.

"There exist, however, inscriptions shewing (what had previously been doubted) that Nebuchadnezzar invaded Egypt, thereby fulfilling, at least in their general sense—for we do not know whether the fulfilment extended to details—the predictions of Jeremiah 43:9-13; 44:30) uttered shortly after 586, and of Ezekiel (29:19 f.; cf. vs. 8-12) uttered in 570. In the Louvre there is a statue from Elephantine, representing Nes-Hor, governor of Southern Egypt under Pharaoh Hophra (Apries: 589-564 b.c.) the inscription on which seems to state that an army of Asiatics and Northern peoples, which had apparently invaded Egypt, intended to advance up the valley of the Nile into Ethiopia; but that this disaster to the district under his command had been averted by the favour of the gods. And a fragmentary (cuneiform) inscription of Nebuchadnezzar himself, now in the British Museum, states that he invaded Egypt in his thirty-seventh year (568 b.c.) defeated the king of Egypt, [Ama] -a (?)

122

EGYPT IN BIBLICAL PROPHECY

-su,—*i.e.* as can hardly be doubted, Amasis (570-526 B.C.)—and slaughtered, or carried away, soldiers and horses." [19]

It is true that the frequent and extended references in these prophecies to Nebuchadnezzar's invasion of Egypt would lead one to expect many more references to this event in contemporary ancient literature, but the fact that there are so few does not prove, as many have assumed, that Jeremiah and Ezekiel were in error. Nebuchadnezzar's invasion was perhaps only an indication of Egypt's impending collapse, since what he began was carried to completion by the Persians who followed him. In the words of Professor Peet, the famous Egyptologist, "There is nothing improbable in such an event." [20]

Notes

1. C. E. Van Sickle: *A Political and Cultural History of the Ancient World.* New York, 1948. Vol. I, p. 131.
2. For a full discussion of this period see *Dressted* Op. "Cip" pages 567-581.
3. R. Payne Smith in *The Bible Commentary (Anglican Commentary)* New York, 1890. Vol. V, p. 533.
4. L. Elliott-Binns: *The Book of the Prophet Jeremiah,* in the *Westminster Commentaries.* London, 1919. p. 326.
5. A. B. Davidson: *The Book of the Prophet Ezekiel.* London, 1916. p. 230.
6. C. F. Keil: *Biblical Commentary on the Prophecies of Ezekiel.* Edinburgh, n.d. Vol. II, p. 4.
7. Keil, *ibid.* p. 7.
8. Henry A. Redpath: *The Book of the Prophet Ezekiel,* in the *Westminster Commentaries.* 1907. p. 159.
9. E. W. Hengstenberg: *The Prophecies of the Prophet Ezekiel.* Edinburgh, 1869. p. 256.
10. Keil, *op. cit.,* p. 8.
11. Keil, *op. cit.,* p. 14.
12. Keil, *op. cit.,* p. 19.
13. James H. Breasted: *A History of Egypt.* 2nd ed., New York, 1909. p. 595.

14. J. K. Cheyne: Jeremiah (in the *Pulpit Commentary*) New York, 1881. Vol. II. p. 208.
15. *Cambridge Ancient History*. Vol. III. 1925. p. 299.
16. Josephus: *Antiquities of the Jews*. X. 9.7.
17. *Cambridge Ancient History*, op. cit., p. 304.
18. The Ancient Near Eastern Texts, ed. by James Pritchard. Princeton, 1950. p. 308.
19. S. R. Driver: *Authority and Archaeology*. New York, 1899. p. 116-117.
20. T. Eric Peet: *Egypt and the Old Testament*, Boston, 1923. p. 187.

7

"OUT OF EGYPT DID I CALL MY SON"

The only reference to Egypt in the four Gospels is of an unexpected nature, for two reasons. Before Herod could carry out his iniquitous purpose to destroy all the babes of Bethlehem, an angel appeared to Joseph and told him to arise, take the young child with his mother and flee into Egypt, and to remain there until he should receive further word. Matthew tells us that the holy family "was there until the death of Herod: that it might be fulfilled which was spoken by the Lord through the prophet saying, Out of Egypt did I call my son' (Matt. 2:15, quoted from Hosea 11:1). In the first place, Matthew quotes an historical statement from the prophecy of Hosea and interprets it as being fulfilled in Christ. In the second place, this mention of African territory is unique in the geographical data of the Gospels, for during His public ministry Christ confined Himself exclusively to Palestine and lower Syria, so that the place farthest from Judaea and Galilee in the incarnate life of the Son of God enters the narrative at the time He was a babe in His mother's arms. Much tradition, and a great number of paintings have arisen from this brief, and, one would almost say, comparatively unimportant aspect of the nativity record. For our purpose, we must hold strictly to the text, and not drift off into mystical and allegorical interpretations.

Let us first consider the statement as Hosea wrote it: "When Israel was a child, then I loved him, and called my son out of Egypt" (11:1). No one denies that the reference is to two major events in Israel's history—her divine call and her deliverance from Egypt. It is sometimes forgotten that Israel is referred to as God's son in Moses' initial challenge to Pharaoh, according to divine instruction: "Thus saith Jehovah, Israel is my son, my first-born: and I have said unto thee, Let my son go, that he may serve me" (Ex. 4:22, 23). The portrayal of Israel as God's son, and as originally a helpless babe is beautifully set forth in the verses immediately following. This concept of Israel's divine election proceeding from the undeserved love of God is a frequent theme in the Book of Deuteronomy. When the years of wandering were about over, Moses reminded Israel of her divine calling: "Out of heaven he made thee to hear his voice, that he might instruct thee: and upon earth he made thee to see his great fire; and thou heardest his words out of the midst of the fire. And because he loved thy fathers, therefore he chose their seed after them, and brought thee out with his presence, with his great power, out of Egypt" (Deut. 4:36, 37; see also 7:13; 10:15; 15:16). Then there is the familiar declaration, "Jehovah did not set his love upon you, nor choose you, because ye were more in number . . . but because Jehovah loveth you" (Deut. 7:7, 8). Pusey quotes a very apt, concise interpretation of Israel as a child from Osorius (a writer otherwise unknown to me): "When did He love Israel? When, by His guidance, Israel regained freedom, his enemies were destroyed, he was fed with food from heaven, he heard the voice of God, and received the law from Him. He was unformed in Egypt; then he was informed by the rules of the law, so as to be matured there. He was a child in that vast waste. For he was nourished, not by solid food, but by milk, that it, by the rudiments of piety and righteousness, that he might gradually attain the strength of a man. So that law was a schoolmaster, to retain Israel as a child, by the discipline of a child, until the time should come when all, who despised not the heavenly gifts, should receive the Spirit of adoption." [1]

In turning to the use of this passage in Matthew, it is necessary to know the context of the announcement for its correct understanding: "And when they were departed, behold, an angel of the Lord appeareth to Joseph in a dream, saying, Arise and take the young child and his mother, and flee into Egypt, and be thou there until I tell thee: for Herod will seek the young child to destroy him. And he arose and took the young child and his mother by night, and departed into Egypt; and was there until the death of Herod: that it might be fulfilled which was spoken by the Lord through the prophet, saying, Out of Egypt did I call my son" (2:13-15). One thing should be clearly understood—the reference here is to a literal geographical area, to Egypt. There is no hint that any place in Palestine is symbolically called Egypt, as Jerusalem was sometimes called Sodom. No one, it seems, has offered any evidence to warrant questioning the geographical literalness of this experience of the holy family. The text, however, gives no indication of where the family took up temporary residence. There are many traditions, but no actual data. The more commonly accepted tradition places this at what is now called Matarieh, six miles northeast of Cairo. One is probably right in assuming at least two things: that the route taken was not along the main coastal highway in Palestine, for there the little party could easily be overtaken by Herod's soldiers, and secondly, that they did not have to go far into Egypt to be safe from this tyrant's jurisdiction.

There are at least four points of similarity between the nation Israel in Egypt and the babe Jesus in Egypt: (1) Both of them are referred to as "sons," one literally, and the other symbolically. (2) While the word *love* is not in the Matthew text, surely we have a right to say that the love God had for the nation Israel was manifested in a superlative way toward His only begotten Son, here the infant child. (3) *By divine direction,* both the nation and the holy family are commanded to go into Egypt. (4) As Israel was brought out of Egypt in God's own time, so also was an announcement made to Mary and Joseph at the appropriate time regarding their return to the land of promise. One aspect of Israel's sojourn in Egypt was not, as far as we know, experienced by the holy family, in that land of pyramids and pagan temples—the oppression and bondage which Israel endured centuries before. Matthew does not merely imply that there are parallels here: he definitely states that the flight to Egypt and the return was accomplished "that it might be fulfilled which was spoken by the Lord through the prophet, saying, Out of Egypt did I call my son."

The words of Keil are so pregnant with meaning and so

indicative of a true insight into the deeper meaning of this passage, that I am taking the liberty of quoting them in full, rather than substituting something less meaningful of my own. "The adoption of Israel as the son of Jehovah, which began with its deliverance out of the bondage of Egypt, and was completed in the conclusion of the covenant at Sinai, forms the first stage in the carrying out of the divine work of salvation, which was completed in the incarnation of the Son of God for the redemption of mankind from death and ruin. The development and guidance of Israel as the people of God all pointed to Christ; not, however, in any such sense as that the nation of Israel was to bring forth the Son of God from within itself, but in this sense, that the relation which the Lord of heaven and earth established and sustained with that nation, was a preparation for the union of God with humanity, and paved the way for the incarnation of His Son, by the fact that Israel was trained to be a vessel of divine grace. All essential factors in the history of Israel point to this as their end, and thereby become types and material prophecies of the life of Him in whom the reconciliation of man to God was to be realized, and the union of God with the human race to be developed into a personal unity. It is in this sense that the second half of our verse is quoted in Matthew 2:15 as a prophecy of Christ, not because the words of the prophet refer directly and immediately to Christ, but because the sojourn in Egypt, and return out of that land, had the same significance in relation to the development of the life of Jesus Christ, as it had to the nation of Israel. Just as Israel grew into a nation in Egypt, where it was out of the reach of Canaanitish ways, so was the child Jesus hidden in Egypt from the hostility of Herod." [2]

I do not recall seeing this in any of the innumerable comments upon this flight into Egypt, but certainly the text emphasizes one fundamental truth that attaches to the significance of Egypt in the Old Testament, namely, that Egypt was a place out from which the people of God must ultimately come. It was no land of promise. It was *visited,* and God often permitted and even commanded such visits, but they were only temporary and preparatory. In itself, Egypt had no contribution to make to the ethical and moral life of the people of God.[3]

Notes

1. E. B. Pusey: *The Minor Prophets.* 1886. Vol. I, p. 109.
2. C. F. Keil: *The Twelve Minor Prophets.* Edinburgh, 1868. Vol. I, p. 137.
3. There are two excellent articles on this subject in the first volume of Hastings' *Dictionary of Christ and the Gospels*—"Egypt," pp. 509-510, and "Flight," pp. 600-602. See also L. S. Fillion: *The Life of Christ.* St. Louis, 1946. Vol. I, pp. 353-355. Early traditions surrounding the flight are set forth in the *Gospel of Thomas,* and, in the *Gospel of the Pseudo-Matthew,* XVII-XXIV, for which see M. J. James: *The Apocryphal New Testament,* Oxford, 1942, pp. 58, 74-76. Also a chapter in F. W. Farrar: *Christ in Art,* pp. 263-273.

8

"THE TONGUE OF THE EGYPTIAN SEA"

The first extended prophecy explicitly involving the *future* of Egypt is found at the conclusion of the 11th chapter of the Book of Isaiah. The paragraph in which Egypt is thrice mentioned is set in the midst of one of the greatest, and for the most part as yet unfulfilled, prophetic passages of ultimate glory and Messianic supremacy contained in all the Scriptures, (Chapters 10 to 12), forming a perfect preface for Isaiah's extended series of prophecies on the future of the nations of the Near East.

While it is true that the preliminary reference in Chapter 10 is to Assyria (the rod of God's anger, which will be used against Judah; a mighty empire that is doomed to destruction; a great tree or, actually, a forest of trees, which will be cut down), there are here also references to a time that has not yet been known on the earth, in which a universal empire will be overthrown, foreshadowed by the destruction of Assyria. God has not yet "performed his whole work upon mount Zion and on Jerusalem" (10:12). History has not yet revealed that blessed hour in Israel's final submission to Jehovah: "And it shall come to pass in that day, that the remnant of Israel, and they that are escaped of the house of Jacob, shall no more again lean upon him that smote them, but shall lean upon Jehovah, the Holy One of Israel, in truth" (10:20).

The 11th chapter is fundamentally Messianic, as both Hebrew and Christian commentators agree. While in His first advent the Spirit of the Lord did rest upon the Messiah, the spirit of wisdom and understanding, and His delight was in the fear of Jehovah, yet at that advent He did not "smite the earth with the rod of His mouth and with the breath of his lips slay the wicked" (11:4). The glorious picture of a renewed and restored earth, in the animal creation and among the nations of the earth, has not as yet unfolded in historic reality: "And the wolf shall dwell with the lamb, and the leopard shall lie down with the kid; and the calf and the young lion and the fatling together; and a little child shall lead them. And the cow and the bear shall feed; their young ones shall lie down together; and the lion shall eat straw like the ox. And the suckling child shall play on the hole of the asp, and the weaned child shall put his hand on the adder's den. They shall not hurt nor destroy in all my holy mountain; for the earth shall be full of the knowledge of Jehovah, as the waters cover the sea. And it shall come to pass in that day, that the root of Jesse, that standeth for an ensign of the peoples, unto him shall the nations seek; and his resting-place shall be glorious" (vs. 6-10).

Let us not allow these words to evaporate before our eyes through some unwarranted principle of hermeneutics which makes them to refer exclusively to a spiritual experience of the Church, and denies the ultimate literalness of their fulfillment. The comment of the eminent scholar Delitzsch is well worth considering here:

"The fathers, and such commentators as Luther, Calvin, and Vitringa, have taken all these figures from the animal world as symbolical. Modern rationalists, on the other hand, understand them literally, but regard the whole as a beautiful dream and wish. It is a prophecy, however, the realization of which is to be expected on this side of the boundary between time and eternity, and, as Paul has shown in Romans 8, is an integral link in the predestined course of the history of salvation (Hengstenberg, Umbreit, Hofmann, Dreschsler). There now reign among irrational creatures, from the greatest to the least—even among such as are invisible—fierce conflicts and bloodthirstiness of the most savage kind. But when the Son of David enters upon the full possession of His royal inheritance, the peace of paradise will be renewed, and all that is true in the popular legends of a golden age be realized and confirmed. This is what the prophet depicts in such lovely colours. The wolf and lamb, those two hereditary foes, will be perfectly reconciled then. The leopard will let the teasing kid lie down beside it. The lion, between the calf and stalled ox, will not seize upon its weaker neighbour. Cow and bear will graze together, whilst their young ones will lie side by side in the pasture. The lion will no longer thirst for blood, but content itself, like the ox, with chopped straw . . .

"We must guard against treating the description itself as merely a drapery thrown around the actual object; whereas it is rather the refraction of the object in the mind of the

133

prophet himself, and therefore a manifestation of the true nature of that which he actually saw . . . The meaning of 'the earth' is also determined by that of 'all my holy mountain.' The *land of Israel,* the dominion of the Son of David, in the more restricted sense, will be from this time forward a paradisaical centre, as it were, of the whole earth —a prelude of its future state of perfect and universal glorification (Ch. 6:3, 'all the earth'). It has now become full of 'the knowledge of Jehovah,' that is, of that experimental knowledge which consists in the fellowship of love, like the waters which cover the sea, that is, the bottom of the sea (compare Hab. 2:14)." [1]

To this description of a glory which the earth is yet to enjoy further details are added throughout Chapter 12, where the people of God, now in the land of promise, unanimously and fervently cry out, "Jehovah, even Jehovah, is my strength and song; and he is become my salvation" (12:2). Israel has not yet fulfilled the promise of the succeeding verse: "Therefore with joy shall ye draw water out of the wells of salvation"; nor has she yet begun to recognize that "great in the midst of thee is the Holy One of Israel." The more one looks at these promises, while turning the pages of the history of Israel and the Church, and then looks about the world today in its fearful hatreds, boastfulness and godlessness, the more one is convinced that these prophecies have not yet been fulfilled on this earth. If the counsels of God stand sure, and the prophet was foreannouncing a triumph for God that must ultimately come to pass, then we have here one of Isaiah's most exalted prophecies of a future glory for this earth.

EGYPT IN BIBLICAL PROPHECY

It is in the midst of such a dramatic setting forth of the ultimate victory of God over the forces of evil, especially in relation to Israel, that we come upon this amazing prediction concerning Egypt. The text itself should be before us: "And it shall come to pass in that day, that the Lord will set his hand again the second time to recover the remnant of his people, that shall remain, from Assyria, and from Egypt, and from Pathros, and from Cush, and from Elam, and from Shinar, and from Hamath, and from the islands of the sea. And he will set up an ensign for the nations, and will assemble the outcasts of Israel and gather together the dispersed of Judah from the four corners of the earth. The envy also of Ephraim shall depart, and they that vex Judah shall be cut off: Ephraim shall not envy Judah, and Judah shall not vex Ephraim. And they shall fly down upon the shoulder of the Philistines on the west; together shall they despoil the children of the east; they shall put forth their hand upon Edom and Moab; and the children of Ammon shall obey them. And Jehovah will utterly destroy the tongue of the Egyptian sea; and with his scorching wind will he wave his hand over the River, and will smite it into seven streams, and cause men to march over dryshod. And there shall be a highway for the remnant of his people, that shall remain, from Assyria; like as there was for Israel in the day that he came up out of the land of Egypt" (vs. 11-16).

Even a superficial examination of these words will reveal an emphasis which would not ordinarily be expected on the part of a prophet of the eighth century B.C. It was Assyria that had destroyed Israel, and it would be from the same direction that Babylon, under Nebuchadnezzar, would come down to destroy Judah and Jerusalem. In this prophecy, however, while Assyria is mentioned both at the beginning and at the conclusion, it is Egypt, and the area about her, which is given the greater prominence. Not only is Egypt put on an equality with Assyria in verse 11, but there are other geographical references: Pathros is southern Egypt and Cush is close by Ethiopia. Then, as not in the case of Assyria, the prophet devotes a long sentence to some future occurrence in this Egyptian area, wherein he says that the Lord "will utterly destroy the tongue of the Egyptian sea." It is to this passage that we must give the most careful attention. Let us remind ourselves, again in the words of Delitzsch, that events about to be described are located at a time when the Lord "will set his hand again the second time to recover the remnant of his people, that shall remain, from Assyria, and from Egypt." "There was no such *diaspora* of Israel at the time when the prophet uttered this prediction, nor indeed even after the dissolution of the northern kingdom; so that the specification is not historical, but prophetic. The redemption which the prophet here foretells is a second, to be followed by no third; consequently the banishment out of which Israel is redeemed is the ultimate form of that which is threatened in 6:12 (cf. Deut. 30:1 sqq.). It is the second redemption, the counterpart of the Egyptian. Observe how, in the prophet's view, the conversion of the heathen becomes the means of the redemption of Israel. The course which the history of salvation has taken since the first coming of Christ, and which it will continue to take to the end, as described by Paul in the Epistle to the Romans, is distinctly indicated by the prophet. At the word of Jehovah the heathen will set His people free, and even escort them

(49:22; 62:10); and thus He will gather again (*asaph*, with reference to the one gathering point; *kibbetz*, with reference to the dispersion of those who are to be gathered together) from the utmost ends of the four quarters of the globe, 'the outcasts of the kingdom of Israel, and the dispersed of the kingdom of Judah.' " [2]

Recognizing that this whole portion of Isaiah's prophecy refers to a time of ultimate splendour, peace, righteousness and recognition of God on the earth, a time when Israel will be back in her land, we should give special attention to this phrase, *Jehovah will utterly destroy the tongue of the Egyptian sea.* Three bodies of water are of major significance in any geographical survey of this North Africa kingdom—the Nile River, the Mediterranean Sea, and the Red Sea. Now the Mediterranean is never, either in the Bible or in secular literature, referred to as "the Egyptian Sea;" and although on rare occasions a large river such as the Euphrates or the Nile might be spoken of as a "sea," all Biblical scholars acknowledge that the body of water here referred to by Isaiah is the western fork of the Red Sea (the eastern fork being known as the Gulf of Akkabah). It is that part of the Red Sea that lies on the eastern shore of Egypt.

But what is meant by "the *tongue* of the Egyptian sea"? Any Bible atlas, or map of Egypt, will show that the northern end of this body of water terminates in what might be called an elongated bay, a smaller, narrower body of water extending from the sea itself. This bay, in turn, leads into a channel which connects with the Bitter Lakes. At this northern end of the Egyptian Sea the Suez Canal begins, at the southern end of which is the city of Suez and at the northern end, on the

Mediterranean, the recently-bombed city of Port Said. That this prophecy, therefore, points to something that would occur in the vicinity of Suez, and the Suez Canal, can hardly be denied. Over a century ago (1846) Joseph Addison Alexander, of Princeton Seminary, in his epochal work on Isaiah, unequivocally affirmed, "The *Tongue* of this sea is the narrow gulf or bay in which it (the Red Sea) terminates to the north-west near Suez." [3] The more recently published *Interpreter's Bible* explicitly declares that this must be taken as the Gulf of Suez.[4] Soon after the Suez Canal was opened, Professor Birks of Cambridge wrote, almost prophetically, in his excellent commentary on Isaiah, "The tongue of the Egyptian Sea is that arm of the Gulf of Suez which was parted in the Exodus and to which attention is now turned by a recent triumph of human labor and skill; but hereafter that man may be humbled in the dust and the Lord alone may be exalted." [5]

This word *destroyed* deserves careful study also. It is the word *haram* or *charam,* commonly meaning to utterly destroy, to devote in the sense of dooming to destruction, with God as the subject, as in Isaiah 34:2 and Jeremiah 25:9. Representing the idea of utter destruction, it occurs forty-one times in the Hebrew Old Testament.

Having examined the individual phrases of the text, we must try to ascertain the over-all prediction set forth by Isaiah in this geographical prophecy. There have been three basic and differing interpretations. One view is that held by those who find in most of the prophecies references to the glory of the Church, an interpretation which spiritualizes the prophecies and denies to them a literal fulfilment. This, of course, would be the position of Calvin, who, in making the entire passage relate to "the future glory of the Church," asserts, "By these metaphors the prophet means nothing else than that nothing will stand in God's way when it shall be His pleasure to rescue His people from captivity." [6] Among many other modern commentators, Kay gives expression to the same idea when he says, "There was such an ingathering at the commencement of the Church's history—Pentecost; we are taught to look for another larger fulfilment." [7]

A second interpretation finds in the passage a reference to a mass ingathering of the Jewish people at the end of the age, but denies that Israel will have any special place in Palestine, or that there will be a state of Israel. This is the view for example, of Albert Barnes: "The time is coming when the scattered Jews shall be gathered to God—not again to their own land but brought again under His dominion, under the administration of the Messiah—and this event shall be attended with a sudden removal of the obstruction to the gospel and to its rapid spread everywhere among the nations. We have every reason to expect that God intends to make great use yet of the Jews whom He has preserved scattered everywhere." [8]

The third view—and the one which the writer of this book would adopt—is that the passage, which must refer to events occurring and conditions obtaining at the end of this age, requires for its fulfilment a reappearance of the principal nations represented here upon the stage of history for its final act. Among those who hold this conviction is Fausset, who says, "In the first restoration Judah alone was restored, with perhaps some few of Israel; in the future restoration both are expressly specified (Ez. 37:16-19; Jer. 3:18). To Israel are ascribed the 'outcasts'; to Judah, the 'dispersed,' as the former have been longer and more utterly cast away." [9] Even George Rawlinson, for many years Professor of Ancient History at Oxford, acknowledges that while there may have been a secondary fulfillment of the gathering of Jews from all quarters into the Christian Church, as in the second chapter of Acts, "it is possible that there may be ultimately a further fulfillment in a final gathering together of Israel into their own land." [10]

This would imply that there will be a strong national entity in the Mesopotamian Valley, where Assyria once was, that there will also be a powerful national sovereignty in Egypt, and that, as in the days of the ancient kingdom of Israel and Judah, so again at the end of the age, Israel will be the third among these nations. Up to a few years ago, such a national alignment would have seemed impossible, and when some prophetic scholars of the 19th century did suggest such as a possibility, they were scoffed at. That day of scoffing has gone. First of all—and this cannot be emphasized too frequently—*Israel* is a state which bears that name, in which reside Jewish people gathered from all over the world, a nation of unusual military power in proportion to its size and population. Then, there is Egypt, now a free nation, no more under the control of, first, the Ottoman empire, then the British empire. Up to the middle of the nineteenth century, Egypt was only a site for archaeological research, a winter resort for the more wealthy British, a center for Mohammedan learning, an area for Protestant mission work, a land of no importance on the checkerboard of international relations. Today Egypt is continually on the front pages of our newspapers; we hear the name every day on the radio, and it has become the dominant theme of the United Nations Assembly. It is possible that all of this can pass, and the trouble in the Near East be resolved, for the time being at least; but this does not alter the fact that Egypt is here as a nation to play her part in world affairs, a role which has been utterly impossible for hundreds of years until the day in which we are living. And what about Assyria. The very month in which this chapter is being written, Iraq ancient called Babylon has announced that she is determined to destroy the State of Israel. This sounds like Babylon of old, and comes from the same area.

The erection of a canal from the Gulf of Suez to the Mediterranean was first undertaken in the XIXth Dynasty in ancient Egypt. A second canal, beginning at the Nile and proceeding in a northward direction to Lake Balla, may be dated in the XIth or XIIth Dynasty. A third canal, cut by Ptolemy II, Philadelphus (285-246 b.c.) "began at the Pelusiac branch of the Nile near the town of Daphnae, crossed the plateau of El Ferdan and Lake Timsah and joined the Canal of the Pharaohs near Bir Abou-Balla or Sabah-Abiar. From this point the old canal was re-excavated and Strabo tells us that Ptolemy constructed a lock with a double gate at its entrance in order to prevent the water of the sea from contaminating the fresh water of the Nile." [11]

Through the years, the Suez Canal has been a boon to Egypt—what it will be for her in the years ahead no one knows. The very fact that Egypt now has possession of it, and can refuse or permit traffic at her own discretion, is likely to be the cause of international disputes and tensions for a long time to come. As far back as 1930, Abbas Hilmi II remarked, "The canal has been the principal cause of Egypt's miseries." [12] At the time of the completion of the canal, there were no automobiles, no airplanes, no demand for petroleum; today, were the canal to be blockaded for a short time, the streets of Paris and London would be almost empty of motor vehicles.

It is significant that it must have been not far from Suez that the waters overwhelmed the pursuing host of Pharaoh, and Israel was at last out of the grip of Egypt's enslavement. Many decades ago, E. J. Palmer in his classic work, *The Desert of the Exodus,* called attention to the fact that the route of the Israelites must be placed within two or three hours' ride from the modern city of Suez. "Two hours' ride from Suez brought us to Ayún Músa, or Moses's Wells, a beautiful little oasis in the desert. It consists of a few springs of limpid but brackish water, small pools with gardens of palms and tamarisks around them, as well as beds of vegetables and culinary herbs. These gardens are kept by a Frenchman and some Arabs, who have provided summer-houses for the convenience of those who resort thither from Suez to enjoy the fresh desert air. They form the market-gardens from which the vegetable supply of Suez is principally drawn. Here tradition places the site of the passage of the Red Sea; and certain it is that, at least within the range over which the eye can wander, the waters must have closed in upon Pharaoh's struggling hosts. The miracle of the passage of the Red Sea is so important in its bearings upon the whole question of the Exodus that many and various opinions have been advanced

both as to its site and character. The obvious route of the
Israelites from Egypt would have been by the ordinary road
to Palestine through the Philistine territory; but we are
expressly told that 'God led them not through the way of the
land of the Philistines, although that was near; for God said,
Lest peradventure the people repent when they see war, and
they return to Egypt: but God led the people about, through
the way of the wilderness of the Red Sea' (Exod. 13:17, 18).
Now this 'way of the wilderness' must also have passed round
the head of the Gulf, and the two routes must have been at
this point coincident." [13]

"The position of Suez was always one of commercial importance, and a succession of towns had risen, flourished, and
disappeared in turn on or near it, as the Red Sea receded
southward to the head of the two Gulfs in which it now
terminates,' and to the westernmost of which Suez gives its
name." [14] The early name for this site was Arisonöe. In the
fourteenth century it came to be called Kolzoum. In 1798
Suez was nearly one-half demolished when the French began
fortifications there, which were never finished. The population in 1859 was approximately 4,000; the building of the
canal swelled this figure to 16,000 in 1868, but during the
next decade it leveled at 11,000. The present population is
50,000. It is interesting to note that as long ago as 1798,
Napoleon in his Instructions to the Directorate on April 12,
issued the following order: "The army of the East shall take
possession of Egypt. The Commander in Chief . . . shall
have the Isthmus of Suez cut through and I shall take the
necessary steps to assure the free and exclusive possession of
the Red Sea to the French Republic."

EGYPT IN BIBLICAL PROPHECY

This statement of Isaiah's, if it is to be taken literally—with the recognition that no such physical judgment has occurred in this vicinity since the prophet's time—certainly warrants our believing that this particular area on the eastern boundary of Egypt will suffer some violent physical convulsion of a destructive nature.

Notes

1. Franz Delitzsch: *Biblical Commentary on the Prophecies of Isaiah.* 1879. Vol. I, p. 286.
2. Delitzsch, *op. cit.*, p. 289.
3. Joseph Addison Alexander: *Commentary on the Prophecies of Isaiah.* Rev. ed., Edinburgh, 1865. Vol. I, p. 262; see also New York, n.d., p. 88.
4. *The Interpreter's Bible,* Vol. V. New York, 1956. p. 252.
5. T. R. Birks: *Commentary on the Book of Isaiah.* 2nd ed., London, 1878. p. 73.
6. John Calvin: *Commentary on the Book of the Prophet Isaiah.* Eng. tr., Vol. I, p. 396.
7. W. Kay in *The Anglican Commentary.* Vol. V, New York, 1890. p. 113.
8. Albert Barnes: *Notes on the Book of Isaiah.* 1867. Vol. I, p. 258.
9. Jamieson, Fausset and Brown: *Commentary on the Old and New Testaments.* Vol. IV, p. 604.
10. George Rawlinson, in *The Pulpit Commentary: Isaiah.* Vol. I, p. 205.
11. Charles W. Hallberg: *The Suez Canal, Its History and Diplomatic Importance.* New York: Columbia Univ. Press, 1931. p. 29. A complete list of all the references in the ancient classical writers to this locality, now known as Suez but then called Arsinoe, will be found in John Ball: *Egypt in the Classical Geographers.* Cairo, 1942.
12. This is quoted by Hallberg from Abbas Hilmi II: *A Few Words on the Anglo-Egyptian Settlement.* London, 1930. p. 33.
13. E. J. Palmer: *The Desert of the Exodus.* New York, 1872. pp. 41-43.
14. J. C. McCoan: *Egypt.* Rev. ed., New York, 1902. p. 88.

9

PROPHECIES OF ISRAEL'S RETREAT TO EGYPT AND HER FINAL SECOND EXODUS

The late Canon Liddon once preached a notable sermon on "The Fascination of Egypt," and surely the history of Israel from Abraham to the period after the destruction of Jerusalem bears testimony to this mysterious magnetic power of the land of the Pyramids, the Sphinx, and the vast temples to the gods of that ancient kingdom. With the rise of Nebuchadnezzar and the threat of the Babylonian invasion and conquest of Egypt, the king of Egypt brought pressure upon Jehoiakim (608-597 B.C.), son of the good king Josiah, to rebel against Nebuchadnezzar. At the same time, Ethbaal II of Phoenicia refused to continue paying tribute to Nebuchadnezzar, an action which compelled the great king to lay siege to the city of Tyre, a city which to his complete surprise resisted his assaults for thirteen years. During this time, Jehoiakim died. His son and successor Jehoiachin reigned for only three months, and was followed to the throne by his uncle, another son of Josiah, and the last king ever to sit upon the throne of Judah, Zedekiah (597-587 B.C.). "Zedekiah may have intended to remain faithful to the oath of fealty which he had taken to his liege lord Nebuchadnezzar, but he had not the strength of will to adhere to his resolution. Rebellious schemes were secretly formed which he, in the seclusion of his palace, did not find out, or, if cognizant of them, was incapable of opposition. This weakness on the part of the king and foolhardiness on the part of the nobles led to the fall of Judah. The nobles appear to have been seized with madness. Egypt, ever false and deceitful, was continually goading the Judaeans on by making brilliant promises of alliance which it seldom kept. In the fourth year of Zedekiah's reign, ambassadors were urging him to break his word and faith, employing all the artifices of eloquence to bring the wavering monarch to a decision." [1]

In such a critical hour, these vacillating captains and lords sought out the prophet Jeremiah to ask if God might have a word for them through his lips as to whether or not they should flee from the impending invasion of Nebuchadnezzar and seek the shelter of the southern Egyptian kingdom. No doubt, they had already determined what they were going to do. For ten days the prophet waited for an answer from Jehovah, and when it came, it was in the form of a clear disapproval of such a scheme, accompanied by dire warnings of what would happen if the plan were carried out. Inasmuch as the chapter has direct bearing upon the theme of our study, it should be quoted in full:

Thus saith Jehovah, the God of Israel, unto whom ye sent me to present your supplication before him: If ye will still abide in this land, then will I build you, and not pull you down, and I will plant you, and not pluck you up; for I repent me of the evil that I have done unto you. Be not afraid of the king of Babylon, of whom ye are afraid; be not afraid of him, saith Jehovah: for I am with you to save you, and to deliver you from his hand. And I will grant you mercy, that he may have mercy upon you, and cause you to return to your own land. But

if ye say, We will not dwell in this land; so that ye obey not
the voice of Jehovah your God, saying, No; but we will go
into the land of Egypt, where we shall see no war, nor hear the
sound of the trumpet, nor have hunger of bread; and there will
we dwell: now therefore hear ye the word of Jehovah, O remnant
of Judah: Thus saith Jehovah of hosts, the God of Israel, If
ye indeed set your faces to enter into Egypt, and go to sojourn
there; then it shall come to pass, that the sword, which ye fear,
shall overtake you there in the land of Egypt; and the famine,
whereof ye are afraid, shall follow hard after you there in Egypt;
and there ye shall die. So shall it be with all the men that
set their faces to go into Egypt to sojourn there: they shall die
by the sword, by the famine, and by the pestilence; and none
of them shall remain or escape from the evil that I will bring
upon them.

For thus saith Jehovah of hosts, the God of Israel: As mine
anger and my wrath hath been poured forth upon the inhabitants
of Jerusalem so shall my wrath be poured forth upon you, when
ye shall enter into Egypt; and ye shall be an execration, and an
astonishment, and a curse, and a reproach; and ye shall see
this place no more. Jehovah hath spoken concerning you, O
remnant of Judah, Go ye not into Egypt: know certainly that I
have testified unto you this day. For ye have dealt deceitfully
against your own souls; for ye sent me unto Jehovah your God,
saying, Pray for us unto Jehovah our God; and according unto
all that Jehovah our God shall say, so declare unto us, and we
will do it. And I have this day declared it to you; but ye have
not obeyed the voice of Jehovah your God in anything for
which he hath sent me unto you. Now therefore know certainly
that ye shall die by the sword, by the famine, and by the
pestilence, in the place whither ye desire to go to sojourn
there (Jeremiah 42:9-22).

This divine declaration fully unfolds a prophecy uttered first
by Hosea 150 years before, that the day would come when

Israel would again go down into Egypt: "They shall return to Egypt. For Israel hath forgotten his Maker, and builded palaces; and Judah hath multiplied fortified cities: but I will send a fire upon his cities, and it shall devour the castles thereof . . . They shall not dwell in Jehovah's land; but Ephraim shall return to Egypt, and they shall eat unclean food in Assyria . . . For lo, they are gone away from destruction; yet Egypt shall gather them up, Memphis shall bury them; their pleasant things of silver, nettles shall possess them; thorns shall be in their tents" (8:13, 14; 9:3, 6).

The message and warning from Jehovah through Jeremiah fell on deaf ears. Leaders in Judah accused him of speaking falsely, declaring, "The Lord our God hath not sent thee to say, Ye shall not go into Egypt to sojourn there; but Baruch the son of Neriah setteth thee on against us, to deliver us into the hand of the Chaldeans, that they may put us to death, and carry us away captive to Babylon" (43:2, 3). Deliberately disobeying the voice of the Lord, "all the captains of the forces took all the remnant of Judah that were returned from all the nations whither they had been driven, to sojourn in the land of Judah . . . every person that Nebuzaradan had left with Gedaliah," including Jeremiah the prophet and Baruch, and went down into the land of Egypt, specifically to the city of Tahpanhes. There in Egypt, as centuries before, Israel became involved in gross idolatrous practices: "Thus saith Jehovah, Wherefore commit ye this great evil against your own souls . . . in that ye provoke me unto anger with the works of your hands, burning incense unto other gods in the land of Egypt, whither ye are gone to sojourn?" (44:8). Hardly any statements in the entire Word of God reveal such

stubbornness of heart in resisting the will of God as those
which the disobedient Israelites insultingly directed at Jeremiah while they were in Egypt:

As for the word that thou has spoken unto us in the name
of Jehovah, we will not hearken unto thee. But we will certainly
perform every word that is gone forth out of our mouth, to
burn incense unto the queen of heaven, and to pour out drink-
offerings unto her, as we have done, we and our fathers, our
kings and our princes, in the cities of Judah, and in the streets
of Jerusalem; for then had we plenty of victuals, and were well,
and saw no evil. But since we left off burning incense to the
queen of heaven, and pouring out drink-offerings unto her, we
have wanted all things, and have been consumed by the sword
and by the famine. And when we burned incense to the queen
of heaven, and poured out drink-offerings unto her, did we
make her cakes to worship her, and pour out drink-offerings
unto her, without our husbands? (44:16-19).

The prophet's reply forms the last message, of which we
have any record, to come from the lips of this faithful servant
of God:

Then Jeremiah said unto all the people, to the men and to
the women, even to all the people that had given him that
answer, saying, The incense that ye burned in the cities of Judah,
and in the streets of Jerusalem, ye and your fathers, your kings
and your princes, and the people of the land, did not Jehovah
remember them, and came it not into his mind? so that Jehovah
could no longer bear, because of the evil of your doings, and
because of the abominations which ye have committed; therefore is your land become a desolation, and an astonishment, and
a curse, without inhabitant, as it is this day. Because ye have
burned incense, and because ye have sinned against Jehovah,
and have not obeyed the voice of Jehovah, nor walked in his

law, nor in his statutes, nor in his testimonies; therefore, this evil is happened unto you, as it is this day.

Moreover Jeremiah said unto all the people, and to all the women, Hear the word of Jehovah, all Judah that are in the land of Egypt: Thus saith Jehovah of hosts, the God of Israel, saying, Ye and your wives have both spoken with your mouths, and with your hands have fulfilled it, saying, We will surely perform our vows that we have vowed, to burn incense to the queen of heaven, and to pour out drink-offerings unto her: establish then your vows, and perform your vows. Therefore hear ye the word of Jehovah, all Judah that dwell in the land of Egypt: Behold, I have sworn by my great name, saith Jehovah, that my name shall no more be named in the mouth of any man of Judah in all the land of Egypt, saying, As the Lord Jehovah liveth. Behold, I watch over them for evil and not for good; and all the men of Judah that are in the land of Egypt shall be consumed by the sword and by the famine until there be an end of them . . . And this shall be the sign unto you, saith Jehovah, that I will punish you in this place, that ye may know that my words shall surely stand against you for evil (44:20-27, 29).

We have very little exact information on the condition of the Jews who fled to Egypt previous to the destruction of Jerusalem and the final deportation to Babylon. The words of Jeremiah seem to imply that none who went down in this hour of disobedience would ever return to Judah, with the exception of a pitiful remnant to which we shall give attention later. "For many years Jewish settlers had come to Egypt in great numbers and of course they would have their full share of the miseries of the Chaldean invasion, but the new-comers would suffer more severely, partly as being gathered chiefly in the border towns, and partly from their want of means. They would have no knowledge of the Egyptian language or ways, would have no friends in the country to aid them and would also be recognized by the Chaldeans as inveterate enemies and mercilessly slain." [2] They were placing themselves under the protection of the "queen of heaven," but were not escaping the wrath of the omnipotent God whom they were resisting. Although there were thousands of Jews in Egypt at the time of Alexander the Great, many of whom may have been descendants of the Jews who went down to Egypt on this occasion, there is no record of any of these Jews, of that generation or even of the next, returning to the land of Judah, as so many did from Babylon.

There is one word of hope here: "And they that escape the sword shall return out of the land of Egypt into the land of Judah, few in number; and all the remnant of Judah, that are gone into the land of Egypt to sojourn there, shall know whose word shall stand, mine, or theirs" (44:28). The fact that we have no historical data regarding the return of such a remnant does not in any way invalidate the accuracy of this prophecy.

The Promise That the Israelites Would Ultimately Be Brought Back from Egypt

It is in the light of the passages just considered that we must interpret those otherwise enigmatic promises and prophecies in the Old Testament which speak of the return of Israel from Egypt *the second time,* of which Jeremiah 44:28 is a mature preliminary prediction. Perhaps it would be well for us to bring together all of the passages that speak of Israel's return from Egypt. The first is near the conclusion of the prophecy of Micah, uttered over one hundred years before the fall of Jerusalem. This passage is so inaccurately translated in the King James version that one would never know it had any reference to Egypt; the later versions correctly (by construing *nāsōr* as equivalent to *Misrayim,* 'Egypt') read as follows: "In that day shall they come unto thee from Assyria and the cities of Egypt, and from Egypt even to the River, and from sea to sea, and from mountain to mountain" (7:12). This verse is placed in the midst of an eschatological utterance which relates to the end of the age, when the nations of the earth shall be confounded and afraid of the Lord. The second utterance, chronologically speaking, is the most extended, and is embedded, as we have noted elsewhere in this volume, in a prediction of a Messianic kingdom on this earth: "And it shall come to pass in that day, that the root of Jesse, that standeth for an ensign of the peoples, unto him shall the nations seek; and his resting-place shall be glorious. And it shall come to pass in that day, that the Lord will set his hand again the second time to recover the remnant of his people, that shall remain, from Assyria, and from Egypt, and from Pathros, and from Cush, and from Elam, and from Shinar, and from Hamath, and from the islands of the sea" (Isa. 11:10-12). The final pronouncement is in the post-exilic prophet Zechariah, which can better be understood in its context: "And I will sow them among the peoples; and they shall remember me in far countries; and they shall live with their children, and shall return. I will bring them again also out of the land of Egypt and gather them out of Assyria; and I will bring them into the land of Gilead and Lebanon; and place shall not be found for them. And he will pass through the sea of affliction, and will smite the waves in the sea, and all the depths of the Nile shall dry up; and the pride of Assyria shall be brought down, and the sceptre of Egypt shall depart. And I will strengthen them in Jehovah; and they shall walk up and down in his name, saith Jehovah" (10:9-12).

Various interpretations have been attached to these collected predictions pointing to a second return to Palestine of the Jews living in Egypt. As one would expect in his treatment of such a prophecy as this, Calvin simply says, "By these metaphors the prophet means nothing else than that nothing will stand in God's way when it shall be His pleasure to rescue His people from captivity." [3] Such a view, of course, denies that these predictions are to be literally fulfilled, or actually that they bear upon Israel at all. Wade, in his volume on Isaiah in the *Westminster Commentary* acknowledges that "the return of the exiles implies a dispersion of a far more extensive character than is likely to have taken place in the eighth century . . . So widespread a dispersion seems to suit an exilic or post-exilic date[4];" thus, he denies that Isaiah 11:11 is an utterance of the eighth century.

A number of modern commentators agree, more or less, in believing that these promises were fulfilled in the spread of Christianity and the conversion of many Jews living in Egypt. "There was such an ingathering," says Kay, "at the commencement of the Church's history on the day of Pentecost . . . We are taught to look for another larger fulfilment of the prophecy," and here he quotes Romans 11:26.[5]

Canon Fausset makes the predictions refer to historical events to take place among the people of Israel at the end of this age: "In the first restoration, Judah alone was restored, with perhaps some few of Israel; in the future restoration both are expressly specified (Ezek. 37:16-19; Jer. 3:18). To Israel are ascribed the 'outcasts,' to Judah, the 'dispersed,' as the former have been longer and more utterly cast away." [6] Both of these views are brought together in a single statement by Canon Rawlinson: "The first fulfilment of the prophecy was undoubtedly the return from the Babylonian captivity. A second fulfilment may have been the gathering of so many Jews from all quarters into the Christian Church (Acts 2:9-41). It is possible that there may be ultimately a further fulfilment in a final gathering together of Israel into their own land." [7] This was written at the close of the nineteenth century.

Still another commentator, Barnes, varies this by insisting that it does refer to the Jews at the end of this age—not to their being regathered into the land of Israel, however, but being brought again under God's dominion, under the administration of the Messiah, "an event attended with a sudden removal of the obstructions to the gospel and to its rapid spread everywhere among the nations." [8]

In concluding this chapter, I should like to set forth my own view of these prophecies, that is, that they do relate to conditions at the end of the age, that they specifically refer to Jews at the end of this age and, finally, that the text seems to imply clearly that there will be a great exodus of Jews from Egypt to Palestine at that time. The interesting contemporary fact bearing upon all this is that here are comparatively few Jews in Egypt at the present time. According to the latest statistics, the total number of Jews in the three North African countries of Algeria, Morocco and Tunisia is 425,000, out of a total population of 22,911,000, or, over two per cent of the population; whereas in Egypt, with a population of 22,934,-000, there are only 40,000 Jews, or 0.2 per cent.[9] To present it in another way, the percentage of Jews in Egypt is about one-tenth that of the other three North African countries. It is true that 40,000 Jews among 23,000,000 is not many, and somehow I do not think that these prophecies refer to so small a group. My own conclusion, then, would be that at the end of this age there will be a great influx of Jews into Egypt, and that out of this augmented group, multitudes will be brought back into Palestine. This is the very antithesis of the situation now prevailing in Egypt, from which land many Jews have already fled. Egypt hates Israel. Even if she drove out every Jew living there today, it would hardly fulfill these sober prophecies of Isaiah and Zechariah. May it not be that at the end of this age, in the days of her tribulation, when dark, ominous clouds of invasion from the north threaten, Israel will seek refuge, in great multitudes, in this restored kingdom on the Nile? This would be my own interpretation of this passage.

Notes

1. Heinrich Graetz: *History of the Jews.* Philadelphia, 1946. Vol. I, p. 309.
2. R. Payne Smith, in *The Bible Commentary (Anglican Commentary)* ed. by F. C. Cook. Vol. V, pp. 525, 528.
3. John Calvin: *Commentary on the Prophet Isaiah.* Eng. trans., Grand Rapids, 1948. Vol. I, p. 396.
4. G. W. Wade: *The Book of the Prophet Isaiah,* in *Westminster Commentaries* series. New York, n.d. p. 86.

Dr. Hertz, former Chief Rabbi of London, believes that this prophecy regarding the return of the Jews to Egypt was fulfilled long ago. "At the destruction of Jerusalem by the Romans, both Titus and Hadrian consigned multitudes of Jews into slavery; and Egypt received a large proportion of those slaves. Those over seventeen years were sent to the mines, etc., but the market was so glutted that though offered at nominal prices, none would buy them." J. H. Hertz: *The Pentateuch and Haftorahs: Deuteronomy.* London, 1936. p. 358. My colleague, Dr. Gleason L. Archer, has suggested that these events of 70 and 135 A.D. were, however, more probably the fulfilment of Deut. 28:26.

5. W. Kay, in *The Bible Commentary*, as above. p. 111.

Some years ago Peters correctly discerned that this phrase, "the second time" in v. 11 "cannot refer either to deliverance from Egypt or from Babylon because in neither case were the Jews recovered from the lands here enumerated; and it cannot refer merely to a conversion (as some hold) of the people because it is linked with 'a cutting off of the adversaries of Judah,' with 'a gathering of the outcasts of Israel and the dispersed of Judah from the four corners of the earth,' with a removal of *the enmity* between the two kingdoms, etc. It must relate to the future, and the miraculous events." George N. H. Peters: *The Theocratic Kingdom of Our Lord Jesus, the Christ.* New York, 1884. Vol. II, p. 62.

6. A. R. Fausset, in the *Jamieson Fausset and Brown Commentary on the Old and New Testaments.* Vol. III, p. 606.

7. George Rawlinson, in *The Pulpit Commentary:* Isaiah. Vol. I, p. 204.

8. Albert Barnes: *Notes Critical Explanatory and Practical on the Book of the Prophet Isaiah.* New ed., New York, 1867. Vol. I, p. 260.

9. *The American Jewish Year Book.* Phil., 1957. p. 225.

Note: On the fascination of Egypt the following paragraph, written by one not particularly concerned with prophecy, will be of interest: "There is a shrub in England, I forget what it is named, but it has a curiously unpleasant smell. If you take a leaf and crush it in your hands the scent is strangely penetrating and you wish that you had not plucked it; yet each time you pass that bush the inclination to crush another leaf and experience the same revulsion of feeling is almost overpowering. Egypt has for me this same uncanny power of attraction and repulsion; there were times when I loathed the place with a bitter hatred, and yet I feel that I shall be drawn back there once more before I die." Major Vivian Gilbert: *The Romance of the Last Crusade.* pp. 70, 71.

10

THE KING OF THE SOUTH

Any attempt at a thorough examination of Egypt in Biblical prophecy demands a careful study; indeed, a mastery, as far as possible, of one of the most difficult chapters in all the prophetic writings, the 11th chapter of Daniel. The words *Egypt* or *Egyptian* do not appear with any great frequency here. Rather, it is the continually appearing title, "the King of the South" that compels us to try to ascertain what this unusual and profound prophet has to say about the experiences Egypt would have in the years subsequent to his ministry, and what her place might be at the end of the age. The chapter is as difficult as it is important. Its significance is indicated, on the one hand, by the fact that it is the only chapter in the entire Book of Daniel which is prefaced by a full chapter of introduction—rare in any of the prophetic writings—and, on the other hand, by the fact that in relation to its teaching, a heavenly messenger twice remarks to Daniel that what he is about to have revealed to him, and he must write, is "the truth" (10:21; 11:2). The chapter is also significant in that it terminates (12:1-3 is a part of this revelation) with one of the few specific references in the Old Testament to a final resurrection.

The difficulties of the chapter are of a three-fold nature. The Hebrew text bristles with difficulty in some places, causing some scholars to believe that two or three passages here are so confused in the original that their exact meaning cannot be dogmatically determined. Secondly, there has been considerable disagreement among Biblical scholars, from the time of Jerome to our generation, as to the historical periods into which this chapter should be divided; where, for example, predictions concerning the days immediately following the time of Daniel terminate, and prophecies regarding Antichrist and the end of the age begin. Thirdly, there has been no little discussion, even when the text is clear, and the historical period to which a passage refers is positively identified, as to the exact meaning of some of the words of this chapter, such as the word translated *fortresses* in v. 38, and the phrase, "the desire of women" in v. 37.

Some Outstanding Characteristics of This Chapter

Before endeavoring to divide the chapter into historical periods, or to interpret its predictions, we should have some general idea of the basic themes that dominate this revelation. This is fundamentally a chapter of *war*, one of the six principal chapters in the prophetic scriptures which depict the struggle of nations, participated in by the enemies of God, against God's people (the other five would be, in my opinion, Jeremiah 50, Ezekiel 38, 39, Joel 3, Revelation 9 and 19) I am of course referring to *prophetic* chapters dominated by war, not *historical* accounts of sieges, etc., as that of the destruction of Jerusalem. Both the vocabulary and the events of the chapter testify to this. Departing briefly from the text I have been using throughout, I would simply list the military terms found in the Westminster Version of the Bible: *army,* vs. 7, 13, 25; *stornghold,* vs. 7, 10, 19, 31, 38; *fortresses,* vs. 24, 39; *great forces,* vs. 10, 31; *forces,* v. 22; *warrior king,* v. 3;

battle, v. 25; *sword,* v. 33; *chariots,* v. 40; *horseman,* v. 40; *troops,* v. 15. The terrible consequences of war are also in the vocabulary of this chapter: for example, *uprooted,* v. 4; *captivity,* vs. 8, 33; *fight,* v. 11; *overthrown,* v. 14; *destruction,* vs. 16, 17; *spoil,* v. 24; *plunder,* v. 24; *spoliation,* v. 33; *broken,* vs. 4, 20. Mingled with these military terms are phrases which reveal the evil aspects of international relations which have been so in evidence through the ages as nation tries to negotiate with nation: "he shall come in unawares and possess himself of the kingdom by smooth sayings" (v. 21); "he shall practice treachery" (v. 23); "the two kings, their heart set on mischief, shall speak lies at one table" (v. 27).

The chapter presents one long series of invasions: two invasions by a southern king of northern territory (vs. 7, 11), and six references to invasions of the South by a northern power, though not necessarily indicating six different invasions (vs. 9-10, 13, 15-16, 25, 29, 43).

As has often happened in the past, to reach a climax at the end of this age, these wars, in what we know as the Near East, or Middle East, will involve the people of God then residing in Palestine, who will behold with their eyes every conceivable desecration of the holy places, and will be compelled to listen to diabolical blasphemies against a Holy God. Over and over again we read, "they shall profane the sanctuary"; "they shall abolish the perpetual sacrifice"; "the king shall speak monstrous things against the God of gods"; "the people shall suffer fire and sword, captivity and spoliation." Here we have in the Old Testament what is more fully set forth in the 13th chapter of the Book of Revelation.

Any student of this chapter must eventually ask himself

why so many details of these invasions are included in the narrative—battles, defeats, victories, and then victories, battles and defeats. Leupold has well said that there is a deep reason why such details as these are worthy of the work of the Spirit of prophecy, "and that is, that what is foretold here is in reality, with minor variations, the pattern into which all history falls. Is there not an appalling sameness about this business of leagues and pacts between rival nations, of disagreements, of wars, of alliances, of political marriages, of recriminations, of treachery, of temporary ascendancy, of defeat and utter downfall, of recovery through some aggressive leader; and then the same thing all over again with a slightly different sequence of events? From this point of view there is a drab sameness about history which allows us to say that, in addition to being a prophecy of a particular period of Syrian and Egyptian history, this may be regarded as a panoramic view of all history in a picture that is idealized, at least to some extent." [1]

To What Periods of History Do These Predictions Point?

The rationalistic view of this chapter, adopted by a number of more liberal critics, is that the chapter does not contain any prophecy at all, that while its utterances are put into a prophetic mold, it actually is a review of certain events occurring in the area surrounding Palestine, especially Syria and Egypt, from the time of the return from the exile under the Persian kings down to the cruel attacks upon Israel by Antiochus Epiphanes in the second century. One holding this view must also insist that the book was not written by Daniel, and in such insistence must frankly acknowledge that the person writing this chapter performed a literary fraud, for he desired his readers to believe that God had given him a fore-knowledge of events to take place centuries after his decease, whereas he is but recording in prophetic phraseology events that had already transpired. It does not fall within the scope of this volume to repudiate this view. It is the view of un-belief, and anyone accepting it forfeits his confidence in the Word of God, even in the teachings of our Lord. Hundreds of pages have been written pointing out the fallacies of such an interpretation, and they need not be summarized in a work such as this in which the writer assumes the Danielic authorship of this chapter.[2]

A second view, quite commonly held, is that while this chapter is a prophecy, the record of a revelation given by a divine messenger to Daniel, possibly in 530 B.C., or later, the predictions carry us down only to the time of Antiochus Epiphanes, about three and one-half centuries later, so that the entire chapter was fulfilled in the second century preced-ing the advent of Christ. Those who accept this view are baffled by the final paragraph (vs. 40-45), the events of which they admit, did *not* actually take place in the life of Antiochus Epiphanes.

A third view, which to me seems equally extreme, is that practically the whole chapter is a prophecy of events to take place at the end of this age! All recognize that verse 2 refers to the period of Persian supremacy, and verses 3 and 4, to Alexander and his immediate successors. Most commentators believe that the major part of the remaining portion of the chapter is a prophecy of the wars between the Ptolemies and the Seleucids, and, in greater detail, a record of some of the more important events in the life of Antiochus Epiphanes, especially as they relate to Israel. However, no less a scholar than Tregelles himself insisted that the remainder of the chapter (vs. 5-45), and the first three verses of the 12th chapter, must speak of events that have not yet occurred on this earth.[3] Tregelles would outline the chapter as follows:

I. Details of Conflicts to take place in the Middle East before the Appearance of Antichrist, vs. 5-20
II. The Appearance of Antichrist and His Initial Activity, vs. 21-30
III. The Covenant of Antichrist with the Jews and his Violation of this Covenant, vs. 30-35
IV. The Power and Blasphemous Characteristics of Antichrist's Reign, vs. 36-39.
V. The Closing Stages of his Career, vs. 40-45.

This view has been adopted in our generation by one of the finest prophetic students, in my opinion, of the twentieth century, Mr. G. H. Lang.[4] In spite of the weight that these names, and others that could be mentioned, might lend to it, the view has not had general acceptance; and while there are some attractive features in the interpretation, I personally have not been able to divorce myself from the more commonly adopted view of this passage held by conservative scholars from the time of Jerome to the present day, a view we shall now examine.

Most Biblical scholars who understand this as a truly prophetic chapter agree that it does carry us down to the end of the age and that the dominating personage, the persecutor and blasphemer, is Antichrist; at the same time, most agree that Antiochus Epiphanes is also revealed here with more detail than is any other one king of the many who are enumerated in this series of invasions and battles. The problem then arises, where does the prediction of Antiochus Epiphanes end, and that relating to Antichrist begin? Jerome, who wrote the most important book on Daniel to the time of the Reformation, placed the division at the end of verse 35, where the phrase, "the time of the end" indicates the presence of a bridge, as it were, between prophecies relating to the ancient world and prophecies regarding the end of this age. His words are worth quoting: "Those of our persuasion believe all these things to be spoken prophetically of the Antichrist who is to arise at the end time. But this factor appears to them as a difficulty for their view; namely, the question as to why the prophetic discourse should abruptly cease mention of these great kings and shift from Seleucus to the end of the world. We hold that it is the practice of Scripture not to relate all details completely, but only to set forth what seems of major importance. Those of our school insist also that since many of the details which we are subsequently to read and explain are appropriate to the person of Antichrist and he is to be regarded as a type of Antichrist, and those things which happen to him in a preliminary way are to be completely fulfilled in the day of Antichrist, we hold that it is the habit of Holy Scriptures to set forth by means of types the reality of things to come, in conformity with what is said of our Lord and Saviour in the Seventy-Second Psalm, a Psalm which is noted at the beginning as being Solomon's and yet not all the statements concerning him can be applied to Solomon." [5]

It is not necessary here to enter into an explanation of the inexhaustible and difficult paragraph embracing verses 36-39, for there is no definite reference to Egypt contained therein.

Some modern scholars contend that no specific mention of Antichrist is made previous to verse 40. As Wright reminds us, the majority of modern critics admit that the events depicted from verse 40 to the end of the chapter did not take place during the time of Antiochus Epiphanes.[6]

The Persian Period

We are now ready to consider briefly the various monarchs and their respective conflicts, as they are successively unfolded in this war-filled chapter. Verse 2 summarizes what might be called the Persian Period: "And now will I show thee the truth. Behold, there shall stand up yet three kings in Persia; and the fourth shall be far richer than they all: and when he is waxed strong through his riches, he shall stir up all against the realm of Greece." While there were thirteen Persian rulers between the time of Cyrus and Darius, only four are mentioned here, so that nine Persian kings are not even considered in this prophecy. We need not haggle over what four men are referred to here, inasmuch as no names are given. The first three monarchs may be identified as follows: Cyrus II, who originally appeared as a ruler of the little province of Anshan in 559 B.C., and who captured Babylon in 539 and died in 529 B.C. (the Cyrus of Daniel 1:21, and also of Ezra 1, where his decree which permitted the rebuilding of the temple at Jerusalem is recorded); Cambyses, successor to Cyrus, who reigned from 529 to 522 B.C., adding Egypt to the Persian empire, a king not named in the Old Testament; and Darius I Hystaspis, 521-486 B.C., who ordered the building of the temple to be resumed. The fourth monarch referred to was either Xerxes I, 486-465 B.C., or Artaxerxes I, 465-424 B.C., the Persian ruler of Ezra 7:11-26, Nehemiah 2:1 and 13:6. Wright is correct in saying that "up to the accession of Xerxes, there were but three Persian kings who had given themselves any concern about Israel." [7] "No man ever stirred up the realm of Grecia as did Xerxes. First of all, he entered into a league with the Carthaginians, who engaged to divert the forces of Greece by attacks on the Greek colonists in Sicily and Italy. Aided with money from Xerxes, Hamilcar hired a great number of mercenaries in Spain, Gaul, and Italy, and brought into that war no less than three hundred thousand men by land and sea." [8]

Alexander and His Immediate Successors

The next two verses, 3 and 4, represent the third prophecy of Alexander the Great (and his immediate successors) set forth in the prophecies of Daniel (see also 7:6; 8:5-8, 21, 22): "And a mighty king shall stand up, that shall rule with great dominion, and do according to his will. And when he shall stand up, his kingdom shall be broken, and shall be divided toward the four winds of heaven, but not to his posterity, nor according to his dominion wherewith he ruled; for his kingdom shall be plucked up, even for others besides these." "The first meeting of Greece and Judea, both of which were in different ways to offer civilization to the world, was of a friendly character, although the one appeared in all her glory and might, the other in her weakness and humility. Judaea became a province which was bounded on the north by Mount Taurus and Mount Lebanon, and on the south was Egypt, and was called Hollow Syria (Coele-Syria) to distinguish it from the higher Syria which lay in the neighborhood of the Euphrates. The governor of this province, residing in Samaria, was Andromachos. The violent resentment of the Samaritans went so far that heedless of the consequences they rose up against Andromachos, seized him and consigned him to the flames (331 B.C.). Alexander, upon his return from Egypt while hastening to conquer Persia, hurried to Samaria, avenged the murder of Andromachos and placed over that territory Memnon. In other ways Alexander appears to have mortified and humiliated the Samaritans, and knowing that they were enemies of the Judaeans, he favored the latter in order to mark his displeasure toward the former." [9]

Alexander the Great died in Babylon in 334 B.C. at the age of thirty-two. Though he had two sons, both were assassinated soon after their father's death, and his twelve generals divided the spoils of the empire among themselves. As the result of fearful struggles for power, Macedonia was assigned to Cassander; Thrace and Asia Minor to Lysimachus; Syria and the lands east came under the rule of Seleucus; and Egypt was assigned to Ptolemy I. It is from the name Seleucus that we get the title for the dynasties ruling in Syria to the times of the Romans, the Seleucidae; and in Egypt, from 30 B.C. to the times of the Romans, the kings were known as Ptolemies. Thus do our history books designate certain eras as the Ptolemaic Period of Egyptian history, and the Seleucid Period of Syrian history. Strange to say, the territories assigned to Cassander and Lysimachus play no part in the prophecies of this 11th chapter of Daniel, which concerns itself entirely with the quarrels and wars between the Seleucidae and the Ptolemies. Some of the names which we will be compelled to mention for the elucidation of this text will be foreign to many readers; still, without specific historical references the chapter cannot be adequately understood.

The First Appearance of the King of the South

An ordinary reading of this chapter by one who has little or no knowledge of the history of the ancient world during the third and second centuries B.C. would lead to the assumption that all references to "the king of the south" must be to the same individual; whereas actually, in fifteen successive verses (5-20) there are six different monarchs of the Ptolemaic period of Egyptian history. Having ambition to extend his territory northward, Ptolemy I Soter (323-285 B.C.) invaded Palestine and Phoenicia in 320 B.C., proceeding as far as Jerusalem, but upon hearing of the approach of Antigonus, commander in chief of all the armies of the Alexandrian Empire (from 322 B.C. onwards), he retired to Egypt. This led Seleucus and Ptolemy to form a league against Antigonus, and in 312 B.C. Antigonus' fleet, under command of his son Demetrius, suffered an overwhelming defeat off the coast of Gaza. Seleucus became the independent ruler of Babylon, and the Seleucid kings dated their era from 312 B.C.

"And the king of the south shall be strong, and one of his princes; and he shall be strong above him, and have dominion" (v. 5). The phrase, "one of his princes," of this verse refers to Seleucus I Nicator (312-281 B.C.). After the defeat of the forces of Antigonus, Seleucus returned to the province which had originally been assigned to him, Babylonia. In 301 B.C., in league with Lysimachus, king of Thrace and Bithynia, he defeated Antigonus at the battle of Ipsus, in which the latter was slain. Thus Seleucus became the most powerful monarch of all those ruling in the once-united empire of Alexander, reigning from Asia Minor to the northwest confines of India, and was acknowledged to be "strong above" Ptolemy.

The text of Daniel passes over the second Seleucid king, Antiochus I Soter (280-261 B.C.), but does speak of a union through marriage of these two royal lines. Perhaps we should have both the text and a detailed comment before us, in order to achieve a full understanding of this otherwise enigmatical passage: "And at the end of years they shall join themselves together; and the daughter of the king of the south shall come to the king of the north to make an agreement: but she shall not retain the strength of her arm; neither shall he stand, nor his arm; but she shall be given up, and they that brought her, and he that begat her, and he that strengthened her in those times" (v. 6). "About 250 B.C., Ptolemy II Philadelphus (283-246 B.C.) brought his long wars with Antiochus II Theos (261-246 B.C.) to an end by giving his daughter Berenice to Antiochus, with the condition that he divorce his actual wife, Laodice. This Laodice was at least Antiochus' half-sister, possibly his full sister. In 277 B.C. Ptolemy II had already married his full sister Arsinoe II, following in the main the practice of the Pharaohs, in keeping the royal, and as it was claimed, divine blood, free from all baser admixture; and Antiochus II may have been following Ptolemy's example. In any case Laodice seems to have retained his affections; and upon Ptolemy II's death in 246 B.C. Antiochus II forsook Berenice and went back to Laodice. Then he died suddenly, probably poisoned by Laodice, who, as St. Jerome tells us, feared from his changeful disposition that he might reinstate

Berenice and her son; these two latter Laodice also caused to be killed, and a number of Berenice's women died with her: 'his seed,' i.e., Ptolemy II's, Berenice and her son." [10]

Another Ptolemy is referred to in verses 7 and 8: "But out of a shoot from her roots shall one stand up in his place, who shall come unto the army, and shall enter into the fortress of the king of the north, and shall deal against them, and shall prevail. And also their gods, with their molten images, and with their goodly vessels of silver and gold, shall he carry captive into Egypt; and he shall refrain some years from the king of the north." The member of Berenice's family here referred to was her brother Ptolemy III Euergetes (246-222 B.C.) who stood in her father's stead by succeeding Ptolemy II. Ptolemy III at once undertook an invasion of Syria, the territory of "the king of the north," and would no doubt have conquered the whole Seleucid empire had he not been forced to return to Egypt upon receiving news of an insurrection in his own kingdom. In a decree of the Egyptian priests issued in 239 B.C. in honor of Ptolemy III—a decree discovered in the Delta of Egypt in the middle of the nineteenth century—mention is made of the sacred images brought back by Ptolemy after being carried off by the Persians in the days of Cambyses (529-522 B.C.). We are told by Jerome that Ptolemy brought home "four thousand talents of silver and twenty-five hundred precious vessels and images of the gods." An attempted invasion of Egypt by the northern king is recorded in verse 9. The northern monarch, who at this time (241 B.C.) was Seleucus II Callinicus, met with defeat and returned north.

The two rulers of Syria referred to in verses 10 and 11 were Seleucus III Ceraunus (226-223 B.C.) and Antiochus III, the

169

Great (223-187 B.C.). The former was soon murdered in a campaign in Asia Minor, while the latter temporarily succeeded in his advance of 219 B.C.; however, the following year the Egyptian army gathered sufficient strength to repel the invasion, and in a frontier town of Palestine, near Raphia, the invader suffered a severe defeat in the spring of 217 B.C. The "king of the south" at this time was Ptolemy IV Philopator (222-203 B.C.) who is said to have had an army of 70,000 infantry, 5000 cavalry, and 73 elephants. "And the multitude shall be lifted up, and his heart shall be exalted; and he shall cast down tens of thousands, but he shall not prevail" (v. 12). The historian Polybius reported the Syrian losses as 10,000 infantry, and 300 cavalry killed and 4000 prisoners taken. Ptolemy did not take advantage of these military victories, however, and "soon returned to his indolent ways."

The Ptolemy just mentioned died in 204 B.C. and was succeeded by his infant son Ptolemy V Epiphanes (204-181 B.C.). This brings us very close to the awful era of persecution under Antiochus Epiphanes, who is the central character of this chapter. Although Antiochus III had experienced a crushing defeat at the hands of the Egyptian king, he had been extending his territory and power in the East, enabling him to return south (the time is twelve years after the events of verse 12) with a vast multitude. "And the king of the north shall return, and shall set forth a multitude greater than the former; and he shall come on at the end of the times, even of years, with a great army and with much substance. And in those times there shall many stand up against the king of the south: also the children of the violent among thy people shall lift themselves up to establish the vision; but they shall fall. So the king of the north shall come, and cast up a mound, and take a well-fortified city: and the forces of the south shall not stand, neither his chosen people, neither shall there be any strength to stand. But he that cometh against him shall do according to his own will, and none shall stand before him; and he shall stand in the glorious land, and in his hand shall be destruction." The phrase, "the children of the Violent," has been given a number of interpretations. It probably is a reference to those who were living in disobedience to the law of God (compare Ezek. 18:10). "The Law was broken in that certain factious ones, evidently thinking that they were fulfilling prophecies, took the side of Antiochus against Egypt." [11] In 198 B.C. Antiochus III defeated the Egyptian army, under Scopas, at Paneion, near the sources of the Jordan, "and this battle may be taken to mark the practically permanent transference of Palestine from the power of the Ptolemies in Egypt to that of the Seleucids in Syria." [12] Verse 16 refers, of course, to Antiochus III, standing "in the glorious land with destruction in his hand," indicating that the determination of Antiochus to engage in battle with the king of Egypt affected the whole land of Palestine, while Antiochus showed himself kindly disposed toward the Jewish people.

A detailed account of the further activities of Antiochus III is contained in verses 17-19: "And he shall set his face to come with the strength of his whole kingdom, and with him equitable conditions; and he shall perform them: and he shall give them the daughter of women, to corrupt her; but she shall not stand, neither be for him. After this shall he turn his face unto the isles, and shall take many: but a prince shall cause the reproach offered by him to cease; yea, moreover, he shall cause his reproach to turn upon him. Then he shall turn his face toward the fortresses of his own land; but he shall stumble and fall, and shall not be found." The commentary of Leupold on these verses is so clear and concise that I am taking the liberty of quoting it in its entirety, without comment. "Since the two main actors on the stage are the king of the north and the king of the south, and since the one under consideration is the king of the north, the 'to one' must refer to the king of the south. It is a fact that is verified by history that Antiochus the Great gave his daughter Cleopatra in marriage to Ptolemy Epiphanes, and that it was the purpose of the father to gain an advantage over the king of Egypt by trusting that his daughter would be her father's ally rather than her husband's. That is what is meant by the infinitive of purpose 'to destroy it,' i.e., the kingdom. The next statement is also verifiable: 'This shall not stand, neither shall it be to his advantage.' The girl felt it her duty to be faithful to her husband and so refused to be a tool in her father's hands . . . Antiochus made this expedition to gain control of Asia Minor and the islands of Ionia, which the Romans sought to control, in addition to assuming a guardianship over the young Egyptian king. This action was, therefore, designed to break the power of Rome. By 196 B.C., he had gotten hold of even a part of Thrace.

"Rome resented this particularly because she exercised a kind of mandate over Thrace. The expedition of Antiochus finally called forth the active resistance of Rome, which led to a battle near Magnesia in 190, in which battle Lucius

Scipio administered such a sound drubbing to Antiochus that the 'presumptuous boastings' of the Syrian were silenced once and for all. Yet Scipio himself was not to make the same mistake that the man whom he had conquered had made. He achieved his victory 'without repaying him with like boasting.' This implies a nobler and a more restrained conduct on the part of the Roman general." [13]

Antiochus III was succeeded by his son Seleucus IV Philopator 187-175 B.C., to whom a single verse is assigned in this chapter (v. 20): "Then shall stand up in his place one that shall cause an exactor to pass through the glory of the kingdom; but within few days he shall be destroyed, neither in anger, nor in battle." The phrase, "the glory of the kingdom" is a reference to Palestine. The raiser of taxes may have been Heliodorus, but more probably this refers to heavy taxes forced upon Seleucus IV by the heavy Roman indemnity. His reign, compared to that of his immediate successors, was insignificant.

It is to Antiochus Epiphanes that the largest single segment of this chapter is devoted, verses 21-25 (some would extend this to verse 29). Some commentators, and in part Jerome, among the Church Fathers, insist that in this verse Daniel begins a description of Antichrist yet to come, but Wright is correct in saying, "It is extraordinary to maintain that so much should be told in the chapter of Alexander the Great and the kings of Syria who followed him, and that just at the very point when the prophecy begins really to touch the interests of the holy nation, it should break off and pass over to the days immediately preceding the Second Advent of Christ." [14] The chapter does speak of Antichrist, and

Antiochus Epiphanes was the most perfect type of Antichrist that appeared in all the centuries of the history of the Jews. My own division of this extended section would be as follows: a general description of Antiochus Epiphanes, vs. 21-24; the first campaign, vs. 25-28; the second campaign, vs. 29-35. The more one studies the life of Antiochus Epiphanes, the more he realizes what a perfect type of Antichrist he was. He deserves our careful attention.

It is significant that during almost the entire third century B.C. Palestine was under the control of the Ptolemies, and it should be noted that as far as our records inform us, the Ptolemies did not attempt to interfere with the Jewish way of life, nor did they endeavor to promote Hellenism by founding Greek cities in non-Greek territories. At the beginning of the second centuries B.C., however, when Antiochus III succeeded in driving Ptolemy V out of Palestine, and added this territory to his Seleucid empire, the status of the Jews underwent a radical and bitter change. After the defeat at Apamea, Antiochus ceded all that he held of Asia Minor beyond the Taurus mountains, and so upset the cultural balance between Greek and Oriental that "now for the first time the Seleucid Empire could fairly be called Syrian." In spite of this loss of territory, the Seleucid realm was still the largest of the Hellenistic empires. It was the policy of Antiochus Epiphanes which ultimately led to the persecutions so vividly described in the First Book of Maccabees. "Geographically straggling and racially heterogeneous, its natural tendency was fissile and centrifugal. To hold it together Antiochus proposed to develop a common religious bond. The inevitable process of syncretism had already made some progress in that direction;

the term 'Zeus,' which had come to mean little more than God, was equated with the pan-Semitic supreme deity, known variously as Hadad or Ba'al. This syncretistic process Antiochus fostered. But he also had the further notion of linking it with the Royal Cult, by the suggestion that he himself was the 'manifestation' in human form of God by whatever name he is worshipped." [15]

Not only did Antiochus attempt to bind the empire together with a syncretistic religion, but he became the first of the Seleucid rulers to claim divine honor in his own lifetime. At the beginning of his reign, he was called simply King Antiochus, but in 169 B.C., he took the title king Antiochus God Manifested; in 166 B.C., he added another title, Nicephorus, that is, "Victorious," and from then on regarded himself as an incarnation in particular of Zeus Olympius. (The word "manifest" is *epiphanes,* which comes from the same root as the New Testament word *epiphany,* referring to the appearance of the Lord Jesus Christ both in His first advent and His second advent). We must again turn to the text in Daniel: "And in his place shall stand up a contemptible person, to whom they had not given the honor of the kingdom: but he shall come in time of security, and shall obtain the kingdom by flatteries" (v. 21). Antiochus, the brother and successor of Seleucus IV, is here called "contemptible," probably to contrast the weaknesses and ultimate viciousness of his character with a title he had given himself, Epiphanes; also, as another has said, "there was much superficiality and even buffoonery in his life and character."

"And the overwhelming forces shall be overwhelmed from

before him, and shall be broken; yea, also the prince of the covenant. And after the league made with him he shall work deceitfully; for he shall come up, and shall become strong, with a small people. In time of security shall he come even upon the fattest places of the province; and he shall do that which his fathers have not done, nor his fathers' fathers; he shall scatter among them prey, and spoil, and substance: yea, he shall devise his devices against the strongholds, even for a time" (vs. 22-24). "The righteous prince" is perhaps a reference to Antiochus, the infant son of Seleucus IV. "The rich places of a province" may be in either Egypt or Palestine, or the eastern parts of the Seleucid empire. The munificent gifts to cities and temples made by Antiochus are often referred to by historians. Many of these gifts were obtained through plunder. Wright most aptly reminds us that in the concluding phrase of verse 24, "and that for a season," we have "an upward glance of the prophet heavenwards, while predicting the days of darkness." [16]

The next four verses consist of an account of the first campaign of Antiochus Epiphanes against Egypt, the King of the South. After the battle at Pelusium, Antiochus overran most of fertile provinces of Egypt and by fraud or force seized the king, Ptolemy Philometor, upon which the Egyptians placed his brother Physcon on the throne. With his sister Cleopatra, Physcon retreated to the fortified city of Alexandria, to which city Antiochus then lay siege, a siege which he had to abandon because of the intervention of the Romans. "And he shall stir up his power and his courage against the king of the south with a great army; and the king of the south shall war in battle with an exceeding great and mighty army; but he shall not stand; for they shall devise devices against him. Yea, they that eat of his dainties shall destory him, and his army shall overflow; and many shall fall down slain. And as for both these kings, their hearts shall be to do mischief, and they shall speak lies at one table: but it shall not prosper; for yet the end shall be at the time appointed" (vs. 25-27). There is no record in secular literature of the treachery alluded to in verse 27. "Then shall he return into his land with great substance; and his heart shall be against the holy covenant; and he shall do his pleasure, and return to his own land" (v. 28). "Antiochus, induced by circumstances to revisit his own dominions, made a virtue of necessity and retired from Egypt before the arrival of the Roman embassy; furthermore, the state of affairs in Judaea at that time demanded his earnest attention." [17] Laden with the spoils of war, after at least a temporary success, Antiochus returned to Syria. In passing through Palestine, he discovered the rumblings of an insurrection, and took this opportunity to plunder the temple in Jerusalem—"his heart shall be set against the holy covenant." Verse 29 records what has been called the second campaign of Antiochus Epiphanes, begun "at the time appointed," which Leupold reminds us is "at a time when Divine providence sees that this step may further its own purposes. So even the deeds of the wicked must contribute to the achievement of the objectives of the Almighty." [18] The prophecy in verse 30 is of a well-known historical event. When a Roman embassy headed by Popillius Laenas encountered Antiochus besieging Alexandria and told him to cease, Antiochus asked for time in which to consider what his reply might be. The

messenger from Rome forthwith drew a circle around Antiochus and told him that he must make his decision before
he stepped out of the marked ring. Antiochus now with-
drew from Egypt for the last time, and in retreating to
Syria, he took vengeance upon the Jewish people. "And
forces shall stand on his part, and they shall profane the
sanctuary, even the fortress, and shall take away the continual burnt-offering, and they shall set up the abomination
that maketh desolate. And such as do wickedly against the
covenant shall he pervert by flatteries; but the people that
know their God shall be strong and do exploits. And they
that are wise among the people shall instruct many; yet they
shall fall by the sword and by flame, by captivity and by spoil,
many days. Now when they shall fall, they shall be helped
with a little help; but many shall join themselves unto them
with flatteries" (vs. 31-34). We have here the second
description in the Book of Daniel of what has become known
as the prophecy of *the abomination of desolation* (see 8:11-
14); there is a third reference to this at the conclusion of the
book (12:11). Certainly there are two fulfilments of this
prophecy: it was fulfilled during the days of Antiochus
Epiphanes, and it is yet to be fulfilled at the end of the
age, for our Lord surely referred to this prediction in Matthew 24:15, and what He spoke of was then still in the
future. This is so important that we ought to have before
us the actual historical record of this awful period from the
First Book of Maccabees.

"And on the fifteenth day of Chislev in the one hundred
and forth-fifth year they set upon the altar an 'abomination
of desolation,' and in the cities of Judah on every side they

established high places; and they offered sacrifice at the doors of the houses and in the streets. And the books of the Law which they found they rent in pieces, and burned them in the fire. And with whomsoever was found a book of the covenant, and if he was (found) consenting unto the Law, such an one was, according to the king's sentence, condemned to death. Thus did they in their might to the Israelites who were found month by month in their cities. And on the twenty-fifth day of the month they sacrificed upon the altar which was upon the altar of burnt-offering. And, according to the decree, they put to death the women who had circumcised their children, hanging their babes round their (mothers') necks, and they put to death their (entire) families, together with those who had circumcised them. Nevertheless many in Israel stood firm and determined in their hearts that they would not eat unclean things, and chose rather to die so that they might not be defiled with meats, thereby profaning the holy covenant; and they did die. And exceeding great wrath came upon Israel." [19]

I personally cannot help but believe that verse 35 brings to a close the prophecy relating specifically to Antiochus Epiphanes, and introduces the prophecy of Antichrist, of whom Antiochus was a perfect type. The verse ends with the significant eschatological phrase, "the time of the end." The end of the terrible persecution just described comes with the death of Antiochus Epiphanes; but this points forward to another termination, of a far greater persecution under Antichrist himself. Even Young admits of (v. 36), "The correct interpretation is given in 2 Thess. 2:4. Only of the Antichrist may the language of Daniel be predicated." [19a]

EGYPT IN BIBLICAL PROPHECY

Our main purpose in studying this 11th chapter of Daniel is to ascertain what it has to say prophetically about Egypt; consequently, I need not go into further detail on these familiar and profound descriptions of the work of Antichrist (available in innumerable commentaries on Daniel) but will confine myself, for the most part, to what the passage says about Antichrist in his relationship to Egypt, and to another character who arises here, the King of the South. One phrase in verse 38, however, bears definitely upon our war-burdened age. In verse 37 we are told that Antiochus had no regard for the God of his fathers, but he had to worship, so he chose to "honor the god of strongholds," which was nothing else than the god of war. "Warlike conquests, the taking of strongholds—that he will engage in. To that he will devote great treasures, even 'gold and silver, precious stones and all sorts of treasures.' That attitude is not hard to understand because history offers so many illustrations of it. But what will make it stranger is the fact that this person will come from a line of ancestors who had no such ambitions and who were devoted to no such god. That fact is stated in the words that this is 'a god whom his fathers knew not.' " [20]

"And he shall deal with the strongest fortresses by the help of a foreign god: whosoever acknowledgeth him he will increase with glory; and he shall cause them to rule over many, and shall divide the land for a price" (v. 39). "Strange, how wars will prevail to the end, and how the Antichrist shall himself be addicted to wars! To bind men to himself he bestows particular honors on those who acknowledge him. He even makes them influential rulers and gives them land grants as favors." Young suggestively says, "He is a god who is characterized by fortresses or strongholds. In other words, his is the personification of war. The Jews had known of war, of course, but they had never deified it. Thus, in the place of any god he will honor war as his god. For religion he will substitute war, and war he will support with all that he has. This thought is figuratively expressed by the words, 'with gold and silver,' etc. This verse does not apply to Antiochus. A far more convincing case can be made out for Herod, but the words best apply to the activities of the Antichrist." [21]

"And at the time of the end shall the king of the south contend with him; and the king of the north shall come against him like a whirlwind, with chariots, and with horsemen, and with many ships; and he shall enter into the countries, and shall overflow and pass through" (v. 40). It is agreed by almost all commentators, whatever be their position in regard to Antichrist, that the events of verses 40-45 never occurred in the life of Antiochus Epiphanes. There is, therefore, only one of two interpretations possible: that Daniel was here led into error and made predictions of events that never took place, or that this is truly a prophecy of the time of the end, that is, the end of the age, when Antichrist will arise with power and engage in convulsing military expeditions. While during the third and second centuries B.C. the king of the south was of the Ptolemaic line, here, though he must be identified with the same territory, Egypt, he of course is not a Ptolemaic king. But that which occurred over and over again in the history of the Near East after the days of Alexander is going to recur at the end of this age, with greater intensity than ever. That is, the power of the north, Syria and probably Iraq, will be involved in war with the southern territory, Egypt, and little Palestine will be caught between these two mighty states, and will be trodden upon, soaked with blood, a martyr on the altar of the god Mars. Actually, verse 40 presents three different powerful characters as being prominent at the end of the age: the king of the south, the king of the north, and "the king who shall do according to his will." Here both the northern and the southern powers attack Antichrist, but the text would imply that Antichrist is victorious.[22] While some countries in that vicinity will escape, for one reason or another, Egypt will not; indeed, she will be plundered once again: "But he shall have power over the treasures of gold and of silver, and over all the precious things of Egypt; and the Libyans, and the Ethiopians shall be at his steps" (v. 43). "So great will be the power of Antichrist in this last fierce thrust that he makes that he shall get control of the resources of this country which are here described as 'the treasures of gold and silver and all the precious things of Egypt.' In this connection the Libyans and the Ethiopians can be intended to describe only the empire of Egypt in its broadest extent, for Libya to the northwest and Ethiopia to the extreme south represented the farthest reaches to which greater Egypt attained. If a major world power falls so completely under his control, Antichrist must surely achieve great power before his end." [23]

With all of his might, however, Antichrist can be in only one place at a time, and the entire Near East will be seething with rebellion, tensions and struggles for preeminence among nations, so that while he is in Egypt, he will hear rumors from the East and from the North, and will be compelled to go back to the territory once ruled by Antiochus, this time with a fury which will drive him "to destroy and exterminate many." This refers primarily to his vengeance toward the people of Israel, who will be in the land of Palestine at this time, for certainly the conclusion of this chapter is set at no other place than the Mount of Olives, from which both the Mediterranean Sea and the Dead Sea can be seen, and upon which he will build his palace, no doubt in a blasphemous attempt to insult the God of the Jews. "But even as in 7:25, 26 the Antichrist reaches a certain point and then encounters the judgment, so that same event is recorded here in a more dramatic fashion. Just when it seems as if the Holy City must fall before him whom none seemed able to resist, there comes the catastrophic overthrow: 'he shall come to his end.' And since that end is the judgment of God, there 'shall be none to help him.' God's judgments cannot be resisted. So again a chapter has closed with the note of comfort and victory for the church and of a definite and final overthrow of the last great enemy of the church on earth." [24] This holy mount between the two seas has had various interpretations, but it can hardly be any other place than Mount Zion, or Mount Scopus, from which can be seen the Dead Sea on the east, and the Mediterranean Sea on the west. On this mountain Antichrist will meet overwhelming defeat. Even Jerome wrote, "No one shall be able to assist the Antichrist as the Lord vents His fury upon him. Our school of thought insists that Antichrist is going to perish in that spot from which the Lord ascended to heaven."

Summary of the Chapter

A prolonged and careful study of this difficult chapter will reveal at least eight basic truths, which might be enumerated here: (1) Throughout the chapter, wars continually occur—from the days of the Persians to the end of this age. This is emphasized in our Lord's Olivet discourse, in many prophetic passages in the Old Testament, and surely in the Book of Revelation. (2) The issues of these wars fluctuate; that is, as always throughout history, a nation that first wins, later suffers defeat at the hands of an enemy renewed in strength or a new power. (3) Of the two primary groups in this chapter, the northern and southern, the northern power generally dominates and, for the most part, initiates these wars. (4) War, force, power are deified in the closing days of the age. (5) Throughout the chapter a hatred of Israel is evident, with frequent desecrations of Jerusalem, and the nation seems helpless as these armies from the north and south move across her intervening territory. (6) As Antiochus Epiphanes in the second century B.C., so at the end of this age a supreme enemy of God will appear, a blasphemer who will persecute the children of God and attempt to annihilate true religion. (7) Egypt will experience a period of humiliation at the end of the age. (8) The supreme, final enemy of God will come to his end on the Mount of Olives.

EGYPT IN BIBLICAL PROPHECY

Notes

1. H. C. Leupold: *Exposition of Daniel*. Columbus, Ohio, 1949. pp. 475, 476. Newton makes the interesting observation that "it is uniformly the case in books of prophecy that minuteness of detail increases in the later unions." B. W. Newton, *op. cit.*, p. 225.

2. A century ago, Auberlen gave expression to his own views on this chapter in words the like of which we seldom hear today: "Of all the predictions contained in the Holy Scripture, this is doubtless the most special and minute, and in order not to be offended at this prophecy, it is necessary to believe in the omniscience and real revelation of God in the prophetic word. Nay, we may assert, of this eleventh chapter, that it is essentially important as a datum for the doctrine of divine prescience in a system of dogmatics. The supposition of some theologians, that God has a prescience of the development of the world in its pure abstractness only, in its final end, and in the most essential points of its evolutions, cannot be reconciled with our passage." Carl August Auberlen: *The Prophecies of Daniel and the Revelations of St. John*. Edinburgh, 1856. p. 61.

A remarkable statement on this chapter by the historian Edward Gibbon, which does not appear in any commentary I have seen, is worth quoting here. The Bishop of Worcester, Richard Hurd (1720-1808), was invited to deliver the Warburton Lectures on Prophecy for the year 1768. When his friend Edward Gibbon, the brilliant opponent of Christianity, heard of this, he wrote to him as follows, which is at least a tribute to the accuracy of the chapter: "There are two reasons which still force me to withhold my assent. I. The author of the book of Daniel is too well informed of the revolutions of the Persian and Macedonian empires, which are supposed to have happened long after his death. II. He is too ignorant of the transactions of His own times. In a word, he is too exact for a Prophet, and too fabulous for a contemporary historian.

"I. The first of these objections was urged, fifteen hundred years ago, by the celebrated Porphyry. He not only frankly acknowledged, but carefully illustrated the distinct and accurate series of history, contained in the book of Daniel, as far as the death of Antiochus Epiphanes; for beyond that period the author seems to have had no other guide than the dim and shadowy light of conjecture. The four empires are clearly delineated; the expedition of Xerxes into Greece, the rapid conquest of Persia by Alexander, his untimely death without posterity, the division of his vast monarchy into four kingdoms, one of which, Egypt, is mentioned by name, their various wars and intermarriages, the persecution of Antiochus, the prophanation of the Temple, and the invincible arms of

185

EGYPT IN BIBLICAL PROPHECY

the Romans, are described with as much perspicuity in the prophecies of Daniel, as in the histories of Justin and Diodorus. From such a perfect resemblance, the artful infidel would infer that both were alike composed after the event." *The Works of Richard Hurd, D.D.,* Vol. V, pp. 365, 366.

3. S. P. Tregelles: *Remarks on the Prophetic Visions in the Book of Daniel.* 5th ed., London, 1883. pp. 135-157.
4. G. H. Lang: *The Histories and Prophecies of Daniel.* London, 1950. pp. 154-175.
5. Jerome, in J. P. Migne: *Patrologie Cursus Completus Series Latina,* Vol. XXV, p. 565.
6. Charles H. H. Wright: *Daniel and His Prophecies.* London, 1906. p. 313.
7. Wright, *op. cit.,* p. 245.
8. William Harris Rule: *An Historical Exposition of the Book of Daniel the Prophet.* London, 1869. pp. 280, 281.
9. S. R. Driver: *The Book of Daniel. Cambridge Bible for Schools and Colleges,* Cambridge, 1912. p. 165.
10. C. Lattey: *The Book of Daniel.* Dublin, 1948. p. 94.
11. See an extended note on this phrase in the volume by H. J. Rose in *The Anglican Commentary,* p. 377.
12. Lattey, *op. cit.,* p. 96.
13. Leupold, *op. cit.,* p. 490-492. With the kind permission of the publishers, the Wartburg Press. Driver quotes an interesting remark by Mommsen: "Never perhaps did a power fall so rapidly, so thoroughly, so ignominiously, as the kingdom of the Seleucidae under this Antiochus the Great."
14. Wright, *op. cit.,* p. 280.
15. Leupold, *op. cit.,* p. 517.
16. Wright, *op. cit.,* p. 284.
17. Wright, *op. cit.,* p. 287.
18. Leupold, *op. cit.,* p. 500.
19. I Maccabees 1:29 ff.
19a. Edward J. Young: *The Prophecy of Daniel.* Grand Rapids: Eerdmans, 1949. p. 248. On V. 36 see an important discussion in Wm Kelly; *Book of Revelation* pp. 296-298.
20. Leupold, *op. cit.,* p. 517. The paragraph beginning with verse 36 has had many different interpretations, some of them strange indeed. The work by the American writer Samuel Parkes, *An Historical Commentary on the XIth Chapter of Daniel* (Binghamton, 1858. pp. 560) makes this chapter to terminate with the Crimean War, and places the "mount between the seas" in Crimea! The author argues that verses 36 to 39 refer to the Roman Catholic Church. Surprising as it may be, Luther held a somewhat similar view in that he believed Antichrist to be the Pope. What, then, does he do

EGYPT IN BIBLICAL PROPHECY

with verse 38? This "represents the power, the ritual created by the Pope through the masses, absolutions, holy water, etc., through which he gathers from all the world gold, silver, precious stones, as well as the power of his 'deity.' And by means of bulls, letters and seals, he has secured his strength and power." Alexander Keith likewise interpreted this as the Roman Catholic Church (*History and Destiny of the World and of the Church According to Scripture.* London, 1861. pp. 256-305).

The best recent interpretation of this passage, assigning it to Antichrist, is in Robert D. Culver: *Daniel and the Last Days.* New York, 1954. pp. 161-172.

21. Leupold, *op. cit.,* p. 518. Young, *op. cit.,* p. 249.
22. See Leupold, p. 521, etc.
23. Leupold, *op. cit.,* p. 522. No less a scholar than the sainted Puritan, Thomas Goodwin understood verse 45 as referring to the British Isles, as "between the two seas." See his *Expositions of the Revelations* in his *Works.* London, 1861. Vol. III, Part 2, p. 66.
24. Leupold, *op. cit.,* p. 524.
25. Jerome, *op. cit.,* p. 574.

How far from the true meaning of the text can even a man like Luther find himself when he forces it to say what it was not meant to say? On verse 45 Luther wrote: "Jerusalem is situated between the Mediterranean and the Dead Seas, but more significant is the fact that Rome lies between two great seas, the Adriatic and the Tyrrhenian. Rome may be called an exalted holy hill, for many thousands of martyrs lie there, and it first was the seat of the very best of churches; great things took place there until the devil located there. Spiritualizing this passage it would mean that the Pope has set himself up as a god in this holy place and set up his kingdom or structure of abominable teaching."

Thirty years ago D. M. Panton, normally a careful student of Biblical prophecy, gave an interpretation of "the king of the South" which may well serve as a warning to all of us of how far from the actual truth one can go in forcing a Biblical prophecy into the mold of some contemporary events. "Of the group of the States which constituted the South under Alexander's successors—namely, Egypt, Palestine, Cyprus, and part of Syria—Cyprus is annexed to Britain; Palestine is under her mandate; and Egypt is subject to her military dominion . . . The critical factor in England mastering Egypt, and thus becoming the Empire of the South, was the creation of the Suez Canal, a vital nexus of her Empire as the highway to India, and which therefore excludes—except by the fall of the British Empire—all others from the Monarchy of the South. Her grip on Egypt, beginning in the dual control of 1882, has culminated in the restoration of a local King of the South, while the real king resides at Windsor; exactly as we find that the King of the South comes 'into the realm of the King of the South but shall return to his own land.'" ("The King of the South," in *Dawn,* Feb. 14, 1925, p. 486.)

EGYPT IN SOME NINETEENTH CENTURY
PROPHETIC LITERATURE

The nineteenth century witnessed the most prolific out-
pouring of literature on Biblical prophecies bearing upon
the end of the age that the Christian Church has ever known.
There was a second outburst of such literature—not of the
same bulk, and not as the result of the same continuous,
careful study undertaken earlier—at the time of the first
World War, particularly in relation to the British capture
of Jerusalem by General Allenby, an event often, though
erroneously, said to mark the beginning of the end of the
"times of the Gentiles." Since then, the pendulum has swung
to the other extreme, so that today we seldom see literature
of any significance relating Biblical prophecy to present
historical movements. Our generation is much in need of
an accurate history, the result of careful research, of all the
literature on this subject, from the beginning of the
Plymouth Brethren movement down to the dawn of the
twentieth century. Much of the literature has, it would seem,
disappeared, including many of the prophetic periodicals
of a century ago.

In a large amount of chaff, there was some wheat. Prophetic students of the nineteenth century saw, and recorded
in considerable detail, the imminent rise of Russia as a

189

world power and enemy of Christianity. These same men also foresaw—though often misinterpreting texts—the fall of the Ottoman empire, and they were unanimous in their prediction of a time of great world wars. Their statements regarding contemporary historical events were often unfounded, and had no direct bearing upon the clear teaching of a Scripture passage. Thus, many of the assertions were, at least in part, responsible for the Church as a whole abandoning the serious study of Biblical prophecies, as they relate to the last days, and to the nations to be involved in these future events.

It is not my intention in this chapter to make a catalog of all the references to Egypt in this voluminous literature. The substance of this chapter is a selection I trust from the more significant titles. Included will be statements that have been proved tragically erroneous, as well as those indicating some true insight into what the Scriptures have to say about certain historical movements to occur at the end of the age.

The most important single work in which the Egypt of the end time, in the light of Biblical prophecy, is set forth with thoroughness is the volume by Benjamin Wills Newton (1807-1899), *Babylon: Its Future History and Doom, with Remarks on the Future of Egypt and Other Eastern Countries*. This was originally published in 1850, but a third, enlarged edition, the one commonly seen today, appeared in 1890, and it is from this edition that I quote here. First of all, Newton rightly affirms, "That Egypt and Greece will be kingdoms at the time when 'the transgressor shall have come to the full,' and Antichrist have been revealed, is certain, if the eighth chapter of Daniel be true; for in that chapter Antichrist is said to arise in the latter time of *their* kingdom words, 'their kingdom,' referring to Egypt, Greece, Syria and the territories immediately contiguous to Constantinople, once held by Lysimachus. The eighth of Daniel declares that the four divisions of the Empire of Alexander the Great (so far as those kingdoms were subsequently subjugated by Rome) will reappear when 'the transgressors shall have come to the full.' Indeed, two of these divisions (Greece and Egypt) have already virtually reappeared as kingdoms, although great efforts were made by England and other European Powers to prevent their severance from Turkey." [1]

Newton lived in a time which witnessed the beginnings of the restoration of Egypt as a national power. "The restoration of Egypt, which is now gently proceeding under Western influences, is an event of solemn interest, as heralding the near approach of the time when that platform is to be constituted which is to be the sphere for the closing developments of the Day of Man. As Egypt was the first channel through which civilization from the East reached Europe, so it is in Egypt that returning civilization is finding the first sphere of its operation in renovating (not indeed according to the ways of God, but of man) Syria and the Euphratean districts. The Nile and the Euphrates are by God's appointment, *the* great rivers of the world. He who can effectually control them and the Mediterranean (a Sea whose 'shores are Empires') will be *the* Master of the Earth. No one nation is able to control them: but a Federation of nations may control them, provided that such confederated nations can be themselves guided and ruled by a competent hand. All men see that what is needed now by the whole

Earth is a strong *central* Government, guided by a strong and able hand." [2]

It is significant that while Newton recognized the seriousness of the problem of the Near East, he was far from the truth in regard to the people who would ultimately reign there. "It is very evident that the Eastern Question, as it is termed, must ere long receive its solution. The welfare and peace of Europe are jeopardised by it. The question is, Shall Asiatic power, or European power, establish itself in those countries that anciently formed the Eastern branch of the Roman Empire? Shall Egypt, and Greece, and Asia Minor, and Syria, be subject to European, or to Asiatic control? Our answer is, They will be subject to European control? As Greece under Alexander prevailed over Persia; and as Imperial Rome under Trajan crossed the Euphrates and established itself in Assyria, so again shall Western institutions and Western power prevail in the East so as for Assyria to be made the seat of European strength, and European civilization. It would be strange, indeed, if Egypt were to revive, and Palestine were to revive, and Assyria remain in desolation." [3]

In the year 1957, it is surprising to note how these prophetic writers of an earlier generation gave to England a permanent sovereign relationship over Egypt, a relationship which we now know to be impossible, and for which assertion there is no real Scriptural evidence. Thus, e.g., Robert Patterson, in his widely distributed brochure, "Egypt in History and Prophecy," went so far as to insist that the prophecy of Isaiah about "a great one" coming to deliver Egypt referred to the British Empire! "But the God of Providence has now arisen. The British cannon thundering in the harbor of Alexandria, and the British government laying its strong hand upon the oppressors of Egypt and seeking to restore law and order in that land, show that divine providence has at this very time raised up 'a great one' for their deliverance, even Great Britain, the mightiest commercial and maritime power in the world, on whose dominion the sun never sets, and under whose government, after ages of misrule, the wounds of Egypt may perhaps be healed, and some degree of security and justice extended to her oppressed people." [4]

Over and over again we come upon passages in these works which affirm a general conviction that missionary activity in Egypt would continue to spread and develop until most of that land was won to Christ—a program which has certainly been interrupted by modern events. To quote Patterson again: "The Lord has been preparing Egypt also for the prevalence of Christianity by the settlement there for over twenty years of English and American missionaries, who have opened schools in Alexandria, Cairo, and almost all the chief towns of Egypt, and have planted churches in many of them." [5]

One of the strangest writings of the latter part of the nineteenth century on this subject was a work published in London in 1887, entitled, *Notes on Some Prophecies Indicating the Probable Relation Between England and Egypt in the Last Days*. The author here makes Ephraim of the Old Testament stand for Great Britain, and consequently, such phrases as "Ephraim shall return to Egypt" (Hosea 9:3; 8:13; 12:1; 7:11-16) are forced to mean that this is a prophecy of England's entrance into, and rule over Egypt. Still, though the author himself is an Englishman, he acknowledges the possibility that England will ultimately be forced out of Egypt. "Although we are now in Egypt, and although England may have some temporary power or supremacy in Egypt, there would seem to be at least four reasons why she should not retain possession or have power over Egypt in the last days." The first reason, taken from Isaiah 19:4, is that Egypt in the last days will be given over to a cruel lord and a fierce king, and, as the author rightly comments, England is neither of these. Secondly, assuming that England is "the king of the south"—a most fantastic interpretation of these passages—as such she will be defeated. Thirdly, England will be identified in the last days with Tyre and Tarshish, and because Isaiah 23:13 prophesies that this power will be overthrown, the English empire also will be overthrown. Finally, the author reasons from Ezekiel 30:8, "Whether England annexes Egypt entirely, which at present seems very improbable, or retains only temporary possession over it, these last words will imply that some great scene of God's judgment must yet happen in Egypt, 'when all her helpers shall be destroyed.' Hence, if this be indeed 'the time of the end,' it is evident that we must be on the eve of some stupendous events of the greatest solemnity to England." [6]

The theme of Egypt in prophecy entered occasionally into the sermons preached in America toward the close of the nineteenth century, most of which never got into print, of course. A series of addresses given by one of New York City's most distinguished clergymen of that time, Dr. Charles S. Robinson, were among those printed in the *Missionary Review of the World* for 1888. Actually, they are not sermons from Biblical texts, but, rather, narratives of some of the things which he himself observed as he traveled through Egypt. Describing the oppression, the poverty, the meager harvests and the lack of rain in that land, he affirms that such conditions must represent a fulfilment of Isaiah's prediction that the Lord would smite Egypt. This smiting was to be accompanied or followed by healing, and Robinson reported seeing signs, especially in Cairo, that Egypt was on the threshold of better days. His words are too optimistic in the light of what we know today: "Civilization is opening the path for gospel grace. The crescent on the Turkish flag is waning rather than waxing. Prayer is offered publicly by converts in dedicated houses of God; missionary work has been prospered marvelously in that unpromising land, and God is fulfilling His covenant rapidly." Then he does what so many others of his day did—he points to England as the nation which would be the means of fulfilling these promises of ultimate blessing for Egypt, in statements which could not be written today, and which had no Scriptural basis then:

"The most practical proof of the divine covenant as to Egypt's ultimate conversion is found in the entrance of the British influence and rule there. The coming in of foreigners is not a curse, but rather a benediction to Egypt. The finances are better managed in these days than they have been for centuries before. The national indebtedness is more firmly provided for; the bonds have risen from seventy to one hundred per cent lately; blood and treasure have not absolutely been wasted on that soil by the best intelligence of Great Britain through these years. Say what we will concerning England's domination in the East, one thing at least is true: no civilized Christian man or woman has visited the lands of the Bible, traveling along among the heterogeneous peoples, and crossing the frontiers of miscellaneous governments, without feeling at the moment when the border-line of any British possession was reached: 'Here is law and order, here is truth and decency and safety! Happy is the nation that hears the tread of a foreigner so beneficent, a stranger so kind, a conqueror so noble!'" [7]

During the first World War, Mr. E. B. Samuel, in a paper read before the Prophecy Investigation Society in London on "Palestine-Turkey-and Egypt," made the following remarks, which, though they have value, indicate how unwise it is to make the fulfilment of any prophecy dependent upon political decisions of a nation not mentioned in that prophecy: "Israel's going back to Egypt has, since the Exodus, been connected with punishment, and the threatening of Deut. 28:68, that they should be taken back to Egypt in ships, has been carried out before in their history and has been fulfilled again lately, when some thousands were compelled to flee there from Palestine.

"Isaiah 10:11 and Zechariah 10:10 make it clear that they will return by way of the land of Egypt. Isaiah 27:13 has reference to the two branches of the nation, the lost ones in Assyria are some of the ten tribes, and the outcasts in Egypt are some of the two tribes: the expression used here is peculiarly suitable to the present Jewish refugees there. Isaiah 11:16 and Micah 7:15 make the Exodus a picture of Israel's future deliverance. The song of Moses at the Red Sea finds an echo in many prophecies concerning their final redemption. For example, 'Jehovah is my strength and my song and is become my salvation,' is re-echoed in the song of praise that is put into the mouth of future Israel both in Isaiah 12:2 and Psalms 118:14. How far God is preparing for their return from Egypt by placing that land under the control of Great Britain one cannot tell; it may be in the interest of this country to place the Jews in Palestine after this war and give them autonomy under the British flag. British statesmen have on several occasions shown themselves friendly to the Zionist movement, which aims at securing for the Jews 'a publicly recognized and legally assured home in Palestine.' Other nations, especially Russia, will not be willing that Palestine shall fall under full British control; while Great Britain will not permit, if she can help it, any great Power to get possession of Palestine, so near to Egypt and the Suez Canal, the gateway to India. The idea of Palestine for the Jews is now finding favour in many quarters. Wonderful as it may appear, it is actually receiving support in Roman Catholic Italy." [8]

Apart from the interpretation of prophetic passages in the Old Testament specifically referring to Egypt, it must be acknowledged that nineteenth century prophetic students (with the exception of B. W. Newton) did not accurately foresee any of the basic situations now prevailing in this nation of the Nile Valley. They were almost unanimously wrong in insisting that Egypt, with the remainder of the Near East, would continue under the control of European nations: they failed to foresee the tremendous convulsions that would follow the rise of nationalism in all the kingdoms of North

Africa and along the eastern boundary of the Mediterranean; and they overestimated the place of England in God's program for the end of the age, even though England cannot be identified specifically with any one prophetic utterance in the Old Testament Scriptures. Secondly, they were overly optimistic in their statements on the progression and influence of Protestantism in Egypt in this twentieth century. I do not know of any prophetic student of the last one hundred years who foresaw the tragic curtailment of missionary activity in Egypt since the rise of Nasser. Thirdly, they could not comprehend the international significance of Suez, and did not know what an important part oil would play in the shuffling of interests and policies in this confused age. Finally, they failed to see that Egypt, even according to the Old Testament prophecies must reassert herself as a powerful and independent national entity. In other words, the prophetic students of the nineteenth century did not exercise the wisdom which should attend prophetic investigation when they considered the place of Egypt in Old Testament prophecy.

Notes

1. Benjamin Wills Newton: *Babylon and Egypt, Their Future and Doom.* 3rd ed., 1890. p. 201.
2. Newton, *op. cit.,* pp. 204, 205.
3. Newton, *op. cit.,* p. 203.
4. Robert Patterson: *Egypt in History and Prophecy.* Boston, 1883. p. 50.
5. Patterson, *op. cit.,* p. 52.
6. *Notes on Some Prophecies Indicating the Probable Relation Between England and Egypt in the Last Days.* London, 1887. p. 325.
7. Charles Robinson, in *The Missionary Review of the World,* Oct., 1888, pp. 749-752.
8. E. B. Samuel, *Palestine, Turkey, and Egypt,* London, n.d.

EGYPT IN BIBLICAL PROPHECY

Note: Other writings on this subject which have come to my attention are J. B. Alexander, "Egypt's Smiting and Healing—Prophecies Fulfilled," in *The Evangelistic Repository*, Vol. LXII, 1890, pp. 92-100 (a work I have been unable to discover in any library in this country); "God's Purpose for Egypt," in *Watching and Waiting* (London) November-December, 1956, Vol. XV, pp. 273-278; C. T. Cook, "Egypt in the Prophetic Scriptures," in *The Christian* (London) September 7, 1956; Arthur W. Kac, "The Present Egyptian Conflict in the Light of Biblical Prophecy," in *The Hebrew Christian*, Winter, 1957, Vol. XLII, pp. 1-8.

12

BIBLICAL PROPHECIES RELATING TO EGYPT
IN MODERN MISSIONARY LITERATURE

It is not my purpose in this chapter to survey the history of Christian missions in the land of the Pharaohs, for this has been done repeatedly by others. Here I would attempt simply to give some indication of the influence of the prophecies we have been considering over missionary thought as it relates to the evangelization of this vast North African land. This chapter can be only fragmentary, for, in spite of the large libraries available to students in our country, the writings and biographies of many of the earlier missionaries to Egypt are not available.

The first missionaries of modern times to enter Egypt were Moravians, in the middle of the eighteenth century, men such as Frederick William Hocker, who labored from 1752 to 1765, George Pilder, of the same decade, and John Henry Danke, 1768 to 1772, with whom John Antes and George Henry Wieninger worked briefly. These men suffered untold hardships for Christ, but due to lack of interest in Europe, discouragement, and, for some, death, the effort was abandoned in 1782. I have not been able to consult the writings of any of these men, nor has any authority on missionary literature in this country been able to guide me to sources of further material.

EGYPT IN BIBLICAL PROPHECY

The Holland Mission in Egypt was established in 1868, as the result of an experience of Dr. Witteveen of Ermelo, Holland. During a period of protracted prayer, Dr. Witteveen, a Dutch pastor, had his mind drawn to Isaiah's prophecy regarding Egypt as set forth in Chapter 17. With the help of the Barman Mission of Germany, he persuaded two brothers named Moory to undertake pioneer work in Egypt, where they arrived in 1868. Within a year one died and the other was compelled to return to Holland because of poor health. The following year saw a new start by Mr. Nyland, an evangelist, who resided in the Baseler Mission House in Cairo. From time to time he was joined by other missionaries, some of whom were compelled to flee because of persecution, while others suffered much in family losses. The Mission closed near the beginning of our century; but it did originate through the influence of this prophecy of Isaiah.[1]

In 1897, Douglas Montague Thornton, a gifted missionary, of the Church Missionary Society of London, wrote to a friend as follows: "I have definitely backed out of Educational Secretary work on 31st July. I am told that C.M.S. would be willing to send me wherever I felt called to go. That means to the Mohammedans certainly. Where? There are three places which all have their attractions, and which from considerable reading now on the Mohammedan question seem to be very important places to occupy— (1) Bombay, (2) Cairo, (3) Hausaland. The first has been in my mind since 1891. The second grows upon me more and more, for I believe prophecy indicates the future importance of Egypt in this question. Hausaland is undoubtedly the opportunity of the hour, and dearly beloved Walter Miller longs for me to go with him. He is offering for this work almost at once. But I think the Lord is leading to (1) or (2). It may be that I should go to the Punjab to learn Urdu first before settling in Bombay. I can't say yet. Arabic, too, must be studied, and where? I need your prayers." [2] Just at the time that Thornton was being moved to action by his study of Old Testament prophecy, seven young men volunteered for service in Egypt under the supervision of the Egypt Mission Band. An account of this endeavor is set forth in a small book edited by William J. W. Roome, *Blessed Be Egypt,* the preface and introduction to which are dominated by references to these prophecies:

"With earnest prayer that the promise, 'Blessed be Egypt,' may be abundantly fulfilled, and many of God's children in the homeland take a deeper interest in that ancient people, and some at least be led by His Blessed Spirit to lay their 'all' on His altar, and go forth at His command, and also that the Lord's dealing with these young men may prove an encouragement to many others to look to the Holy Spirit of God alone for guidance in their daily life and supply of their every need, is this little book sent in the name of our Risen Saviour . . .

"The Scripture of truth tells us that He has wondrous purposes of grace towards Egypt and the Soudan. When these purposes have been fulfilled 'Israel shall be the third with Egypt and with Assyria, the work of my hands, and Israel mine inheritance.' We may gather from this passage that Israel, Egypt, and Assyria are to be blessed contemporaneously. For several years past God has been dealing wondrously, both politically and spiritually, with the dry bones of Israel. His political dealings with Egypt have been no less wonderful, and as we seek to interpret these dealings by the prophetic writings, we cannot doubt that the set time to favour Egypt, the Soudan, and Asia Minor is dawning. The 18th, 19th, and 20th chapters of Isaiah reveal to us some of the blessings in store for Egypt, Cush, and 'the land beyond the rivers of Cush.'

" 'The burden of Egypt. Behold, the Lord rideth upon a swift cloud, and shall come into Egypt: and the idols of Egypt shall be moved at His presence, and the heart of Egypt shall melt in the midst of it. And I will set the Egyptians against the Egyptians: and they shall fight everyone against his brother, and everyone against his neighbour; city against city, and kingdom against kingdom. And the spirit of Egypt shall fail in the midst thereof; and I will destroy the counsel thereof: and they shall seek to the idols, and to the charmers, and to them that have familiar spirits, and to the wizards. And the Egyptians will I give over into the land of a cruel lord; and a fierce king shall rule over them, saith the Lord, the Lord of Hosts . . . In that day shall there be an altar to the Lord in the midst of the land of Egypt, and a pillar at the border thereof to the Lord. And it shall be for a sign and for a witness unto the Lord of Hosts in the land of Egypt: for they shall cry unto the Lord because of the oppressors, and He shall send them a Saviour, and a great one, and He shall deliver them' (Isa. 19:1-4, 19, 20).

"Christian men and women, you who desire to dwell in the secret place of the Most High, and thus learn the secret of the Lord, will you not begin from this day to pour out your soul for Egypt and the Sudan? As the nations 'rush' madly along, and we see the day approaching, let us 'so much the more' enter into our chambers and shut the door, and pray to our Father who seeth in secret, and we shall soon see the blessing coming upon the missionaries, missions, rulers, and peoples of Egypt and Ethiopia. May we be strengthened with might by His Spirit in the inner man for this 'work' of believing prayer! Brethren, the time is short! The Lord has promised to heal Egypt (Isa. 19:22); but for this He will be enquired of by His believing people." [3]

The periodical issued by the United Presbyterian Church since the beginning of this century carried an article as early as 1906 entitled "Prophetical Interpretation. Wanted a Book!" in which the author speaks autobiographically in the following paragraph: "For many years it has been my deep conviction that vast tracts of prophetical Scriptures lie barren to us through our imperfect knowledge of history, especially the history of the Near East . . . I cannot but think that our interpretation of the prophecies have not been keeping pace with the increased knowledge of Orientalists in the history of the nations concerned; and that if a careful student of history, who also had the gift of spiritual insight, were to carefully collect all the historical data, and minutely compare them with the prophecies, we would have as results (1) Fresh proof of the marvelous inspiration of the Scriptures. (2) A correct historical interpretation, which surely is the only way to arrive at their true spiritual teaching. (3) We would have a stimulus for missionary work in these lands and we should surely find glorious promises for the future which are yet to be fulfilled." [4]

The following year, Dr. Charles Watson concluded his important work, *In the Valley of the Nile,* with this challenge: "Why may not Egypt be speedily evangelised? Political barriers have been largely removed. Moslem hostility has been considerably abated. Prosperity has lifted the nation out of the degradation of extreme poverty. Missionary experience has tested and proved the best methods of work. Strategic centers, ready to be occupied, abound and even invite occupation. The Church is abundantly able, in both men and means, for the accomplishment of the task. God Himself hath declared for our encouragement, 'Jehovah shall be known to Egypt, and the Egyptians shall know Jehovah in that day.' And Christ's own word unto His Church is, 'Say not ye, There are yet four months and then cometh the harvest? Behold, I say unto you, Lift up your eyes, and look on the fields, that they are white *already* unto harvest.' We say it reverently, *Deus vult.* And, ere the present generation pass away, Christ may be made known in either city and town, in every village and hamlet of the Nile Valley, if the Church of Christ be also willing." [5]

Some years later, Rev. Arthur T. Upson, Field Director of the Nile Mission Press, addressed a gathering in London on the most intriguing subject, "Isaiah's Survey of the Moslem World and the Nile Mission Press Response to that Call." Specific references to the Isaianic prophecies were made, as follows: "I rubbed my eyes the other day when I discovered that the map of the Moslem world was reproduced in the Book of Isaiah. Since prophecy is fulfilled twice or three times, it is highly probable that every country of which Isaiah prophesied it should fall, has fallen and will fall again. I will

EGYPT IN BIBLICAL PROPHECY

first run through those prophecies in Isaiah and then speak of Persia, the Anglo-Egyptian Sudan, Algeria and the Sahara, leaving Egypt, Assyria and Israel for tonight . . .

"Fifth burden—Isaiah 19:1 speaks of the 'burden of Egypt.' How was God going to punish Egypt? He says: 'And the Egyptians will I give over into the hand of a cruel Lord.' May that not be Cambyses, King of Persia. Or is it Islam?

"Sixth burden—Isaiah 21 speaks of 'the burden of the desert of the sea.' Which is the desert of the sea? It may be the Great Sahara, though a reference in the next few verses implies that there is a connection with Elam, and that is part of Persia. The Sahara may be the desert of the sea, or it may not.

"So you see how God made Isaiah see in telescopic vision the whole of what we now call the Moslem world." [6]

Surely what the Holy Spirit revealed to Isaiah has not yet been accomplished. Apart from the Christians who are in the Coptic Church of Egypt—I do not attempt to evaluate here the work of the Roman Catholic Church in that country—it has been estimated that in the forty years of missionary labor, from 1854 to 1894, only seventy-five Mohammedans were baptized into the Christian faith. The latest statistics on missionary work in Egypt reveal that twenty-two different societies are represented, four of which are British, two continental, seven North American, and nine "national churches." Included in the last group is the largest mission work in Egypt, once known as the United Presbyterian Church of North African Egypt, but now called the Evangelical Church in Egypt, Synod of the Nile. These twenty-two societies have 547 places of worship, 256 of which belong to the Evangelical Church of that land. Of the approximately 67,000 communicant members of the Protestant church, the Evangelical Church in Egypt claims 26,000.[7] The present Egyptian government has placed restrictions on missions in that land more severe than have been known for nearly a century; for example, a recent decree states that if mission schools are to be retained, they must teach the Koran to all students enrolled from Mohammedan homes. Even since I began writing this volume, the entire missionary situation has changed in Egypt. All British missionaries have been compelled to leave their work in the Nile Valley—and they were doing a good work—as have all missionaries with any French connections; in fact, the Protestant missionary effort in Egypt has been more severely crippled in the last two years than at any time since the Protestants began laboring in that land. But the Word of God standeth sure, and some day these ancient prophecies, which have quickened many of God's servants and have driven them out into inconceivably difficult fields for Christ's sake, will lay hold of a new body of consecrated men and women, and in God's own time will be gloriously fulfilled.

In 1948, Miss Irene Naish significantly based the narrative of her booklet, *Wonders in Egypt,* on the words of Jeremiah 32:20, "Thou . . . the mighty God . . . hast set signs and wonders in the land of Egypt even unto this day." For the concluding chapter she chose as a text Revelation 3:7, 8: "These things saith He that . . . hath the key . . . He that openeth, and no man shutteth, and shutteth, and no man openeth . . . Behold I have set before thee an open door . . ." Miss Naish continued in an optimistic vein: "This seems to be the key to future missionary work in Egypt. At the moment, owing to the general world unrest and the rising tide of nationalism in that land, it is impossible to foresee developments. We are told, however, not to look at 'things seen' but to endure as seeing Him Who is invisible, and that One has not, as yet, rescinded His command to His disciples to go and preach to every creature, which includes the Moslems of Egypt. There is a glad readiness to recognise the Master's Almighty power to open, but the corollary is 'and no man shutteth.' We are told also that it is He Who shuts, and man is powerless to open. It is well·to keep this two-fold aspect of Our Lord's actions before our eyes as the key to the otherwise heart-breaking obstacles which have confronted, and still are confronting, the proclamation of the Gospel in lands under Islam's sway. Let us believe God's Word, which tells us that the hearts of kings are in His rule and governance to dispose and turn as seems best to Him. Thus we may get beyond earthly governmental actions and rest assured that, in the mystery of His inscrutable wisdom, any rebuffs we may meet are part of His ultimate purpose." [8]

Although some of his statements regarding the fulfilment of prophecy are rather fantastic, Boutros' concluding paragraph in *The Soul of Egypt* is worth quoting: "These are wonderful days in which we live, and in spite of the hardness of Islam and the indifference of the Church to the challenge, we are asking again a token: one hundred Moslem converts to stand together; let us have faith that He will answer in the dawn of this brighter and fairer day. We have seen some of the promised 'Princes that shall come out of Egypt' (Ps. 68:13) and we take them as a foregleam, feeling there is no incentive to service comparable to this calling a people to 'return unto the Lord'—whom He has declared *will* return, and in infinite grace has called 'Blessed be Egypt My people.' " [9]

Notes

1. H. J. DeJong Schouwenberg, "The Holland Mission in Egypt," in *The Moslem World*. April, 1924, Vol. XIV, pp. 148-151. An extensive search for further details on this experience of Dr. Witteveen has been in vain. A search of the biography of Dr. Witteveen, by J. H. Gunning (1891) graciously loaned by the library of the University of Amsterdam fails to add any other data.
2. W. H. T. Gairdner and D. M. Thornton: *A Study in Missionary Ideals and Methods*. New York, 1918. pp. 50, 51.
3. J. W. Roome: *Blessed Be Egypt*. London, 1898. pp. viii, ix, 12, 13.
4. G. S. (possibly Girgus Sayoufee) "Prophetical Investigation. Wanted a Book!" in *Blessed Be Egypt*, July, 1906, Vol. VII, p. 107.
5. Charles Watson: *In the Valley of the Nile*. New York, 1908. pp. 235, 236.
6. Arthur T. Upson, "Isaiah's Survey of the Moslem World and the Nile Mission Press Response to the Call," in *Blessed Be Egypt*, July, 1927, Vol. XXVII, p. 77.
7. See *The World Christian Handbook*, 1952 edition (London, 1952) pp. 178-179; and the *Directory of World Missions*, edited by Joseph I. Parker, 1938, pp. 148-149.
8. Irene E. Naish: *Wonders of Egypt: The Story of the Egypt General Mission*. London, 1951. p. 47.
9. Allison Douglas Boutros: *The Soul of Egypt*. p. 178.

Note: Those interested in the subject of missions in Egypt will want to consult the exhaustive work by Andrew Watson, *The American Mission in Egypt* (1897); also Charles R. Watson: *Egypt and the Christian Crusade* (1907), and *In the Valley of the Nile* (1908); Julius Richter: *A History of Protestant Missions in the Near East* (Edinburgh, 1910) pp. 337-363; and the concluding chapter of Montague Fowler: *Christian Egypt, Past, Present, Future*. London, 1901.

13

THE STRANGE CULT OF THE PYRAMIDISTS

About one hundred years ago a British writer, John Taylor, launched in his book *The Great Pyramid* (1859) the strange idea that the Great Pyramid of Gizeh is a monument divinely intended to prophetically reveal a mass of chronological data, a vast stone structure that would, when properly understood, indicate the years, and sometimes the months and very days of the major events in the redemptive program of the world.[1] The theory caught the attention of a famous astronomer Charles Piazzi Smyth, about whom we shall have more to say later, and from that time to the present, scores of books and thousands of articles have been written to support this fantastic concept. Inasmuch as their scheme involves a prophecy concerning Egypt which we have already considered, it would seem that a study of our subject must necessarily include some discussion of this strange view. First of all we might consider the Pyramid of Gizeh itself, then briefly summarize the history of this prophetic interpretation, examine with some detail the views set forth by these men, and, finally, point out some of the inconsistencies and contradictions of the theory.

There are about seventy different pyramids up and down the Nile Valley, of which thirty-three are classified in the latest authentic work on this subject as the "major Pyramids of the Old and Middle Kingdoms." [2] The earliest of these was

THE GREAT PYRAMID

(The words in parentheses are designations by those holding this pyramidal theory.)

KING'S CHAMBER

QUEEN'S CHAMBER

(World War)

GRAND GALLERY
(Grace)

(Passion of Christ)
(Law)

PIT

the Step Pyramid, built under Zoser about 2815 B.C., in the
IIIrd Dynasty, located at Sakkara. The Great Pyramid of
Gizeh (also spelled Giza) was erected in the IVth Dynasty by
Cheops, about 2650 B.C. The last, also at Sakkara, was built
during the XIIIth Dynasty under King Khenjer, about 1777
B.C. So we note that Pyramids were built in Egypt over a
period of a thousand years, and that the erection of the last
one was undertaken just as Israel began her sojourn in Egypt.
The Pyramidists all agree that of these numerous structures,
only one is to be thought of as having any prophetic significance. This assertion in itself is rather strange, inasmuch as all
of the Pyramids follow a somewhat similar architectural design. As one of the Pyramidists himself has said, "While
Egypt has many Pyramids, the Great Pyramid of Cheops at
Gizeh is the only one having any astronomical, prophetical or
messianic significance. All the others, some quite large, are
but inferior imitations of the incomparable Cheops master-
piece." [3]

The Pyramid of Cheops, the largest of all Pyramids in
Egypt, and generally acknowledged to be the largest structure
ever built by man, covers 13.1 acres at the base. Its measurements are as follow: 755.3 feet on the north, 756.08 feet on
the south, 755.88 on the east, 755.77 on the west, and 481.4
feet in height. The angle of slope is 51° 52'. Into this vast
mound, built on solid rock, 2300 separate blocks of stone were
placed averaging two and one-half tons each, though some of
them weigh as much as fifteen tons. Some idea of the enormity
of this structure may be had in the fact that within this
Pyramid could be placed all the houses of Parliament and
St. Paul's Cathedral in London. It is with the inner structure

of the Pyramid that we are primarily concerned, and for a better understanding of the argument, we must have before us a chart. The north entrance to the Pyramid (1) is 55 feet above ground level and 26 feet east of the center. I would like to use here the exact words of Mr. Edwards in his excellent, compact work on the Pyramids:

"From the entrance a corridor, measuring about 3 feet 5 inches in width and 3 feet 11 inches in height, descends at a gradient of 26° 31′ 23″ first through the core of the Pyramid and then through the rock. At a distance of about 345 feet from the original entrance, the corridor becomes level and continues horizontally for a further 29 feet before terminating in a chamber. On the west side of the level section of the corridor, near the entrance to the chamber, there is a recess, the cutting of which was never completed. The chamber also is unfinished, its trenched floor and rough walls resembling a quarry. A square pit sunk in the floor may represent the first stage in an unfulfilled project for deepening the chamber. According to Vyse and Perring, who measured the chamber in 1838, its dimensions are: height, 11 feet 6 inches; east-west, 46 feet; north-south, 27 feet 1 inch." [4]

When the decision was made to alter the original plan and to create a burial chamber in the body of the Pyramid instead of in the basic rock, a hole was cut in the roof of the Descending Corridor, about 50 feet from the entrance, and a new (3) Ascending Corridor was cut of the same width and height as the Descending Corridor, and 129 feet in length, with a gradient of 26° 2′ 30″. At the lower end of this corridor are three large granite plug blocks, placed one behind the other, whereas those in the upper part are parallel with the gradient of the corridor, with the exception of the "girdle-stones," which were placed at regular intervals of 17 feet and two feet. We again pick up Edwards' description:

"When the Ascending Corridor was being constructed, the builders probably intended the burial-chamber to occupy a position in the centre of the superstructure and at no great height above ground-level. Such a chamber was actually built at the end of a passage leading from the top of the Ascending Corridor. Called by the Arabs the 'Queen's Chamber'—a misnomer which it has retained—this chamber lies exactly midway between the north and south sides of the Pyramid. Its measurements are 18 feet 10 inches from east to west and 17 feet 2 inches from north to south. It has a pointed roof, which rises to a height of 20 feet 5 inches. In the east wall there is a niche with corbelled sides; its original depth was only 3 feet 5 inches, but the back has now been cut away by treasure-seekers. Its height is 15 feet 4 inches and the width at the base 5 feet 2 inches. Presumably it was designed to contain a statue of the king, which may, however, never have been placed in position.

"There are many indications that work on the Queen's Chamber was abandoned before it had been completed. The floor, for instance, is exceedingly rough; if the chamber had been finished it would probably have been paved with finer stone. Again, in the north and south walls there are small rectangular apertures from which shafts run horizontally for a distance of about 6 feet 6 inches and then turn upwards at an angle of approximately 30°. These apertures were not cut at the time when the chamber was built—an omission which can only be explained on the hypothesis that the chamber was never finished . . .

"The abandonment of the Queen's Chamber led to the construction of two of the most celebrated architectural works which have survived from the Old Kingdom, namely the Grand Gallery and the King's Chamber. The Grand Gallery was built as a continuation of the Ascending Corridor. It is 153 feet in length and 28 feet in height. Its walls of polished limestone rise vertically to a height of 7 feet 6 inches; above that level each of the seven courses projects inwards about 3 inches beyond the course on which it rests, thus forming a corbel vault of unparalleled dimensions. The space between the uppermost course on each side, measuring 3 feet 5 inches in width, is spanned by roofing slabs, every one of which is laid at a slightly steeper angle than the gradient of the gallery.

"At the foot of each wall a flat-topped ramp, 2 feet in height and 1 foot 8 inches in width, extends along the whole length of the gallery. A passage measuring, like the roof, 3 feet 5 inches in width runs between the two ramps. At the lower end of this passage there is now a gap, caused by the removal of the stones which formerly linked the floor of the passage with that of the Ascending Corridor and also covered the mouth of the horizontal passage leading to the Queen's Chamber. In the gap, the lowest stone in the western ramp has been removed, revealing a shaft which descends, partly perpendicularly and partly obliquely, first through the core of the Pyramid and then through the rock, until it emerges in the west wall of the Descending Corridor. Its apparent purpose and the significance of some other peculiar features in the Grand Gallery will be considered after the King's Chamber has been described." [5]

A high step at the end of the Grand Gallery gives access to a low, narrow passage leading to the King's Chamber, which, built entire of granite measures 34 feet 4 inches from east to west, 17 feet 2 inches from north to south, and 19 feet 1 inch in height. "In the north and south walls, at a height of about 3 feet above the floor, are the rectangular apertures of shafts which differ from those of the Queen's Chamber only in penetrating the core of the Pyramid to the outer surface, the northern at an angle of 31° and the southern at an angle of 45°. The object of these shafts is not known with certainty; they may have been designed for the ventilation of the chamber or for some religious purpose which is still open to conjecture. Near the west wall stands a lidless rectangular granite sarcophagus which once contained the king's body, probably enclosed within an inner coffin of wood. In appearance it is rough, many of the scratches made by the saw when cutting it being still clearly visible. Sir Flinders Petrie discovered that the width of the sarcophagus was about an inch greater than the width of the Ascending Corridor at its mouth; he therefore concluded that it must have been placed in position while the chamber was being built." [6]

The innumerable details found in any account of the Pyramids regarding these various plugs, blocks and aperture are not essential to the purpose of this chapter, and for the most part would only confuse a reader, unless he were making a prolonged study of the subject.

As indicated at the beginning of this chapter, a brief note about the distinguished Pyramidist, Charles Piazzi Smyth is in order in our treatment of this subject, Smyth (1819-1900) was the Astronomer Royal of Scotland from 1845, and the Professor of Astronomy at Edinburgh University. Many of his papers were published in the *Edinburgh Astronomical Observations* (Vol. XI-XV), and his discoveries in the area of astronomical research were numerous and important. Enamored with Taylor's theory regarding the Great Pyramid, Smyth went to Egypt to examine this monument personally, and, as a result, issued a work which has since served as the foundation for Pyramidal studies, *Our Inheritance in the Great Pyramid* (1864; 5th ed., 1890). Later he published his *Life and Work at the Great Pyramid.*[7] Oddly enough, Smyth himself had an almost feverish hatred for all the pagan temples and structures of ancient Egypt, developing, as it were, an anti-Egyptian attitude, and insisting that only the Great Pyramid, among all of that land's marvelous monuments of antiquity, had ever been divinely designed. The father of the famous archaeologist and Egyptologist, W. Flinders Petrie, was converted to this Pyramidal theory of revelation by reading Smyth's work and made plans to go to Egypt with his son to undertake further investigation at Gizeh. The father was unable to make the journey, however, and the son's visit there launched him upon a career that may well be said to mark a new era in archaeological research. The younger Petrie developed an aversion to the whole concept of Pyramid prophecies, and while the Pyramidists have always proudly used his scheme of measurements, they must recognize that he was their uncompromising antagonist.[8]

The literature following the books of Smyth has been vast in quantity. Some of the volumes are large, with complicated drawings, expensive, and in many places difficult to understand. Several years ago Mr. Adam Rutherford established an Institute of Pyramidology in London, appointed himself president, and began to issue a Journal. The majority of Pyramidists soon identified themselves with the Anglo-Israelite group, and vice versa, so that in most works defending the British-Israel heresy, there are chapters on the prophetic teachings of the Pyramids. A very learned journal devoted to the Pyramid teachings, *Destiny,* is published at Haverhill, Massachusetts regularly.

Some Basic Teachings of the Pyramidist School of Interpretation

A chapter on this theory of prophetic teaching must set forth certain references to specific factors in the architectural design of the Pyramid as they relate to these prophecies and, wearisome as this may seem to some, it is necessary to enter into this subject—though with all possible brevity. There are literally hundreds of minutia in the various publications on this theme, especially those by Davidson, which must be passed over here. The entrance to the Pyramid gives immediate access to what is known as the Descending Passage, which extends in a straight line for 345 feet, and then levels off for 30 feet, leading to a chamber to which we shall refer soon. The passage is 4 feet high and $3\frac{1}{2}$ feet wide, and slopes at an angle of 26° 18′ 10″. It is generally taken to be "a graphical representation of man's gravitation to lower moral and spiritual levels, and finally into hell, unless he is rescued by Divine power." [9] At a distance of approximately 40 feet from the entrance is a straight knife-edge line cut from the roof to the floor on each side wall. At night, the Pole Star, or North Star shines down the passageway to these Scored Lines. The astronomer Herschel determined that in the twenty-second century B.C., the Pole Star or Dragon Star would shine all the way down this Descending Passage, and Smyth ascertained that at that time Alcyone, the chief star of the Pleides, was in exact alignment with the Scored Lines. Both of these stars were in the precise required positions simultaneously in 2140 B.C. Thus the Pyramidists believe that these lines in the Descending Passage mark the ancient year 2140 B.C., or by modern reckoning, the autumn of 2141 B.C.[10]

About fifty feet beyond the Scored Lines is the entrance to a passage leading upward, known as the First Ascending Passage, extending 628 Pyramid inches from the Lines, the aperture itself extending 59½ inches. Taking these inches as years, we are brought to 1453 B.C., which the Pyramidists say "marks a time when some people or nation must have been taken out of the rut of the world in general," which would be the Exodus.[11] Working backwards from the First Ascending Passage to the entrance, 481⅝ Pyramid inches, we arrive at the year 2622 B.C., at which time, so these men say, the Pyramid must have been built.

Let us turn again to the Descending Passage, which leads to an enclosed chamber supposedly symbolizing the great time of trouble which shall come upon the earth. The distance across the subterranean cavity is 322⅝ inches. Here the inches are made to represent months of thirty days, not years, and the Pyramidists say that this has reference to the period from July 28, 1914 to January 25-26, 1941, so that in 1941 "we may expect the rounding up of the last of the rebellious

Gentile nations by Israel, operating under the power of God." [12] In other words, while this Descending Passage is supposed to lead to hell, in this symbolism, it does not lead there at all, but rather to a chamber which is supposed to represent the last tribulation period of the nations of the earth, a period so dated that it should have already been completed.

The first Ascending Passage extends 90 feet, to a large passageway known as the Great Gallery, 156 feet long and 28 feet high. Just at the point at which the First Ascending Passage terminates in the Grand Gallery, there is a horizontal passage extending for 1510.96 Pyramid inches, at the end of which is a room known as the Queen's Chamber. At the place at which the First Ascending Passage, the Grand Gallery and the horizontal passage meet, a Well Shaft, leading deep into the solid rock, connects with the Descending Passage. The significance of this can best be interpreted by one of the Pyramidists: "The horizontal ledge at the top of the Well-Shaft is on the same level as the floor of the Queen's Chamber, and the horizontal plane in which both of these lie intersects the floor of the Law Passage at a point $33\frac{1}{2}$ inches back from the end. As Jesus was $33\frac{1}{2}$ years of age when He was crucified, this point therefore marks the date of His birth $33\frac{1}{2}$ years previously. Furthermore, the vertical plane of the end of the Law Passage intersects the above-mentioned horizontal plane 30 inches from the point representing Jesus' birth, and 30 years was Christ's age at His baptism when He began His $3\frac{1}{2}$ years' Ministry." [13]

With the Horizontal Passage, all established categories break down, as the Pyramidists themselves admit. This passage, they claim, "gives a panoramic view of human history right down to the termination of the Millennium when the nations are prepared to enter into their grand destiny." [14] Thus, the Horizontal Passage, with the Queen's Chamber, "portrays the whole plan of God for the world in a nutshell." So say the Pyramidists to escape all kinds of problems here: "It is obvious that it is constructed on a greatly reduced scale, for its entire length is much less than that of the Grand Gallery, which represents the Christian Age only. While in this case an inch does not represent a specific unit of time, such as a year or decade or century, yet the Passage is constructed to scale . . . a year being represented only by a small fraction of an inch." [15] They then proceed to find here two different periods of time determined by the depth of the Passage which increases toward the end, but into these details we need not enter here. This long passage, then, is made to represent the period from Adam, 4007 B.C., to the beginning of the inaugural period of the millennial reign of Christ, A.D. 1953, "after which humanity will begin rapidly to be relieved of the heavy yoke that has distressed them so long." [16]

As depicted on the chart, there are three specific chambers within this Gizeh Pyramid, at different elevations. The first, to which the Descending Passage leads, has been interpreted, as we have noted, as hell. The two chambers to which the Ascending Passage and Grand Gallery lead are Chambers of Life, in contrast to the lowest one, the Chamber of Death. These chambers, says Lt. Kenney-Herbert, "must represent the final state—the end of things temporal, whether life or death . . . They must represent two different aspects of the same destination, the heaven of the graph of the ascent, and so, whatever the true interpretation of the Queen's Chamber Passage may prove to be, we may conclude that it is not an extension of the dispensation of the Law. And further, as this Passage leads directly to a Chamber of Life it cannot symbolize a nation temporarily 'cast away' until the fullness of the Gentiles be come in (Rom. 11:15)." [17] The various minute measurements of these chambers need not be set forth here.

At the end of the Grand Gallery is the King's Chamber, which has always been interpreted by the Pyramidists in the greatest detail and with words of exuberance and joy. This is 1881½ Pyramid inches long and therefore, inasmuch as it begins with A.D. 33, must lead up to the fall of 1914. Since the Great Gallery terminates in a level passage known as Tribulation Passage, at the base of the King's Chamber, this should mean that the tribulation period began in 1914. No one denies that the first World War burst upon us at that time, but the world has not been in continual tribulation since then, and the Biblical tribulation period, with the reign of Antichrist, certainly has not begun. A paragraph from Rutherford will indicate to what extremes these theorists go:

"While the Law Passage is low and contracted, being only about four feet in height, and bound in by great Girdles, the Grand Gallery on the other hand is exceptionally high, being about seven times the height of the Law Passage. Throughout the entire length of the passage and midway between the roof and the floor, on each of the side walls, runs a groove or slide suitable for a sliding partition, which thus divides the Grand Gallery into two portions, an upper and a lower, which fittingly represent the two phases of Abraham's seed, the spiritual (the upper) and the natural (the lower). Owing to seven overlappings at regular intervals up the walls of the Grand Gallery, the upper portion is slightly shorter and narrower than the lower. The upper part is therefore built inside the limits of the lower, thus symbolising that the Election of Grace is within the Election of Race." [18]

So here we have what the Pyramidists believe to be the basic teachings of this ancient pagan structure. The conclusions can be reached only through a convenient shift in the scheme of measurement, from a year, to a month, to a day. There is no inscription, no legend, no indication in any of the hundreds of feet of Pyramid passages that they were ever intended to depict time periods in God's redemptive program. Again and again, as we have noticed, there is an alteration in the original architectural scheme for these passages. Finally, it must be emphasized that all these predictions concerning events to take place in the twentieth century have proved false. Although this subject has been dealt with only briefly here, it should be remembered that thousands of pages have been written expounding these fundamental measurements.

Some Fundamental Criticisms of the Prophetic Interpretation of the Pyramid

My initial criticism of the entire concept of finding prophetic truth in this Pyramid is that the Pyramidists have never explained why, of all the many similar structures along the Nile River, it should be this one and no other that has prophetic significance. Although it is the largest and its inner design the most complicated, there were Pyramids constructed on similar plans before and after it, and there is nothing in the Great Pyramid of Gizeh itself to indicate that it alone has a mystical, esoteric significance. One fact which, in my opinion, would seem to completely eliminate any theory that God intended this Pyramid to serve as a perfect revelation of future events to the end of this age is that the plan for the passageways and burial chambers of the Pyramid was changed repeatedly, as we have seen in the paragraphs taken from Edwards' work. This is not the way God works: He does not start in one direction, then change His mind, and finally alter the whole scheme of structure. There were no such vital changes in the plans for the Tabernacle or the Temple. Thirdly, these Pyramidists are definitely in error in assigning the erection of this particular monument to various Old Testament characters, or to some non-Egyptian race. Cottrell follows many others in declaring that the builder was no less a person than Enoch, directing attention to the fact that in the *Egyptian Book of the Dead* the Pyramid is called "the Pillar of Enoch." [19] There is no hint anywhere in Egyptian history that this Pyramid was conceived by any other but Egyptian architects; nor is there the slightest hint in Biblical literature that Enoch had anything to do with the erection of some great monument in Egypt.

In the most unfortunate book that he ever wrote, Seiss sets forth the theory, echoed by others, that this Pyramid was built by Job, whom he identifies with Melchizedek, on the basis of Job's being called "the greatest of all the men of the east." [20] Those holding this view must then try to connect some passage in the Book of Job with this particular structure, and choose Job 38:1-7. These verses do contain some architectural terms, but they relate to "the foundations of the earth," and not to some building in Egypt, as all other commentators agree. The builder of this Pyramid was no other than Cheops, as the monuments of Egypt testify, and there is not a shred of evidence anywhere in the Scriptures that this was the work of Enoch, Melchizedek, Job, or any other Biblical character. Nothing is to be gained by these men in assigning the erection of the Great Pyramid to one of the patriarchs, but it just represents one of the many fantastic ideas incorporated with the major piece of fancy, that the Pyramid has prophetic significance.

Chronological Contradictions and Mistaken Pronouncements

It is when the Pyramidists begin to cite dates derived from an architectural survey of these passages, corridors, chambers, etc., that they reveal the folly of their entire system. One writer contradicts another in relation to dates of events now long past; e.g., Rutherford asserts that Adam was created in 5394 B.C., but Davidson insists that the year was 4000 B.C.; Rutherford places the Exodus from Egypt at 1493.

It is, however, when we come to the actual predictions of these Pyramidists that we are forced to conclude—and one would think they would be forced also to admit—that there is something definitely wrong in a system which leads them to make predictions proved false by time. Rutherford says that the year 1936 marks the time that "we begin to enter into our destiny. Not only is 1936 marked by the end of Israel's Tribulation Passage in the Pyramid, but it is an outstanding date in Biblical prophecy regarding the final deliverance of Israel." [21] By Israel, Rutherford of course means Great Britain. Instead of Great Britain being delivered from anything in 1936, she has found her power and empire gradually diminishing, and her economic structure in more perilous condition than ever in the history of modern times. Rutherford continues, "This does not mean that all Britain's troubles will be ended then, but it does mean that deliverance will begin at that time, and that after September, 1936, our nation will be increasingly victorious in her troubles mainly through divine intervention." [22] In the same work, he names 1941 as a year of climax in world history: "The power of all other nations is to be broken after 1936, and they are to be humiliated in order that they may be brought into a contrite spirit . . . This simultaneous delivering of Israel and crushing of Gentile power will culminate in Armageddon, the crisis of which appears to be due in the year 1941, according to the indications of the Pyramid and Biblical prophecy." [23] Toward the conclusion of the volume, our author states that this date, A.D. 1941, is the one "indicated by the end of the Great Subterranean Chamber in the Pyramid as marking the end of the Time of Trouble and the beginning of the world sway of Israel and Judah combined, this being due to become universal within the following twelve years, A.D. 1941 to 1953." [24]

In another work, Rutherford asserts that in 1953 the cleansing of the sanctuary is due, for he says this is "the final date revealed in the King's Chamber, and it indicates that by then the divine organization will be complete and ready for beginning the cleansing of the sanctuary and rectification of Israel's constitution in harmony with the divine laws." [25]

As everyone knows, these things have not come to pass. Britain's troubles are not over; Britain has not been delivered, nor Israel either; the cleansing of the sanctuary has not begun; the battle of Armageddon has not been fought, and the world is in greater peril today than ever from great leading powers which are in themselves godless. It is difficult to understand how one can retain confidence in a scheme of interpretation which leads to such erroneous predictions as these. Another writer in this group, Lt. A. Kenney-Herbert, in his *Problem of the Pyramid,* definitely states that the Lord would return before 1944.[26]

An addendum to the sixth edition of Davidson's massive volume, *The Great Pyramid, Its Divine Message* (London, 1937) reads, "There are no grounds for the interpretation that after September 16, 1936, there will be no more war. The King's Chamber period, from September 16, 1936 to August 20, 1953, is defined as the period of the Judgment of the Nations, of the Unveiling of 'The Mystery of the Open Tomb' and of the return to the Plane of the Divine Centre. It is also defined as the period during which the nations of the New World order, of which the English-speaking peoples form the nucleus, are brought safely through the dangers and difficulties which beset them; and as the period during which the forces of war and disorder will be ultimately subdued by Divine Intervention." [27] Davidson is recognized everywhere as a leading authority on the prophetic interpretation of the Pyramid, but here again his calculations are revealed to be in error, for August 20, 1953, has passed and the forces of war and disorder have not been subdued.

Similar fantastic theories are introduced by one author or another in this particular school of pseudo-prophetic study. Seiss, for example, says that the Hebrew word translated *altar* in Isaiah 19 means "the lion of God," and that one reason this passage refers to the Pyramid of Gizeh is that "the Great

Pyramid is pre-eminently the lion among all earthy buildings." [28] It is not necessary to comment on such a guess as this. He even presumes to identify this vast tomb structure in idolatrous Egypt with "the mountain of God" in Ezekiel's description of Zion, though of course Zion is never attached to any geographical location in Egypt. Once drawn to this type of interpretation these Pyramidists claim to find strong hints of the prophetic significance of the Gizeh Pyramid even in the New Testament; e.g., this is the stone, according to Seiss and others, which the builders rejected (Acts 4:11) none other than the Lord Jesus Christ, as in I Peter 2:4-8. In other words, the Great Pyramid does not only contain prophetic teaching, but it has Messianic significance—though there was no Messianic doctrine in the religion of Egypt at the time this Pyramid was built. Perhaps the most far-fetched of all suggestions is that the total value of the letters of the Hebrew words of Isaiah 19:19, 20, is 5449, which, so the exponents of the theory insist, is identical to the height of the Pyramid, expressed in Pyramid inches.[29]

Let me here, then, summarize the results of our study, and make one or two additional comments. The fundamental Biblical passage used by the Pyramidists, that in Isaiah, has always been understood by the Christian Church to be a prophecy of what God was yet to do, whereas the gizeh Pyramid was erected centuries before Isaiah's ministry. There is no reason why one Pyramid rather than another should contain a prophetic revelation, but these men acknowledge that it is only in Great Pyramid of Gizeh that they find any prophetic revelation. It should never be forgotten that, whatever the Pyramidists may say, these vast tombs were built by idolatrous

Gentiles who had no knowledge of the true God; and it is contrary to all we know of the methods God has used in revealing deeper truths to men that He should reveal to ungodly Gentiles what He withheld from His chosen prophets and from those who were ordained by Him to be the authors of the Holy Scriptures. There is no hint anywhere in the Word of God that an architectural structure might contain chronological truth in the realm of prophecy. Three buildings were erected in the Old Testament according to divine instruction, the tabernacle, the temple of Solomon's day, and the post-exilic temple. All of these structures have rich typical significance, but no Biblical scholar advances the idea that their measurements embrace chronological prophecies. This is also true—whatever else it may mean—of the description of the millennial temple in the concluding chapters of Ezekiel. If these structures for which details were given by God, built by God's chosen people, did not contain prophetic chronological revelation, it is ridiculous to expect such truth to emanate from a vast pile of brick constructed by idolatrous pharaohs, not for purposes of sacrifice or worship, but for burial.

The Pyramidal body of interpretation is identified with many other strange concepts wholly unacceptable to sound Biblical scholars, for example, that Britain is the chosen race. The Pyramidists differ among themselves as to the exact meaning of many of the passages of the Pyramid of Gizeh. Finally—and this cannot be over-emphasized—the predictions which these men continually set forth in their writings have proved false, and therefore we must recognize (and they should admit) that even if the Great Pyramid does embody

chronological prophecies they have not yet discovered a
method for accurately interpreting them.

Notes

1. John Taylor: *The Great Pyramid.* 1859; new ed., London, 1864. This work
   of almost 450 pages was published by no less a firm than Longmans, Green.
2. I. E. S. Edwards: *The Pyramids of Egypt.* London: Penguin Books, 1947.
   pp. 243-244. I am indebted to the publishers of this work for permission
   to quote so extensively from it.
3. George R. Riffert: *Great Pyramid: Proof of God.* Haverhill, Mass., 1932.
   p. 26.
4. Edwards, *op. cit.* p. 88.
5. Edwards, *op. cit.* p. 89 ff.
6. Edwards, *op. cit.* pp. 94, 95.
7. That Smyth did write some authoritative works in the area of astronomy
   is evident from the fact that the Catalog of Printed Cards of the Library
   of Congress lists nineteen titles from his pen in metrology, astronomy,
   and spectroscopy. His well-known work on the Pyramid, *Our Inheritance
   in the Great Pyramid*, with maps and plates, was first issued in 1864; a
   fourth edition, greatly enlarged, with 25 plates, appeared in 1880. The
   later *Life and Work at the Great Pyramid During the Months of January,
   February, March and April, A.D. 1865*, was published in three volumes in
   1867, and, I think, obtains a very high price today.
8. These details are taken from a most interesting chapter, "The Great
   Pyramidiot," in *The Mountains of Pharaoh*, by Leonard Cottrell. London:
   Robert Hale, 1956. For additional material, see W. M. Flinders Petrie:
   Seventy Years in Archaeology.
9. Riffert, *op. cit.* p. 51.
10. Adam Rutherford: *Anglo-Saxon Israel.* 2nd ed., London, 1935. See chart
    opposite p. 222.
11. Rutherford, *op. cit.* p. 245.
12. Rutherford, *op. cit.* p. 310.
13. Rutherford, *op. cit.* pp. 250, 251.
14. Rutherford, *op. cit.* p. 300.
15. Rutherford, *op. cit.* pp. 301, 302.
16. Rutherford, *op. cit.* p. 303.
17. A. Kenney-Herbert: *The Problem of the Pyramid.* London, n.d. pp. 123,
    124.
18. Rutherford, *op. cit.* p. 271.
19. For a discussion of this *Book of the Dead* in relation to the Pyramid, see

EGYPT IN BIBLICAL PROPHECY

D. Davidson and H. Aldersmith: *The Great Pyramid: Its Divine Message.* 7th ed., London, 1937. pp. 383 ff., 395 ff.

20. Joseph Seiss: *A Miracle in Stone, or The Great Pyramid of Egypt.* 14th ed., New York, 1910. This is perhaps a reprint of the 4th edition dated September, 1878. pp. 114-120 and 207-227.
21. Rutherford, *op. cit.* pp. 279, 280. See also Worth Smith: *The Great Pyramid.* New York, 1937. p. 146.
22. Rutherford, *op. cit.* p. 280.
23. Rutherford, *op. cit.* p. 319.
24. Rutherford, *op. cit.* p. 319.
25. Adam Rutherford: *A New Revelation in the Great Pyramid.* London, n.d. (1946) pp. 14, 15.
26. Kenney-Herbert, *op. cit.* p. 137.
27. Davidson, *op. cit.* p. IX.
28. Seiss, *op. cit.* p. 119.
29. As another example of a most fantastic interpretation, which present-day events make more ridiculous than ever, I quote the following paragraph:

"Britain possesses the 'gate' of its enemies, i.e., the strategic point which commands the entry in the foreign countries. Gibraltar is the gate to the countries on the shores of the Mediterranean. Who possesses it? Great Britain! Aden is the gate to the countries whose shores border the Indian Ocean. To whom does it belong? Great Britain! Singapore is the gate to the countries of the Far East. Who holds it? Great Britain! The Cape of Good Hope and the Falklands each constitute an important gate in the Southern Seas. Who occupies them? Great Britain! Several minor gates also belong to Great Britain—such as Malta, Cyprus, Hong Kong. And Britain itself occupies the commanding position in the Atlantic! (Lord Fisher said: 'There are five keys to the world, viz., the Straits of Dover, the Straits of Gibraltar, the Suez Canal, the Straits of Malacca and the Cape of Good Hope, all of which we hold.') Thus the 'gate' to all the great continents of the World is held by Great Britain. In no other nation is this part of the Divine Promise to Abraham being fulfilled; this further demonstrates that the British nation is Abraham's earthly seed. The Divine Promises to Abraham form the summary of the History of the World; upon these the whole superstructure of prophecy and history is built." (A. Rutherford: *Anglo-Saxon Israel.* p. 53-54).

Even journals not devoted to this scheme have made foolish statements based on these Pyramid calculations. For example, the *Prophetic News and Israel Watchman*, Jan., 1896, carries an article entitled "The Great Pyramid pointing to about A.D. 1908 as the end of this age and the beginning of the Millennium."

14

"BLESSED BE EGYPT"—EGYPT'S
FINAL REDEMPTION

By this time we have discovered three principal prophetic themes of the Old Testament bearing upon Egypt. The first embraces a series of prophecies promising a deliverance of God's people from Egypt, beginning with the announcement to Abraham (Gen. 15:13-16) and fulfilled in the exodus from Egypt. Then there is the statement of Hosea (11:1), referred to by St. Matthew (2:15) as being fulfilled in the Holy Family's return from Egypt. Finally, there are the numerous predictions that God would bring Israel out of Egypt *the second time* (Deut. 28:68; Isa. 11:11-16; Zech. 10:10). These predictions relate not only to events that have already occurred, but to Israel's future as well.

The second theme is Egypt's conquest by her enemies, particularly by Nebuchadnezzar, to which much space is devoted in the later prophecies, as in Jer. 43:8-13; Ezek. 29 -31; Isa. 7:12; Micah 7:12. The third major theme covers Egypt's entire history, from the time of her fall as a powerful empire apparently to the end of the age, when she is called "the basest of kingdoms" (Ezek. 29:13-16; Zech. 11:11).

We consider now the fourth, and happiest of all prophecies concerning Egypt: that of ultimate blessedness, of a return to the Lord, and of a time when she will be at peace with those whom she now hates. The most extended passage on this subject, and one of the most familiar prophecies in all of the Old Testament, as well as one of the more difficult, concludes the first of Isaiah's oracles regarding the nations:

"In that day shall five cities in the land of Egypt speak the language of Canaan, and swear to the Lord of hosts; one shall be called, The city of destruction. In that day shall there be an altar to the Lord in the midst of the land of Egypt, and a pillar at the border thereof to the Lord. And it shall be for a sign and for a witness unto the Lord of hosts in the land of Egypt: for they shall cry unto the Lord because of the oppressors, and he shall send them a Saviour, and a great one, and he shall deliver them. And the Lord shall be known to Egypt, and the Egyptians shall know the Lord in that day, and shall do sacrifice and oblation; yea, they shall vow a vow unto the Lord, and perform it. And the Lord shall smite Egypt: he shall smite and heal it: and they shall return even to the Lord, and he shall be intreated of them, and shall heal them. In that day there be a highway out of Egypt to Assyria, and the Assyrian shall come into Egypt, and the Egyptian into Assyria, and the Egyptians shall serve with the Assyrians. In that day shall Israel be the third with Egypt and with Assyria, even a blessing in the midst of the land" (Isa. 19:18-24).

One hardly knows where to begin an examination of these words—so differing are the basic assumptions of commentators, and so varying their interpretations. On one great truth, however, all must agree: it is predicted here that *Egypt will have a revival of true religion;* she will turn to God, will be blessed of God, and will be at peace with her neighbors. The mere enumeration of the phrases persuades us of this: "five cities . . . shall swear to Jehovah of hosts"

(v. 18); there shall be "an altar to Jehovah in the midst of the land of Egypt, and a pillar . . . to Jehovah" (v. 19); "a sign and for a witness unto Jehovah of hosts; they shall cry unto Jehovah because of oppressors; he will send them a saviour, and a defender, and he will deliver them" (v. 20); "Jehovah shall be known to Egypt; the Egyptians shall know Jehovah in that day; they shall worship with sacrifice and oblation, and shall vow a vow unto Jehovah" (v. 21) "they shall return unto Jehovah, and he will be entreated of them, and will heal them," (v. 22); "Jehovah of hosts hath blessed them, saying, Blessed be Egypt my people" (v. 24).

The first question to be faced in considering this passage has to do with the period referred to by the prophet. Have these promises been fulfilled, or do they still await their historical confirmation? Before answering this question, we might pose another: Do not these words depict a situation of flourishing, true religion in Egypt that is more or less permanent, a final condition, as it were, the consummation of God's purpose for this people in blessing them? If this is true, these verses cannot be said to have been fulfilled, for Egypt today is about as far away from knowing Jehovah, and being blessed by Jehovah, as any nation in the Mediterranean area. She is predominantly Mohammedan, and even in the last two years she has initiated an opposition to missionary effort, including stringent laws governing missionary schools, which bring the evangelization of Egypt to the lowest level it has known for the last century.

A common interpretation is that of Hengstenberg: "It is scarcely necessary to point out how gloriously this prophecy

234

was fulfilled; how at one time there existed a flourishing church in Egypt. Although the candlestick of that church be now removed from its place, yet we are confident of and hope for a future in which this prophecy shall anew powerfully manifest itself. The broken power of the Mohammedan delusion opens up the prospect, that the time in which this hope is to be realized is drawing nigh." [1] It must be noted, in relation to this view, that there is nothing in the prophecy which would lead us to believe that the great revival would be followed by a prolonged period of apostasy and the abandonment of the worship of Jehovah, preceding a second major revival of true religion. The passage in Isaiah speaks of one time and of one consummation—not of two periods of marked spiritual quickening, separated by a long period of unbelief. All Christians must regret that such a hope as this expressed by Hengstenberg, which can be paralleled in many writings of a century ago, has not been fulfilled. It is true that the power of the Ottoman Empire has been broken, but this has not resulted in any great spiritual upsurge or growth in the Christian Church in those lands. For example, today in Turkey, where a century ago some of the outstanding missionaries of that generation were laboring, the government forbids anyone declaring his intention to preach the gospel to come into that territory to live; and in Egypt, now free from any external influences, the devotion to Islam seems more fervent than it was one hundred years ago, and the larger number of missionaries have been compelled to leave because of the Suez crisis. Of course, these conditions are only temporary: the situation in the Near East today is

EGYPT IN BIBLICAL PROPHECY

an altogether different matter, economically and spiritually, from that of a decade ago, and radically different from fifty years ago. Tomorrow may be different from today.

One phrase found at the opening of each paragraph in this section seems to demand that we look to the end of the age, the time of *the day of the Lord,* for the fulfilment of these promises. Keil is right when he says, "It is not the future in general, but the last times, that is, the Messianic future, that is pointed out." [2]

In attempting an interpretation of the specific phrases of this passage, we are confronted by a number of theories. For example, in the statement that the day will come when there will be "five cities in the land of Egypt that speak the language of Canaan, and swear to Jehovah of hosts," there is no hint as to what these five cities might be. Hengstenberg is probably correct in assuming that this phrase means "a goodly number of cities." [3] With his interpretation of the passage as a whole, nevertheless, one might easily disagree: "When viewed more deeply, the language of Canaan is spoken by all those who are converted to the true God. Upon the Greek language, for example, the character of the language of Canaan has been impressed in the New Testament. That language which, from primeval times, has been developed in the service of the Spirit, imparts its character to the languages of the world, and changes their character in their deepest foundation." [4] A somewhat similar view is set forth by Kay: "The language which had once been that of the debased Canaanites, but which had been rescued out of its corruption and sanctified by being employed as the vehicle for the communication of God's purposes to mankind . . . was no doubt largely spoken in Egypt by numerous Jewish settlers; and there it transfused its spirit into the Greek forms of speech." [5] In his helpful commentary, Alexander remarks, "Of all the explanations, the simplest is the one proposed by Calvin which supposes the whole verse to mean that for one town which shall perish in its unbelief, five shall profess the true faith and sware fealty to Jehovah." [6]

Verses 19 and 20 have also been given varying interpretations. We have already considered one of these—that which arose in the middle of the nineteenth century, which made these words refer to the building of the Pyramid of Gizeh. These verses played an important part in the erection of a Jewish temple by Onias at Leontopolis, about twenty miles from Memphis in lower Egypt. The entire episode is recorded by Josephus in Book XIII of his *Antiquities of the Jews,* and is so interesting that we would do well to have it in our text:

"When this Onias saw that Judea was oppressed by the Macedonians and their kings, out of a desire to purchase to himself a memorial and eternal fame, he resolved to send to King Ptolemy and Queen Cleopatra, to ask leave of them that he might build a temple in Egypt like to that at Jerusalem, and might ordain Levites and priests out of their own stock. The chief reason why he was desirous so to do, was, that he relied upon the prophet Isaiah, who lived about 600 years before, and foretold that there certainly was to be a temple built to Almighty God in Egypt, by a man that was a Jew. Onias was elevated with this prediction, and wrote the following epistle to Ptolemy and Cleopatra: 'Having done many and great things for you in the affairs of the war, by the assistance of God, and that in Celesyria and Phoenicia, I came at length with the Jews to Leontopolis, and to other places of your nation, where I found that the greatest part of your people had temples in an improper manner, and that on this account they bore ill-will one against another, which happens to the Egyptians by reason of the multitude of their temples, and the difference of opinions about divine worship. Now I found a very fit place in a castle that hath its name from the country, Diana; this place is full of materials of several sorts, and replenished with sacred animals: I desire, therefore, that you will grant me leave to purge this holy place, which belongs to no master, and is fallen down, and to build there a temple to Almighty God after the pattern of that in Jerusalem, and of the same dimensions, that may be for the benefit of thyself, and thy wife and children, that those Jews who dwell in Egypt may have a place whither they may come and meet together, in mutual harmony one with another, and be subservient to thy advantages; for the prophet Isaiah foretold that 'there should be an altar in Egypt to the Lord God'; and many other such things did he prophesy relating to that place.'

"And this was what Onias wrote to King Ptolemy. Now any one may observe his piety, and that of his sister and wife Cleopatra, by that epistle which they wrote in answer to it; for they laid the blame and the transgression of the law upon the head of Onias. And this was their reply:—'King Ptolemy and Queen Cleopatra to Onias, send greeting. We have read thy petition, wherein thou desirest leave to be given to thee to purge that temple which has fallen down at Leontopolis, in the Nomus of Heliopolis, and which is named from the country Bubastis; on which account we cannot but wonder that it should be pleasing to God to have a temple erected in a place so unclean, and so full of sacred animals. But since thou sayest that Isaiah the prophet foretold this long ago, we give thee leave to do it, if it may be done according to your law, and so that we may not appear to have at all offended God herein.'

"So Onias took the place, and built a temple, and an altar to God, like indeed to that in Jerusalem, but smaller and poorer. I do not think it proper for me now to describe its dimensions, or its vessels, which have been already described in my seventh book of the Wars of the Jews. However, Onias found other Jews like to himself, together with priests and Levites, that there performed divine service. But we have said enough about this temple." [7]

On the meaning of the phrase, "I will send them a Saviour and a defender, and I will deliver them," a number of differing views have been set forth. Victorinus thought that this referred to Alexander the Great, who, by his invasion of Egypt delivered that land from its oppressors and corrupt government.[8] Most of the early Church Fathers, however, especially Lactantius, regarded this as a Messianic prophecy.[9] It is strange that while the passage occurs here and there in some of the Ante-Nicene writings, there is no reference to it, as far as I know, in all the subsequent Church Fathers down through Chrysostom. This is one of many evidences we have that the second century gave a great deal of attention to eschatology and Biblical prophecy, while the later eminent divines, Origen, Augustine, Jerome and Chrysostom revealed a spirit of indifference toward this important area of study. Personally, I think that here Alexander is right when he says, "Even if the language of this verse by itself might seem to point to a particular deliverer, the comprehensive language of the context would forbid its reference to any such exclusively. If the chapter is a prophecy, not of a single event, but of a great progressive change to be wrought in the condition of Egypt by the introduction of the true religion, the promise of the verse before us must be that when they cried God would send them a deliverer, a promise verified not once but often, not by Ptolemy or Alexander only, but by others, and in the highest sense by Christ himself." [10]

Verses 21 and 22 only repeat what has been set forth in the preceding verses, and require no additional comment. We have observed in earlier chapters many passages stating that Egypt would be smitten by a judgment from God, but here is a promise that healing would follow the smiting. While this may be an economic healing, the reference is primarily to a spiritual healing of Egypt, the termination of idolatrous practices, and the abandonment of whatever false religion may be mastering her when the day of the Lord shall come.

The prophet concludes his oracle on Egypt by introducing two other nations: Assyria and Israel. As many commentators admit, Assyria may sometimes refer to Syria, immediately north of Israel. Israel has always been located between these two empires: Assyria to the north, and Egypt to the south. She was in bondage to the southern power at the beginning of her history, and was in captivity to the other at the end of her kingdom days. Between those two periods, at various times, she has been harassed and invaded, now by an enemy from the south, then, at other times, from the north. The end of the age will see all these rivalries, antagonisms and conflicts terminated. "In that day shall Israel be the third with Egypt and with Assyria"—all three bound together with open lines of communication—"a highway out of Egypt to Assyria." As Rawlinson reminds us, "The highway was to facilitate the return of the Israelites to their own land." Now the object is perfectly free communication between the three peoples." [11] The roads on which Old Testament conquerors had so often marched are now to serve for the peaceful intercourse of the nations admitted into the kingdom of God." [12]

There is some difference of opinion as to whether or not Isaiah meant to assign to Assyria any special honor among these three nations. Nagelsbach insists that "Israel retains the name of honor, 'mine inheritance,' for thereby it is characterized as the actual son of the house and head of the family," [13] but Alexander repudiates this, affirming rather that here Isaiah's "very object seems to be to represent the three united powers as absolutely one in privilege, and it cannot be supposed that he would wind up by saying that they are not absolutely equal after all." [14] Alexander, however, held the view that there was no particular future for Israel as a nation on earth at the end of this age, and this would account for his rejection of the idea of any special privilege being assigned to God's ancient people. This is the only passage in all the Old Testament in which God assigns to two Gentile nations a place in a trinity of nations that includes Israel, giving to each *a third.* Someone has

241

aptly said, here we have the promise of blessing upon the three great divisions of the human race, the Semitic, Japhethic, and Hametic. Alexander says that when Isaiah "describes these representatives of heathenism as received into the covenant and sharing with the church of God its most distinctive titles, we have one of the clearest and most striking predictions of the calling of the Gentiles that the word of God contains." [15]

The peaceful relationship prevailing among these three nations promised for the end of the age is the very reverse of the conditions now prevailing there.

In commenting upon these words, a distinguished missionary to Egypt in the early part of this century well said, "Isaiah has revealed the will of God for Egypt. There can be no doubt about it. To realize this will, God needs men. This is the price of His victory and ours." [16] Today the place and destiny of Egypt, and other Near East countries, is being determined by the present ruler of Egypt, by economic influences, by the significance of the Suez Canal, by Europe's need for oil, by deliberations of the United Nations, by the recently-announced Eisenhower Doctrine offering help to those countries of the Near East that are threatened by Communism, by the infiltration of Russian influences. Religion is playing no part in these considerations, and the Christian faith, instead of being increasingly accepted, is being more and more pronouncedly rejected. But the day will come when God will intervene in this area of the earth, whether through human agencies and economic distress or by some unforeseen miraculous event, and this nation of Egypt which for centuries has experienced humiliating weakness, and is now refusing to submit to the verdicts and decisions of any collective voice, and is legislating against the Christian institutions within its borders, will reverse the course of its history and, in turning to God, will be the recipient of a divine blessing far beyond anything it has ever known. "When Israel is mentioned as 'the third,' it does not mean the third in power or rank, for it is in the context particularly denominated God's 'inheritance' (thus showing its supremacy) but that these three—once so hostile and at enmity—shall be united and friendly, having familiar intercourse. It is a representation of that unity between the Jewish nation and other nations which results in preventing rivalry and contention, crushing war and its attendant evils." [17] Peace will come to that troubled area of the world, and the northern power, the state of Israel, and the nation to the south will enjoy undisturbed confidence and uninterrupted communication. God's promise stands— Egypt will be blessed!

There is one supplementary prophecy in the Old Testament, of a spiritual revival to occur in Israel, apparently at the end of the age, that will be more or less permanent. In this prophecy concerning the observance of the feast of tabernacles by the nations of the earth, found at the end of the Book of Zechariah, Egypt is the one Gentile nation specifically named: "And it shall come to pass, that every one that is left of all the nations that came against Jerusalem shall go up from year to year to worship the King Jehovah of hosts, and to keep the feast of tabernacles. And it shall be that whoso of all the families of the earth goeth not up unto Jerusalem to worship the King Jehovah of hosts, upon them there shall be no rain. And if the family of Egypt go not up, and come not, neither shall it be upon them; there shall be the plague wherewith Jehovah shall smite the nations that go not up to keep the feast of tabernacles. This shall be the punishment of Egypt, and the punishment of all the nations that go not up to keep the feast of tabernacles" (14:16-19). The feast of tabernacles was the concluding harvest festival of joy and thanksgiving celebrating the ingathering of the crops, announced as one of the major annual feasts for Israel (Ex. 23:16; 34:22; Deut. 16:13; Lev. 23:33-44). Commentators of every age unite in declaring that there is something universal about this feast which will be consummated in the millennium, when the knowledge of the glory of God will cover the earth and nations will walk in His sight.

According to the King James Version, the particular punishment for Egypt, if she refuses to go up to the feast of tabernacles, is that she shall have no rain. However, this phrase is italicized, indicating that these words do not actually appear in the Hebrew text. The Revised Version does not interpret this punishment, simply reading, "neither shall it be upon them." This has been generally understood to refer to rain; thus, God will withhold all rain from this land whose Nile River depends entirely upon the equatorial rains for its flow. As in the prophecy of Isaiah, so here, "Egypt the ancient oppressor of Israel is united with Judah as one in the same worship of God." [18]

Of one great truth these prophecies clearly speak—that there is a day coming when Egypt will turn to Jehovah, and know a blessedness throughout her land beyond anything she has ever experienced on her many long centuries of troubled history.

Notes

1. E. W. Hengstenberg: *Christology of the Old Testament*. Edinburgh, 1872. Vol. II, pp. 145-146.
2. C. F. Keil: *Commentary on Isaiah*. Vol. I. p. 123.
3. Hengstenberg, *op. cit.*, p. 153
4. Hengstenberg, *op. cit.*, p. 143
5. W. Kay in *The Bible Commentary*, edited by F. C. Cook. New York, 1890. Vol. V, p. 138. The statement by G. W. Wade involves many problems, and I am giving it without comment: "The conversion of Egypt will begin with the adoption of the Hebrew faith and language by a few cities." (*The Book of the Prophet Isaiah*. London, n.d., p. 129.
6. Joseph Addison Alexander: *Commentary on the Prophecies of Isaiah*. New ed., edited by John Eadie, Edinburgh, 1865. Vol. I, p. 365. Alexander later remarks, "What appears to be meant is that five-sixths, that is, a very large proportion, shall profess the true religion, while the remaining one-sixth persists in unbelief." p. 357. Delitzsch suggestively adds, "Five cities are very few for Egypt, which was completely covered with cities; but this is simply a fragmentary commencement of Egypt's future and complete conversion." (p. 362.)

One phrase in this prophecy has had so many varying interpretations that I thought it preferable to discuss it here rather than in the text proper. Isaiah says that one of the cities of Egypt "shall be called the city of destruction." The marginal note of the Revised Version is suggestive of the manifold difficulty of this phrase, "Or, *Heres;* or, according to another reading, *the sun.*" The Hebrew word here is *Ir-ha-heres*, that is, "the city of overthrow," but if a slight change is introduced, making it *Ir-ha-cheres*, it means "the city of the sun," which of course would be the great city of Egypt, Heliopolis. The Septuagint does not lean to either of these interpretations, but translates the phrase, "the city of righteousness." Wade is perhaps right in saying that it refers to "a city wherein idolatrous symbols are to be demolished in consequence of its conversion to the true God . . . It is perhaps the destruction of the Temple of the Sun at Heliopolis that the passage especially contemplates." (*Op. cit.*, p. 130). Heliopolis was the city of the sun god, Ra, northest of Memphis, called On in other passages of the Old Testament and Aven in Ezek. 30:17. Delitzsch significantly notes that *haras* is the word commonly used to signify "the throwing down of heathen altars" (Judges 6:25; I Kings 18:30; 19:10, 14).

A paschal letter issued by Theophilus in A.D. 402 was sent by Jerome to two of his correspondents with a letter beginning, "Once more with the return of spring I enrich you with the wares of the east and send the treasures of Alexandria to Rome. Now truly is Isaiah's prophecy fulfilled: 'In that day shall there be an altar to the Lord in the land of Egypt.' They who fostered the infant child now with glowing faith defend him in his manhood; and they who once saved him from the hands of Herod are ready to save him again from this blasphemer and heretic (Origen)." *The Nicene and Post-Nicene Fathers*, 2nd series, New York, 1893. Vol. VI, p. 187. See also Jerome's long letter (CVIII) to Eustochium in the same volume, p. 202.

7. Josephus: *Antiquities of the Jews*. Book XIII, Ch. 3. This Onias was Onias IV. The temple maintained essentially the same worship as was the practice at the temple of Jerusalem. It was destroyed by Vespasian in A.D. 73. See W. M. Flinders Petrie: *Egypt and Israel* (1911) pp. 99-110; and, with detail, Albert *La Religion des Judeo-Arameens D'Elephantine*. Paris, 1937.

8. This interpretation of Victorinus is referred to in G. H. N. Peters: *The Theocratic Kingdom of Our Lord Jesus Christ;* I have not been able to discover such a statement in Victorinus. This is, however, the interpretation of the generally-dependable scholar T. R. Birks in his *Commentary on the Book of Isaiah*. London, 1871.

9. See, e.g., Lactantius: *Divine Institutes*, Book IV, Chap. 13, and his *Epitome of the Institutes*, Chap. LXIV, in *The Ante-Nicene Fathers*, Vol. VII, pp. 112, 239; also Justin Martyr's *Dialogue with Trypho*, Chap. CXXIII, in *The Ante-Nicene Fathers*, Vol. I, p. 261.

10. Alexander, *op. cit.*, p. 361. This view was held as early as Theodosius who wrote, "Accordingly He sends forth at one time prophets and another apostles to be saviours of men." *Ante-Nicene Fathers*, Vol. VIII, p. 45.

11. George Rawlinson in *The Pulpit Commentary: Isaiah*, Vol. I, p. 316.

12. G. F. Oehler: *Theology of the Old Testament*. New York, 1883. p. 520, note 6.

13. Carl W. E. Nagelsbach: *The Prophet Isaiah*. 1890. p. 230.

14. Alexander, *op. cit.*, p. 364.

15. Alexander, *op. cit.*, p. 364. The Septuagint translators, not pleased with Isaiah's assignment of a place of equality to these three nations, made the passage to read, "In that day shall Israel be a third with the

Egyptians and the Assyrians, blessed in the land which the Lord of Hosts hath blessed saying, Blessed by my people that is in Egypt and that is among the Assyrians and Israel Mine inheritance."

16. Charles R. Watson: *Egypt and the Christian Crusade*. Phil., 1907. p. 259.
17. George N. H. Peters: *The Theocratic Kingdom*. Vol. II, p. 94.
18. The best treatment of this passage known to me is in the epochal work by David Baron: *The Visions and Prophecies of Zechariah*. 3rd ed., London, 1919. pp. 520-530.

OLD TESTAMENT PROPHECIES RELATING TO EGYPT IN THE APPROXIMATE ORDER OF THEIR DELIVERANCE

I. IN THE PENTATEUCH AND THE PSALMS

1. The coming time of oppression in Egypt. Genesis 15:12-16. (The name Egypt does not occur, but the reference is undeniable.)
2. "And Jehovah will bring thee into Egypt again." Deuteronomy 28:68
3. "Princes shall come out of Egypt." Psalms 68:31

II. EIGHTH-CENTURY PROPHETS

A. Joel. "Egypt shall be a desolation." 3:19
B. Hosea
   1. Ephraim shall return to Egypt, to her shame. 7:11-16; 8:13; 9:3, 6; compare Isaiah 52:4
   2. "He shall not return into the land of Egypt, but the Assyrian shall be his king." 11:5
   3. I "called my son out of Egypt," 11:1; used in reference to Christ in Matthew 2:15
C. Isaiah
   1. The Lord will "the second time recover the remnant of his people from Assyria, Egypt," etc. 11:11-16
   2. "The Lord shall utterly destroy the tongue of the Egyptian Sea." 11:15
   3. "This burden of Egypt—" Chaps. 19, 20
      a. civil war, confusion, drought. 19:1-16
      b. "the land of Judah shall be a terror unto Egypt." 19:17

248

    c. "five cities in the land of Egypt shall speak the language of Canaan." 19:18

    d. "there shall be an altar to the Lord in the midst of the land." vs. 19:19, 20

    e. "The Egyptians shall know the Lord." vs. 19:21, 22

    f. Israel a third with Egypt and Assyria. vs. 19:23, 24

D. Micah— "In that day shall they come unto thee from Assyria and the cities of Egypt" 7:12

III. SEVENTH-CENTURY PROPHET—JEREMIAH

1. Nebuchadnezzar will conquer Egypt (43:8-13), when the Jews who fled to Egypt will be slain (42:15-18, 22; 44:11-14, 24-30).

2. Egypt (and all the nations) will be drunken, 25:15-29

3. Jeremiah's major prophecy concerning Egypt, Chap. 46

    a. Egypt will be conquered by Nebuchadnezzar, vs. 1-26a; see above, also #3 under Ezekiel.

    b. "afterward it shall be inhabited," v. 26b

    c. Israel will be punished but preserved, vs. 27, 28

IV. SIXTH-CENTURY PROPHETS

A. Ezekiel—Chapters 29—32

1. Desolation of the land, for a period of forty years, 29:1-12.

2. Restoration to the land, but "it shall be the basest of the kingdoms," 29:13-16.

3. To be conquered by Nebuchadnezzar, 29:17-21; 30:1-26; 31:1-13; 32:1-15. See Jer. 43:8-13, etc.

4. Pharaoh is depicted as entering Sheol, 31:14-18; 32:16-32.

5. In R. V. and R. S. V., 38:5 begins, "Persia, Cush, and Put." Cush is Southern Egypt, above the First Cataract; but is now recognized as a late name for the area adjacent to the Nile Delta. Thus Egypt will be allied with the Northern Power in this particular invasion.

B. Daniel—11:5-45

From v. 5 through v. 20, there are *five different* rulers referred to as "the king of the South," (which all agree must be Egypt, the word actually occurring in v. 8). These extend from Ptolemy I Soter, 323-285 B.C., to Ptolemy V Epiphanes, 204-181 B.C. Verses 21-35 refer to the wars of Antiochus Epiphanes 175-164 B.C. The king of the South here, v. 25, is Ptolemy VI Philometor. Apparently, the final section, vs. 36-45, refers to events to occur at the end of the age, in which Egypt will be involved.

C. Zechariah

1. "I will bring them again out of the land of Egypt," 10:10; compare Isa. 11:11-16.
2. "The sceptre of Egypt shall depart away," 11:11.
3. Egypt must go up to Jerusalem to attend the Feast of Tabernacles, or suffer divine discipline, 14:18, 19.

INDEX TO NAMES AND SUBJECTS

251

INDEX TO NAMES AND SUBJECTS

INDEX TO NAMES AND SUBJECTS

INDEX TO NAMES AND SUBJECTS

INDEX OF BIBLICAL REFERENCES

255

INDEX OF BIBLICAL REFERENCES

Map of The Land of Goshen
and The probable Route of
The Exodus
as far as The passage of The Red Sea

Plate VIII   in :   An Atlas of Ancient Egypt.

Special Publication of The
Egypt Exploration Fund, London, 1894.

MAP OF ANCIENT EGYPT

THE DELTA TO BENI SUÉF.

LONGITUDE EAST OF GREENWICH

UNIV. OF CHICAGO / DT 48 . 32 ORIENTAL INST.
Tracing from: An Atlas of Ancient Egypt
Special Publication of The Egypt
Exploration Fund. London, 1894. Plate III

Scale of English Miles

Biblical Names Underlined in **BLACK**

MEDITERRANEAN SEA

DESERT

DESERT

DESERT

DESERT

Gulf of Suez

Bitter Lakes

Suez

Lake Timsâh

RÁQETY
Alexandria
. Iskenderieh

Sand Hills

LAKE BURLUS

Sand Hills

Lake Menzaleh

SIN
Pelusium
Migdol
Zaru
Sile
Tell abu Séfeh

Bahr Faraoni Canal

Saghaiyer Canal

Bahr es

El Buhîyeh Canal

Bahr el Mehalleh

Nût Yesîr Canal

Radâbeh Canal

Er Riyashât Canal

Zân
Tanis •

Bahr Mu'izz

Daphnae •
Tahpanhes

Pelusiac Arm

Pithom

Tell el Maskhûteh
Canal

Tell Rotab

Pibeseth

Goshen

Menaggi Canal

R. Nile

R. Nile

ON

ÁNU
Heliopolis •

Men-Nefer
MEMPHIS   NoPH

Birket el
Qurûn

R. Nile

Beni Suêf

33°

32°

32°

31°

30°